SUGAR IN THE MORNING
ALL GOOD CHILDREN
A LILY IN LITTLE INDIA
THREE MONTHS GONE

Donald Howarth

FOUR PLAYS

SUGAR IN THE MORNING
ALL GOOD CHILDREN
A LILY IN LITTLE INDIA
THREE MONTHS GONE

introduction by
Ian McKellen

OBERON BOOKS
LONDON

All Good Children, *A Lily in Little India* and *Three Months Gone* were first published by Samuel French Ltd.

This collection first published in 2000 by Oberon Books Ltd. (incorporating Absolute Classics)
521 Caledonian Road, London N7 9RH
Tel: 020 7607 3637 / Fax: 020 7607 3629
e-mail: oberon.books@btinternet.com

A catalogue record for this book is available from the British Library.

ISBN: 1 84002 098 9

Cover illustration: Andrzej Klimowski
Typography: Richard Doust

Printed in Great Britain by Antony Rowe Ltd, Reading.

For John Hodgson

Contents

INTRODUCTION

Ian McKellen

In the autumn of 1965, we were rehearsing the first production of *A Lily in Little India* at the original Hampstead Theatre Club, whence new plays, boosted by good reviews, often shot to the West End. Donald Howarth directing his own play was understandably more apprehensive than the cast; although to be more nervous than Jill Bennett was not easy. She and I were tackling the text of one of our scenes together and there must have been some hesitation in the flow of rehearsal when the author/director gave me a note of advice. With callowness. I over-reacted: 'If I'm not saying the line properly it's because it's a bloody awful line anyway.' Although Donald can't now remember, I can: he jumped onto the stage and slapped me. 'Donald! That hurt!' 'Well, you just hurt me,' he said, smiling and grimacing simultaneously.

The tiff was over and I don't recall it here because it was typical of Donald. Indeed a gentler, lovelier man never was. Rather, its significance is my learning that writing plays is akin to giving birth and that it must be very hard to hand over the baby to actors and producers and the rest of the team who are needed to transfer words from the page to the stage. Certainly I have ever since tried to act (particularly in new plays) with the same sort of love and affinity for the character that the author feels. *A Lily in Little India* was a hit with the Hampstead audiences and then at the St Martin's Theatre when it transferred.

My gratitude to its author extends beyond teaching me a lesson, beyond even giving me my first leading part in the West End and the friendships I made, particularly with Jill Bennett and my understudy David Cook. I had spent three years' apprenticeship after university, working in regional theatre companies. *A Lily in Little India* welcomed me into the world of London theatre, then as now a stage actor's Mecca and the work place where ever since I have felt most at home. Not that I forgot the world elsewhere. One of the first plays

I directed at the Liverpool Playhouse was the sequel, *Three Months Gone*, the third play of the trilogy; *All Good Children*, commissioned by George Devine for the Royal Court in 1959, being the first.

The English drama of the fifties and sixties, beginning with John Osborne and developed more resoundingly by Harold Pinter (and other now less revered playwrights), chased Terence Rattigan's Aunt Edna from her comfy front-stall seat, sending her matinée tea-tray, served during the interval, clattering to the ground. Middle-class audiences, bred on the snobbish diet of light comedies, were now served with less digestible fare straight from the kitchen sink, with the *Observer* newspaper's critic Kenneth Tynan as maître d. A revolution was taking place in London theatre by 1959, when *Sugar in the Morning*, Donald's first full length play, was produced on a Sunday night without décor. Tynan wrote 'Unless managers are mad, this play will surely embark before long on a successful public run. The multiple jokes and insights are as warmly sardonic as we have come to expect from the new invaluable school of provincial intellectuals.' The play was subsequently restaged by another of these new radicals: William Gaskill, under the artistic direction of George Devine, who had established a theatre that truly cared for its writers in the same building where Bernard Shaw and Granville Barker once had their new work first produced.

The revolution was in part political. Dramatists who had benefited from free postwar education (and the drudge of national service) railed against the Establishment and pushed their often working-class characters centre stage. Not all of them, of course, and there is no socialist agenda in Donald Howarth's writing. Yet, without insistence, rather with the wry humanity which defines his work and his personality, he mixes the social classes and introduces outsiders to the stage. For instance in *Sugar in the Morning*, long before Gay Liberation waved its flag, we meet a bisexual West Indian who 'prefers whites'. This is the first publication of this play.

Looking back, far removed from old Labour's invitation to local authorities to spend a 'six penny rate' on arts provision and a theatre community ambitious to lead social change, we are left with the harvest of plays of which Donald Howarth's are a prime crop. What now seems to connect the new radicals of the period is their style not their substance. There were not many advances, despite the influence of Bertolt Brecht, in presentation. The young men were not angry about the form of theatre and in the main stuck with the naturalism of scenery and text. Donald Howarth's very detailed stage directions are in themselves fascinating historical reports of how his plays were to be staged.

His work survives fresh as new paint and worthy of revival because of its speeches. Therein lies his originality. His contemporaries too found their own distinctive voice. Osborne hectored, Wesker argued and Pinter paused – all of them eager to give their characters a chance to be heard and understood. Howarth's men and women, old and young, world-weary and innocent make us laugh still and move us too because they are allowed to be true to themselves and be honest, worthy of our attention. They sound like real people but there is a poetic weft underlying their speech – nothing like versification thank goodness but a slight heightening, as if they know they are on display. Howarth gives them a rhythm, phrasing and vocabulary that lifts them out of the ordinary and into the light.

His speeches are a gift to alert actors. I'm sure, at Hampstead, I deserved that admonitory slap. I now envy those who may, having read this very welcome edition, decide to let us hear his words once more from the stage.

Ian McKellen
London 2000

SUGAR IN THE MORNING

Characters

DOUGLAS KENDRICK
in his twenties

GABRIELLE BROADBENT
a widow

KEVIN BROADBENT
her young son

JACK TUBBS
a bachelor

LENA WATTS
childlike, not gormless

ERIC WATTS
her husband

ANNE CLEGG
nineteen and in love

JOHN CLEGG
the same, her husband

GRANNY SILK

NORTHERN CLEMENT GENTLES
from Barbados, prefers whites

The play was first performed at the Royal Court Theatre for one performance on Sunday 14 September 1958 under the title of *Lady on the Barometer,* with the following cast:

DOUGLAS KENDRICK, Eric Thompson
GABRIELLE BROADBENT, Patricia Jessel
KEVIN BROADBENT, Meurig Wyn-Jones
JACK TUBBS, John Gatrill,
LENA WATTS, Jeanne Watts
ERIC WATTS, Ronald Barker
ANNE CLEGG, Anne Bishop
JOHN CLEGG, Alfred Lynch
GRANNY SILK, Hilda Barry
NORTHERN CLEMENT GENTLES, Keefe West

Directors, Miriam Brickman and Donald Howarth

Sugar in the Morning was subsequently performed in the main bill on 9 April 1959, with the following changes to the cast:

DOUGLAS KENDRICK, John Fraser
GABRIELLE BROADBENT, Margaret Johnston
KEVIN BROADBENT, Peter Wood
JACK TUBBS, Toke Townley
ERIC WATTS, Frank Finlay
JOHN CLEGG, Ray Smith
NORTHERN CLEMENT GENTLES, Irvin Allen

Director, William Gaskill

A note about the staging. An apparent confusion of furniture on various levels, one, two or three feet high, the ground, first and second floors of 305 Marlborough Terrace, Manchester. The zigzag route between them conveys the staircase. The imagined privet hedge grows across the front of the house, an invisible barrier.

ACT ONE

The front door of a large house opens. The light from the hall clashes with the darkness outside. A man carrying a suitcase runs out and to the gate. He looks back, agitated. A woman wearing a cocktail dress appears.

MRS BROADBENT: I'll post your books on to you at the infirmary, doctor…

(The man, DOUGLAS KENDRICK, goes into the night. MRS BROADBENT listens for a reply. Silence returns. She goes into the house, shutting out the dark, locking the light in the hall. Distressed, she goes upstairs and is lost in the shadows. The house is suspended in the gloom. As KENDRICK speaks, sunlight warms it, bringing it to life.)

KENDRICK: Three hundred and five Marlborough Terrace. A pleasing grotesque Victorian residence in the suburb of an industrial town. This semi and completely detached redbrick villa with its clay pot chimneys roofing it on drab grey slates, its bay windows, daisied lawn, stained glass, iron gate, miniature drive and untamed privets is the home of Mrs Gabrielle Broadbent.

(KEVIN launches three paper aeroplanes into the garden from a first-floor window and runs downstairs.)

The home, too, of her eleven-plus son, Kevin, and six lodgers. I was one of them for nearly a year. It was June – the eleventh. I was looking for a room on a Saturday. It was warm and I carried my coat on my shoulder…

(A paper aeroplane lands in front of KENDRICK. He carries a suitcase and two anatomical charts. He reads from a scrap of paper. KEVIN retrieves two of the planes. KENDRICK picks up the third.)

Three hundred and five?

KEVIN: Yes. *(He takes the dart.)* Thank you. Mummy isn't in.

KENDRICK: Is this Mummy's house?

KEVIN: Yes it is.

KENDRICK: And when will Mummy be back?

KEVIN: It used to be Daddy's house till he died and gave it to her. I'm going to have it when she dies.

(JACK TUBBS leans out of his window.)

TUBBS: Hullo. Are you looking for someone?

KENDRICK: I'm looking for a room.

TUBBS: Oh, are you. Well. Yes, there is one. Well. Missus is
out. She won't be long, she said. She said if anyone
called I'd to show it to them. It's two pounds. Alright? A
lot i'n't it. It's right at the top an' all. Course, I pay a lot
more for this, ground floor you see and there's a wash
basin. 'S alright like, you know. I'll let you in, then.
Hold on while I get the key. *(He trespasses into MRS
BROADBENT's room.)*

KEVIN: Mummy's gone to Grandma's to clean her kitchen.
Grandma's dirty.

KENDRICK: Is she?

KEVIN: And she's funny.

KENDRICK: Oh.

KEVIN: She's common, that's why she's funny. She isn't
funny really and you shouldn't laugh at her. I do though.
Are all old ladies dirty?

KENDRICK: How old's your mother?

KEVIN: About twenty-one.

TUBBS: She's funny who she takes in, you know, but I'm
sure you'll be alright. What do you do?

KENDRICK: Casualty officer at the hospital.

TUBBS: Oh aye? Aye, I'm sure you'll be alright.

KENDRICK: What do you do?

TUBBS: Who? Me? Oh. I'm a packer. Good clean job.
I answer the phone too. Then I watch TV, you know, sit
back, the old feet up. Can't beat it.

KENDRICK: Can't you?

TUBBS: Er, Missus told me to ask any callers what they did
before I let them in you see, you didn't think I was being
nosy did you? No. She doesn't take in the riff-raff. She
likes to keep a tone about the place. You've only got to
look at me to see that, haven't you eh? Eh? *(He laughs.)*
No but she likes me, you know, she's alright really, isn't
she Kevin, your mum? She likes me because I keep to
myself, like. Oh, what's your name Mister –

KENDRICK: Kendrick.

TUBBS: Oh. I'm Jack. Jack Tubbs. Awful name. Well, Mister Kendrick come in, then. Just for yourself, is it?

KENDRICK: Yes.

(*LENA WATTS comes from her kitchen carrying a cereal packet stuffed with refuse and goes into the hall as TUBBS and KENDRICK go upstairs.*)

TUBBS: At the infirmary, are you?

KENDRICK: Yes, I am.

TUBBS: That'll be handy – in case of emergency – a doctor in the house – eh? Doctor in the house. (*He laughs.*) Hullo, Mrs Watts.

LENA: Hullo.

TUBBS: If you ever want anything wrapped up, packing, you know where to come. No trouble.

LENA: Hullo. (*He dumps the refuse in a dustbin behind the house and returns.*)

KEVIN: Hello, Mrs Watts.

LENA: What's that?

KEVIN: Flash Gordon's space rocket ship.

LENA: He-hee! Flash rocket.

KEVIN: Watch. (*He throws and retrieves it.*)

LENA: He-hee! Alright i'n't it. No propellers though.

KEVIN: Rocket's don't have, silly. It goes further than that if there's a wind.

LENA: 'Ey, let's have a go.

KEVIN: Don't crash it.

LENA: Course I won't crash. It's only paper, anyway.

KEVIN: You have to flick it to zoom off into the universe.

(*MRS BROADBENT comes along the pavement.*)

LENA: Flick it. (*She flicks it.*) Hoowhooh-ho-ho. That weren't very good.

KEVIN: You have to practise. Oh, you've bent the tail fin.

MRS BROADBENT: What are you doing Kevin?

LENA: He-he. Space rocket (*She goes indoors.*)

KEVIN: Mummy, there's a man inside upstairs.

MRS BROADBENT: Who let him in?

KEVIN: He's a doctor…

MRS BROADBENT: Is someone ill?

KEVIN: Mister Tubbs – he's from the hospital.

MRS BROADBENT: Mister Tubbs –

KEVIN: He wants to live in the room upstairs.

MRS BROADBENT: Live in – oh – I thought someone would call today. As soon as I turn my back. What's he like?

KEVIN: He asked how old you were.

MRS BROADBENT: Did he!

KEVIN: I said you were twenty-one.

MRS BROADBENT: Kevin!

KEVIN: Nearly.

MRS BROADBENT: You'd no right to say anything to him.

KEVIN: Well, he asked me.

MRS BROADBENT: I've told you not to speak to anyone you haven't seen before.

KEVIN: He asked me.

MRS BROADBENT: Do you do everything I ask you to? No. Here. Help Mummy and take these. (*She gives KEVIN shopping.*)

KEVIN: Yes, Mummy.

MRS BROADBENT: There's a good boy. (*She checks herself in the hall mirror before starting to go upstairs.*)

TUBBS: Is that you, Missus?

MRS BROADBENT: Mister Tubbs.

TUBBS: I thought it was. There's a bloke for a room. I've just showed it to him. (*He returns the key.*)

MRS BROADBENT: Thank you, Mister Tubbs.

TUBBS: 'S alright Missus. (*Introducing.*) Mrs Broadbent.

KENDRICK: Thank you.

MRS BROADBENT: Good afternoon, er…

KENDRICK: Good afternoon.

MRS BROADBENT: Doctor er…?

KENDRICK: Kendrick. Douglas.

MRS BROADBENT: My son Kevin told me. I'm sorry I wasn't here when you arrived, I do apologise. Is the room suitable for you?

KENDRICK: The room's fine.

MRS BROADBENT: Yes, it's quite a nice room. I always liked it. No wash basin, I know, but that's why it's only a modest rent.

KENDRICK: Two pounds.

MRS BROADBENT: I think that's reasonable. I like my
tenants to be professional people. You are single, of
course?

KENDRICK: I am.

MRS BROADBENT: There are no restrictions. Visitors out
by ten thirty and quietness about the house is all I ask.
When would you like to move in?

KENDRICK: It is vacant, isn't it?

MRS BROADBENT: Oh yes.

KENDRICK: I'll stay from now on, if you don't mind. I've
been living in at the hospital for the past year. Now I'm
casualty officer I can live out.

MRS BROADBENT: Oh I see, really, how exciting for
you. Splendid.

KENDRICK: Would you like the rent in advance?

MRS BROADBENT: It is usual. As a matter of fact, I spent
my widow's allowance on a new blazer for Kevin for the
autumn term, so I'm a little short of cash. Rooms four and
five have been vacant for over two months now – I miss
the income, naturally.

KENDRICK: Naturally.

MRS BROADBENT: Plenty of enquiries but they're mostly
Irish or – not the sort of people we like to have about
the house, sharing facilities. Would you like a receipt?

KENDRICK: Let's shake on it.

*(As they go upstairs one of the anatomical charts KENDRICK
is carrying unrolls in front of MRS BROADBENT. A life-
size male. Blue veins meander and red muscles interlock like
the spurs and rivers on a contour map of the Trossachs.)*

MRS BROADBENT: What a horrible picture.

KENDRICK: You prefer the conventional nude, with skin?

MRS BROADBENT: I like watercolours best.

KENDRICK: Still life.

MRS BROADBENT: Well, I won't keep you doctor.

KENDRICK: You can't afford to till you've let all your rooms.

MRS BROADBENT: Er, no, I'm, oh, well, I'm sure you'll
be very successful in your chosen career. I've always

admired those who devote themselves to medicine and caring for the sick. A hard life. A challenge, but you're the sort of man who'll succeed. Let me know if there's anything you need – if I can help in any way whatsoever… (*Etcetera as they climb the stairs. The dark returns.*)

(*Two months later. ERIC WATTS fills in his football pool coupon in a ground-floor room.*)

WATTS: West Brom, Preston. Blackpool and Hull.

LENA: How much are you putting on this week, Eric?

WATTS: A lot.

LENA: I don't know why you bother to send them. You've never won yet, have you?

WATTS: I've as much chance as anyone else.

LENA: Yes. Can I do a line for you?

WATTS: Don't be silly, you know nothing about it.

LENA: I stand a chance, don't I though, like anyone else?

WATTS: No, you don't.

LENA: I know what to put – home and away – it's like noughts and crosses. I can do that.

WATTS: Look you can't, will you be told, you can't do it. Now shurrup and let me concentrate for five minutes will you.

LENA: Yes, I'll be quiet. I shan't know whether you've come up this weekend, shall I?

WATTS: No you won't.

LENA: I hope you do. Let me know. Write to Mrs Broadbent.

WATTS: I'll do that.

LENA: What time you going, Eric?

WATTS: Seven.

LENA: In the morning?

WATTS: Tomorrow night. Have my tea in good time.

LENA: I always do have don't I? What would you like?

WATTS: I'll leave it to you.

LENA: Alright. (*The light fades.*)

(*MRS BROADBENT waits for KEVIN to finish his Horlicks.*)

MRS BROADBENT: Clean pyjamas on your pillow.
(*She takes KEVIN's mug and kisses him. WATTS, wearing an overcoat, hurries about in his room. LENA shadows him, empathising.*)

LENA: Did you like your tea, Eric?

WATTS: Very nice. Did you do my sandwiches?

LENA: Yes, I've done them, they're all ready.

WATTS: Well, wrap my toothbrush and stuff up while I go and pay Mrs Broadbent.

(*He goes into the hall with his suitcase and the rent book. He leaves the case by the front door. MRS BROADBENT calls up to KEVIN on his way to bed.*)

MRS BROADBENT: Brush your teeth and say your prayers, Kevin.

KEVIN: Yes, Mummy.

MRS BROADBENT: Good night darling.

KEVIN: Good night.

MRS BROADBENT: Ah, Mister Watts.

WATTS: Just coming to settle up for the next two weeks.

MRS BROADBENT: That'll be six pounds.

WATTS: Six pounds.

MRS BROADBENT: I wish I could deduct something as you'll be away but I'm afraid I have the bills to pay just the same.

WATTS: Oh yes, yes, no you can't deduct anything that wouldn't be right.

MRS BROADBENT: Thank you. I'll just bring it up to date.

WATTS: Give it over to Lena, would you. I haven't quite finished packing. I'll see you in a minute. (*He goes back to his room.*)

LENA: You'll have to get some toothpaste, we've only got one tube.

WATTS: Well, you know where the chemist is, don't you?

LENA: I buy it in Woolworths.

WATTS: It's all the same. (*He grabs the toothpaste.*)

LENA: Yes. I wonder what's on at the pictures. Do you know what's on at the pictures?

WATTS: No.

LENA: Are you looking for something?

WATTS: Look out the window and tell me when the taxi gets here. Books, that's all.

LENA: You haven't told me when you'll be back yet.

WATTS: I'll drop you a card. It all depends. Depends on the firm. They might keep me away a week or a month or –

LENA: A month!

WATTS: (*To himself.*) Or a couple of years.

LENA: Couldn't I come and stay with you?

WATTS: And keep me company?

LENA: Aye, if you like.

WATTS: You can't leave your job at the canteen.

LENA: They'd let me go back.

WATTS: No. We can't afford it. You know we're saving up.

LENA: We've been saving up for years. What are we saving it up for, Eric?

WATTS: To spend. Go away and spend it. To go away and never come back.

LENA: How much longer will we have to go on saving, Eric?

WATTS: When I come back there won't be any need for you to save again. There's just about enough now.

LENA: Ooh, Eric. How much is there?

WATTS: Nearly two thousand.

LENA: Two thousand pounds? We could buy a house couldn't we?

WATTS: We could.

LENA: And we could have a young'un.

WATTS: You could have whatever you liked.

LENA: You'll not have time to read all those books, will you?

WATTS: I don't suppose I will. You can't read, anyroad, so you won't miss 'em.

LENA: You're taking a lot, aren't you?

WATTS: I told you, I don't know how long the job'll take.

LENA: I hope it –

WATTS: Are you going to the pictures tonight?

LENA: Yes, I think I will. Can I have some money?

WATTS: Have you spent your wages already?

LENA: No, but I have to go to the shops tomorrow.

WATTS: There's ten shillings.

LENA: Ooh, I shan't want that much.

WATTS: There's five then.

LENA: You'll want some change for the taxi. 'Ey, he's here, I think.

WATTS: That's him. Well. I'm going now.

LENA: Well. Come on. Give us a kiss. I'll have to make it last, won't I?

WATTS: You will.

LENA: Make it a good one, then.

(*WATTS kisses her.*)

Why do you always put your tongue out? It makes me want to laugh at you.

MRS BROADBENT: (*Knocking.*) Your taxi's here, Mister Watts.

LENA: He's coming. 'Bye, love. I'll not come to the gate, it's cold, I'll wave to you from the window.

WATTS: Cheerio, Mrs Broadbent.

LENA: (*From the window.*) He's just coming, driver.

WATTS: See that she looks after you.

MRS BROADBENT: You are funny. I'll be alright with Mister Tubbs and the doctor about. I shall miss you, though. Who'll do my odd jobs while you're away?

WATTS: Jack'll see you through. Oh and tell young Kendrick I took his advice.

MRS BROADBENT: Oh?

WATTS: Aye. He said I ought to give myself a break from married bliss, have a bachelor's honeymoon, combine business with pleasure, like.

MRS BROADBENT: I don't blame you.

WATTS: Realise my potential. I bet you wish you were coming with me.

MRS BROADBENT: I'll be thinking of you.

WATTS: You do, right. Keep me in the back of your mind.

MRS BROADBENT: Have a nice change.

WATTS: Aye, well, a change is as good as a rest.

MRS BROADBENT: Let me know when you're coming back.

WATTS: Yes. Yes, of course.

(*He takes the hand MRS BROADBENT offers, holds it a moment, then kisses her slowly on the cheek.*)

LENA: Eric. You're keeping him waiting. Eric. Eric.

(*ANNE CLEGG has come through the gate and reached the kissing couple in the doorway.*)

ANNE: Excuse me.

LENA: Eric?

WATTS: I'd better be off. (*He sets off with his case.*)

MRS BROADBENT: Goodbye, Mister Watts.

ANNE: I didn't mean to interrupt.

WATTS: Cheerio.

MRS BROADBENT: *Au revoir.*

ANNE: Ta-ra.

MRS BROADBENT: Can I help in any way?

ANNE: You can if you're Mrs Broadbent. I've come in answer to the advert in the board down the road, for a double room. Is it still vacant?

MRS BROADBENT: I'm afraid it isn't.

ANNE: Ooh no, what a shame. I'm always just too late. Well, I don't know what we're going to do. My husband's coming home tomorrow for the weekend and I promised him I'd have a place by then. He's in the army. He'll be ever so annoyed if we have to stay at my auntie's again. We haven't had our honeymoon yet – ooh it's so complicated, you see my auntie's only got a folding bed that turns into a table to put against a wall – it won't take both of us, so John, my husband, has to sleep on the sofa afterwards. I promised him I'd find a place this weekend.

(*KENDRICK has come downstairs and stands behind MRS BROADBENT.*)

MRS BROADBENT: I'm sorry I can't help you.

ANNE: So am I.

MRS BROADBENT: Good night.

ANNE: Do you know anyone I could try?

MRS BROADBENT: I'm afraid I don't.

KENDRICK: Evening.

ANNE: Good night.

MRS BROADBENT: Oh, doctor – just a moment – I have a message I've been asked to convey to you. Good night Mrs – I'm sorry we can't accommodate you. Would you close the door, doctor please. (*She goes in.*)

ANNE: Good night, then.

KENDRICK: Looking for a room?

ANNE: Yes – a double.

KENDRICK: Come in, close the door and wait. (*He joins MRS BROADBENT in the kitchen.*) What's the message?

MRS BROADBENT: Well, nothing to speak of. Mister Watts. He's taking a busman's holiday on your advice and would I thank you.

KENDRICK: Oh.

MRS BROADBENT: He's going to realise his potential, so we can expect him back tomorrow. There, a cup of tea.

KENDRICK: I can't stop now, I'm late.

MRS BROADBENT: It's sugared.

KENDRICK: The young woman who wanted a double room.

MRS BROADBENT: I told her there wasn't one.

KENDRICK: I told her there was.

MRS BROADBENT: We can't have a newly married couple here. Think of Kevin.

KENDRICK: Think of the rent.

MRS BROADBENT: Fancy getting married with nowhere to live.

KENDRICK: Give them a home.

MRS BROADBENT: I'll have a talk with her if she calls again. Now drink up.

KENDRICK: (*Taking the cup and saucer.*) She's waiting in the hall. (*He goes to the door.*) What's your name?

ANNE: Mrs Clegg.

KENDRICK: Mrs Broadbent, Mrs Clegg. Mrs Broadbent's just made a cup of tea for you. Sugared. She'd like to talk to you about room number four.

ANNE: Ooh, thank you Mrs Broadbent. I haven't had any tea, as a matter of fact. Trailing around looking for a place. You know there isn't one room to let with a double bed in it. All singles or twin divans.

MRS BROADBENT: I'm afraid number four hasn't got a double bed, Mrs Clegg. Mister Watts has the only double in the house.

KENDRICK: He's away for at least a fortnight. Swap the beds over and give Mrs Clegg time to find somewhere else. Alright?

ANNE: Yes. Ooh that'd be marvellous. Would you do that?

MRS BROADBENT: When?

27

ANNE: Well, tomorrow you see. My husband has a weekend pass. It'd be wasted if we had to stay at my auntie's.

KENDRICK: Good night. (*He goes.*)

MRS BROADBENT: Good night.

ANNE: And thank you. He's very nice isn't he.

MRS BROADBENT: He's a very kind gentle man.

ANNE: How much is it?

MRS BROADBENT: Two pounds ten shillings.

ANNE: Yes, that'll be alright.

MRS BROADBENT: Single.

ANNE: Oh.

MRS BROADBENT: Three pounds double occupancy.

ANNE: Only at weekends.

MRS BROADBENT: In advance plus a deposit.

ANNE: Will a pound be alright?

MRS BROADBENT: One pound ten shillings. Fifty per cent. (*Money exchanged, they go to the front door.*)

ANNE: See you tomorrow, then. 'Bout one o'clock.

MRS BROADBENT: Very good, Mrs Clegg.

ANNE: Thanks for the tea.

MRS BROADBENT: Good night.

ANNE: *Au revoir.*

(*She goes. LENA is making her face up. MRS BROADBENT gets sheets from a cupboard. TUBBS is watching TV but not for long. MRS BROADBENT knocks.*)

MRS BROADBENT: I'm sorry to disturb you, Mister Tubbs.

TUBBS: 'S alright, Missus.

MRS BROADBENT: Would you do me a favour?

TUBBS: Aye. What?

MRS BROADBENT: Help me move a double bed upstairs.

TUBBS: Oh. Aye. Hold on.

(*MRS BROADBENT knocks on LENA's door.*)

LENA: Yes. Hello?

MRS BROADBENT: Mrs Watts.

LENA: Who is it? Come in. (*She waits. Nothing happens. She opens the door.*) Oh, hullo. It's you. I thought I heard you knocking. I was just –

MRS BROADBENT: I need your bed for some new tenants, Lena dear. You won't mind a single for a while, will you?

They're very young and not the sort we like to have about the house but, as the doctor says, I must let the rooms.

LENA: Yes of course you must.

MRS BROADBENT: You'll have more space with a single bed. When my Roger was alive we always kept to our own beds, much healthier as well as being more comfortable. More hygienic, too, in some marriages. Up in number four, Mister Tubbs.

TUBBS: What?

MRS BROADBENT: The single to come down. Men these days getting married, very silly of them. They have no idea of security. Roger wouldn't have let me marry him under such circumstances.

LENA: What a shame. I am sorry.

MRS BROADBENT: He's a soldier during the week which isn't too bad but they give him weekend passes, that's why they must have a double bed to enjoy their honeymoon – otherwise they wouldn't have come if I hadn't promised them one big bed. You don't mind? You've passed the honeymoon stage by now I should think.

LENA: Ooh, yes, well passed. We go to sleep some nights as often as not. Eric can read in bed now and wear pyjamas.

MRS BROADBENT: I'll get him a single when he returns.

LENA: I shan't be able to kick him when he snores.

MRS BROADBENT: You'll be able to throw things at him instead.

LENA: H-ooah-ha!

MRS BROADBENT: Would you take the bedding off? (*TUBBS struggles with the single.*) You shouldn't have tried to do it by yourself, Mister Tubbs.

TUBBS: I can manage.

MRS BROADBENT: Good. Well done. I'll help clear the way. (*Confusion.*) You see I need the – eiderdown – Lena's double for a couple move it – moving in – I wouldn't have done it – not on the floor – in normal circumstances – when you've got the mattress – I must get on top –

29

financially essential – to let it – down – the room – hold on – immediately – take the other end –

LENA: He's a soldier and she's a –

MRS BROADBENT: Lampshade – hurt your hand?

TUBBS: And foot.

LENA: A honeymoon bride.

MRS BROADBENT: Don't talk.

LENA: No. Do you mind if I go off to the pictures now, please, the big feature starts –

MRS BROADBENT: No, off you go, Mrs Watts. We'll manage, won't we, Mister Tubbs?

TUBBS: Aye.

MRS BROADBENT: Then you must have a little drink with me.

LENA: Don't get squiffy will you, though.

MRS BROADBENT: Good night, Mrs Watts. I'll leave the bedding for you to make up, alright, dear?

LENA: Yes, won't take me –

TUBBS: Enjoy your picture.

LENA: – a minute or two, I will, cheerio.

MRS BROADBENT: Now all we have to do is take the double up.

TUBBS: Aye.

(*The house becomes a moonlit silhouette as LENA closes the front door behind her. Cinema background music is heard.*)

KENDRICK: And so Lena went to the pictures alone. Deserted. The cool night air, the stillness of the garden, the thought of sleeping in a single bed made her uneasy. She hurried on to the comforting chrome of the Odeon. The music and the flickering warm dark calmed and soothed her.

(*'Around the World In Eighty Days' plays on MRS BROADBENT's console in the corner of her mini-cocktail bar-lounge. The bed moving has been completed.*)

MRS BROADBENT: Thank you, Mister Tubbs, so kind.

TUBBS: Any time, Missus.

MRS BROADBENT: A little whisky?

TUBBS: I see you're insisting.

MRS BROADBENT: Quite right I am. Ginger?

TUBBS: As it is, Missus.

MRS BROADBENT: I wish you wouldn't call me that. Missus. Makes me sound like a landlady.

TUBBS: You are. Mrs Broadbent's too long. Cheers.

MRS BROADBENT: *Skol.*

TUBBS: Very good. Do you mind if I finish it off in my room? I'm missing a programme I wanted to see.

MRS BROADBENT: Of course not. Let me fill you up before you go.

TUBBS: Whoa! Thanks.

MRS BROADBENT: Thank you.

TUBBS: Good night – Mrs B. How's that?

MRS BROADBENT: Better.

(*TUBBS goes to his room.*)

KENDRICK: And so Gabrielle was left alone. Deserted. The cool night air, the stillness of the garden, the quiet of the whole house, the thought of being single in a single bed made her surrender to a self-pitying frustration which consumed her life away. Neither the warmth of the whisky nor the soundtrack she played were enough to soothe her discontent. She went to bed with a thick head. (*Light and music fade as MRS BROADBENT goes upstairs, glass in hand. A tall West Indian, NORTHERN CLEMENT GENTLES, whose ancestors had smuggled rum and sugar into Canada in exchange for grain about the time of the Molasses Act is passing by 305 Marlborough Terrace. LENA is scrabbling for her keys in her handbag in the light from a street lamp. She finds them, drops them and can't find them.*)

GENTLES: Here.

LENA: Thank you.

GENTLES: You been crying.

LENA: I – No – Yes – (*She half laughs.*)

GENTLES: Now you laughing. (*She stops.*) Something wrong?

LENA: I've been to the pictures, have you?

GENTLES: Noa. I pay no mind to pictures.

LENA: I pay two and sixpence.

GENTLES: He-he! The silver screen don't interess me none. How you call yourself?

31

LENA: Eh?

GENTLES: Your name, what your name?

LENA: Lena Watts. Why d'you want to know for?

GENTLES: Jus' like to know, that's all.

LENA: How do you call yourself?

GENTLES: My name Gentles. Northern Clement Gentles.

LENA: That isn't a name, is it? Northern and Gentles?

GENTLES: It my name.

LENA: He! I'm cold, are you?

GENTLES: Me. Noa. I'm real hot. (*He smiles.*)

LENA: You haven't got your coat on.

GENTLES: You like to walk some way with me?

LENA: Ooh, no, I must get in, I'm cold.

GENTLES: Perhaps you like to come home wit' me?

LENA: (*Going to him.*) It's late.

GENTLES: No, it's early.

LENA: What time is it?

GENTLES: Ten – eleven, maybe. It's early.

LENA: It's late for me. I'm usually in bed by now.

GENTLES: So that's good. You have a late night now for once.

LENA: Ooh! I've just remembered I have to make up my bed.

GENTLES: Let me help you. I'm very good at it.

LENA: No, I'm sorry. I must go, Good night. Thank you.
Good night…
(*GENTLES shrugs, makes a splishing noise with his teeth
and strolls on. LENA glances back before entering the sleeping
house. GENTLES sees the light go on in LENA's room. The
curtains and the window are open from earlier in the evening
when LENA called out to the taxi driver. GENTLES
hesitates, then turns back. LENA takes her coat off and starts
to make the bed up. GENTLES moves into the slant of light
that falls on to the grass. He stands by the window. LENA
stills as she sees him. He sits astride the sill. They stay looking
at each other. He swings his leg inside and stands up. He
takes the sheet from her and spreads it like a picnic tablecloth.
LENA passes him a blanket and they carry on making the
bed together. He hands her a pillowcase. She holds it apart at
the top and he fits the pillow into the case. He takes it from*

her and rests it at the head of the bed. He sits there, leans against it and beckons her to him with a move of his head. She goes to him. He tells her to kiss him. Mesmerised, she does and his arm circles her thighs. With his other hand he reaches for the bulb in the lamp and takes it from its socket.)

('Sugar In The Morning', sung by JOHN CLEGG backed by the sound of cutlery and crockery being washed up and disposed of, is heard in the darkness before daylight reveals ANNE and JOHN CLEGG, eight months into their honeymoon. JOHN wears his khaki army trousers, belted so the material below the waistband pleats three inches deep above it. Matching combat-green singlet and socks complete his outfit. ANNE wears an apron to protect her lace-fronted underslip. JOHN is trying to start a portable electric turntable. Dinner is being prepared on a small bedsit Belling cooker.)

ANNE: Aw – don't purrit there, love.

JOHN: Aw – don't purrit there, love. Where would you like it?

ANNE: Won't it go on t'bed?

JOHN: Won't play there. It's not level any more.

ANNE: Well, I don't know. Purrit on t'floor then… Go on, I shall walk on it there.

JOHN: You'd better not.

ANNE: I shall.

JOHN: See what you get if you do.

ANNE: No, give o'er or I'll thump you.

JOHN: Huh-he-ha!

ANNE: I will.

(She holds up a fishslice. JOHN feints with his right hand as if to knock the slice away and delivers a mock blow to her womb with his left.)

Aw – stop it. Move it now, come on love.

JOHN: Come on, love. *(He holds ANNE round the waist.)*

ANNE: Don't you want your dinner? It's burning.

JOHN: Awhugh!

ANNE: We'll be thrown out. Awhugh!

JOHN: Awhugh!

ANNE: Gerroff.

JOHN: Gerroff.

(*ANNE wipes the greasy slice across his cheek. He lets go. She throws a dishcloth at him to wipe his face with, laughing.*)
Aw, Anne.

ANNE: I told you.

JOHN: Aw.

ANNE: Aw. You're still beautiful.

JOHN: You wait while tonight.

ANNE: No hurry.

(*JOHN pulls a suitcase out from under the bed and stands the player on it.*)

JOHN: What do you want?

ANNE: Owt you like.

JOHN: 'Rock-hard Rock' – 'Teddy Boys Picnic' – 'Cry for Me Baby' –

ANNE: 'Ey, put that quiet one on.

JOHN: Err, it's too soppy.

ANNE: Well, I like it.

JOHN: Don't know why you bought it.

ANNE: I like it. Don't you like it honest?

JOHN: Not bad.

ANNE: Don't purrit on if you don't want, love.

JOHN: Special request. Housewives' choice.

(*He plays 'Little Things Mean A Lot'. Picks up an army boot and starts to spit and polish it. ANNE croons to him in a breathy twilight soprano.*)

ANNE: 'Blow me a kiss from across the room,
Say I look nice when I'm not –'

JOHN: You look nice. 'Terch my hair as you pass my chair –'

ANNE: Don't spoil it.

JOHN: (*Sweetly.*) 'Little things mean a lot…' (*He gathers momentum, extending his army-booted hand.*) 'Give me your hand when I've lost the way, Give me your shoulder to cry on – '

ANNE: You should be discovered.

JOHN: Reckon they'd go for me?

ANNE: Course they would.

JOHN: 'Give me your heart to rely on.' The one and only Johnny Ray Clegg. Mobbed by a thousand cats and sexy kittens… Lovely.

ANNE: 'Ey, they better hadn't.

JOHN: Lovely. Five hundred a week. 'Don't have to buy me diamonds or pearls, Champagne, sables or such...'
(*MRS BROADBENT knocks on their door.*)

ANNE: Turn it down. I knew she'd come up

MRS BROADBENT: Are you there, Mister Clegg?

JOHN: Old mother square.

ANNE: Ey, put your shirt on.

JOHN: Like hell, give her a thrill. (*He takes his belt off before showing himself.*) Yes, Mrs Broadbent?

MRS BROADBENT: I'm sorry to disturb you.

ANNE: You didn't.

JOHN: Just interrupt us. (*He buckles up.*)

MRS BROADBENT: I wouldn't have to if you weren't disturbing everybody else. I don't want to spoil your – fun, but you must try and –

JOHN: Be a little quieter.

MRS BROADBENT: Could you, please?

ANNE: Yes, of course, I'm sorry.

MRS BROADBENT: It is Sunday. A day of rest for most of us.

ANNE: We didn't think Mrs Broadbent.

MRS BROADBENT: I'm sure you didn't, dear. No one would dispute that. I have asked you before to consider other people, haven't I?

ANNE: Yes, Mrs –

JOHN: You did, yes.

MRS BROADBENT: There's Mister Tubbs underneath you. I'm sure he thinks the ceiling's coming in on him sometimes. Those army boots are heavy I know. So you will try –

JOHN: And be quiet –

MRS BROADBENT: Otherwise –

JOHN: Very hard, yes.

MRS BROADBENT: If I should let the room next door to this, they wouldn't stay a week.

JOHN: No, who could blame them if –

MRS BROADBENT: I'm glad you understand. Oh, Mrs Clegg, are you there?

ANNE: Yes.

MRS BROADBENT: Would you mind not hanging your washing in front of the window. Doesn't look very nice from the outside, does it?

ANNE: Oh, I'm sorry.

JOHN: Looks very nice from the inside.

MRS BROADBENT: Not from outside, Mister Clegg, it makes the place look – well – slummy and today is Sunday as I reiterate.

ANNE: I'll take them down, Mrs Broadbent.

MRS BROADBENT: Thank you, dear. I don't like to nag. Everything else alright?

JOHN: Fine, thank you.

MRS BROADBENT: You're not too cold up here, undressed like that?

JOHN: No. No. Are you, Anne?

MRS BROADBENT: Good. Must keep him fighting fit for his army duties.

ANNE: Oh, Mrs Broadbent, that reminds me, I'm afraid a castor came off the bed and we can't get it back on again.

JOHN: Yes it did, I had a go but –

MRS BROADBENT: Oh dear, now how did that happen? No. Perhaps it was loosened when it was brought upstairs. I'll have it seen to. Lunch smells nice.

JOHN: She's a good cook.

ANNE: I need to be.

MRS BROADBENT: With a big young man to feed, my word yes. You will remember about the noise.

JOHN: She doesn't hold back.

ANNE: Yes I'll keep him quiet.

JOHN: I'll shut her up, make her wear a gag.

MRS BROADBENT: There's good children.

JOHN: Afternoon.

ANNE: Goodbye Mrs Bro…

(*MRS BROADBENT goes. JOHN and ANNE fold up, convulsed. JOHN takes ANNE's briefs from the light flex washing-line.*)

JOHN: Would you mind not displaying your passion pants in the window. We don't want a queue to form on the pavement.

ANNE: 'Ey, leave 'em alone.

JOHN: 'I'm afraid a castor's come off our bed.'

ANNE: Well, I had to tell her.

>*(JOHN goes behind her, stretching the briefs across her groin.*
>*He holds them in place, digging his fingers into her pelvis.)*

JOHN: The bosun's grip.

ANNE: Now behave, for the last time. I said I'd keep you quiet and I will. (*She faces him.*) Put one of these in your mouth and be quiet for a while.

>*(They kiss, each holding both plates. JOHN puts them on the*
>*table and sits, tucking the briefs into his vest as a napkin.*
>*ANNE brings lemonade, pours two fizzing drinks, snatches*
>*the briefs and sits.)*

>For what you are about to receive I hope you're truly grateful.

JOHN: I'll say that to you tonight when I put the light off.

ANNE: So long as we take precautions. I don't want gettin' pregnant for a bit at my age.

JOHN: You'll get what's coming.

ANNE: I shan't.

JOHN: Oh, resistance. I'll need reinforcements.

ANNE: I want to keep my figure so you can hold on to my hips with your vice-like bosun's grip.

JOHN: More to get stuck in to.

ANNE: I don't want to get all fat and horrible like her downstairs. Poor Lena.

JOHN: I wouldn't run off like he did.

ANNE: I shan't risk it.

JOHN: Fat chance. (*He sings the first few lines of 'Sugar in the Morning'.*) Oh – Have they found him yet?

ANNE: They're still looking as far as I know.

>*(They eat. LENA appears in her room, eight months pregnant,*
>*moving cautiously, like a penguin on ice. A telephone rings in*
>*MRS BROADBENT's kitchen. KENDRICK appears on the*
>*pavement. During his speech MRS BROADBENT answers*
>*the telephone, then goes to LENA's room. She and LENA move*
>*to the front door and wait to welcome a prodigal ERIC.)*

KENDRICK: Some months after Eric had left on what should have been a lifelong holiday, Mrs Broadbent's suspicions that another Watts was on the way were confirmed and she took it upon herself to trace the runaway Eric so that he could take it upon himself to fulfil his parental responsibilities. Authorities were informed, and after a nationwide search organised by a daily newspaper in collaboration with the police and the missing persons squad, Mister Watts was found on the Isle of Wight and told the happy news he was to be a father before Christmas. They gave him a one-way ticket to Marlborough Terrace. Overjoyed with despair, he put himself on a slow train back to his pregnant wife.

(*ERIC, with luggage and umbrella, appears.*)

His boss, magnanimous and short of engineers, took him back into the firm and offered him a reduction in salary. He accepted it and the deceptive situation without grace or gratitude. His nightmare had become reality and it was terrible to behold.

(*MRS BROADBENT and LENA are on the doorstep to greet him. The light fades as they enter.*)

(*KEVIN does his homework in the kitchen. GRANNY SILK sets off for the lavatory. LENA comes from her room carrying refuse, ashamed to be seen. She goes to the dustbins round the back. The lid clatters. The baby is expected very soon. A kettle starts to whistle. MRS BROADBENT makes tea for three and checks the time. KENDRICK puts his coat on, reading a book. He picks it up, and goes downstairs. MRS BROADBENT puts an empty milk bottle on the front step. She hears KENDRICK coming and dallies, checking her reflection.*)

MRS BROADBENT: Just off?

KENDRICK: Just off.

MRS BROADBENT: You're in good time.

KENDRICK: It's our busy night.

MRS BROADBENT: Cup of tea before you tend the sick?

KENDRICK: No, thanks.

MRS BROADBENT: I've just made one.

KENDRICK: I've just had two.

MRS BROADBENT: Oh – would you post two letters for me on your way?

KENDRICK: I don't pass a post office.

MRS BROADBENT: A pillar-box will do. There's one by the bus-stop. Will you do that for me?

KENDRICK: Have you got them?

MRS BROADBENT: In the kitchen.

KENDRICK: The post's gone.

KEVIN: Can I watch TV, Mummy?

MRS BROADBENT: Not tonight darling.

KENDRICK: If you post them tomorrow they'd still arrive Monday.

MRS BROADBENT: Of course. Here they are. Shame you have to work on Saturday evenings.

KENDRICK: Our best time, lots of good opportunities to practise. It's the one night of the week when you can't ignore the ordinary man in the street. Saturday. When he enjoys himself. Plenty of black eyes, broken jaws, lips to stitch and dislocated elbows to reset. Cosh boys cosh, fractured skulls – their girlfriends get drunk and disorderly in the back streets or in the backs of cars involved in smash-ups, multiple lacerations, fractured ribs, the occasional miscarriage, haemorrhage, suicide attempts are popular after midnight, slit wrists or bottles of aspirin swallowed with disinfectant, usually jealous or jilted lovers, stomach pump if they're lucky, otherwise… Saturday night – Sunday morning, climax of the working week. Eight hours of valuable experience in Emergency.

MRS BROADBENT: Thank you for taking my letters.

KENDRICK: Good night.

MRS BROADBENT: Looks as though it might rain. Good night. (*She watches KENDRICK go.*) Finished your homework, Kevin?

KEVIN: I have nearly. Three more sums, then I'll have done.

MRS BROADBENT: Then you will have finished.

KEVIN: Then I will have finished doing it.

MRS BROADBENT: When you have finished you may watch the television for ten minutes. Then you must go to bed.

KEVIN: Thank you – Mummy.

MRS BROADBENT: Good boy.

(*KENDRICK rings the front door bell. GRANNY SILK comes from the bathroom, down into the kitchen and switches on the television.*)

Forgotten your keys again?

KENDRICK: Afraid so.

MRS BROADBENT: You overwork your brain too much in other directions, worrying about your exams, that's what it is. You've been at it for ten months now without a break. I'll lend you mine to save you going all the way upstairs again. Come in a moment.

KENDRICK: It won't take a minute to get them.

MRS BROADBENT: I wish you studied as hard as Doctor Kendrick, Kevin. You'd pass with flying colours then, I'm sure.

KENDRICK: I haven't got a television set to seduce me.

MRS BROADBENT: Hear that Kevin? (*She switches it off.*)

GRANNY SILK: You want a new roll up there.

MRS BROADBENT: Have a cup of tea now you're here.

(*She pours it.*)

GRANNY SILK: I said –

MRS BROADBENT: I know, I've left one out.

GRANNY SILK: I just switched it on.

MRS BROADBENT: Mother?

GRANNY SILK: What time is it? Yes, I'll have one. Mustn't miss –

KEVIN: Half past seven, Grandma.

GRANNY SILK: Mustn't miss the ten to. Yes, I will have a cup of tea.

MRS BROADBENT: Here we are. (*Giving tea to KENDRICK.*) I put two in.

GRANNY SILK: Haven't you done those sums yet?

MRS BROADBENT: Are you catching the ten to?

KEVIN: I've nearly done.

GRANNY SILK: You've always nearly done.

KEVIN: Nearly done finished doing.

GRANNY SILK: You're too slow.

KENDRICK: I've missed the half past.

MRS BROADBENT: Better to be slow and accurate.

KENDRICK: I'll get the twenty to.

GRANNY SILK: He takes too long.

MRS BROADBENT: Piece of cake, Mother?

KEVIN: I'm quicker at English.

MRS BROADBENT: Go on with your work, Kevin dear.

GRANNY SILK: Yes, I'll have a piece. What's on telewishun?

MRS BROADBENT: Television.

GRANNY SILK: So you ought to be quicker at English if
your mother has owt to do wi' it. She talks war na'
Queen, doesn't she?
(*KEVIN laughs.*)
Don't you? Hi-hee! Caraway. Which bus did you say you
were catching – er…?

KENDRICK: Twenty to.

GRANNY SILK: Wait for me and go on ten to. He-hee,
aye, you tried to get in while I were up there, di'n't ya?

MRS BROADBENT: Mother.

GRANNY SILK: Good job I put bolt on. Look well if he'd
copped me, hi-hee!

KENDRICK: I must catch the next one. Thank you for the –

MRS BROADBENT: Pleasure. Leave it on the hall table.

KENDRICK: I will.

GRANNY SILK: Aren't you going to escort me then?

KENDRICK: Sorry, Mrs Silk. Another time. Good night.
(*He goes.*)

GRANNY SILK: Righto.

MRS BROADBENT: Say Good night, Kevin.

KEVIN: Good night.

MRS BROADBENT: You shouldn't have to be asked. Good
night.

GRANNY SILK: What sort of a doctor is he?

MRS BROADBENT: Casualty Officer in Charge at the
Infirmary.

GRANNY SILK: In charge.

MRS BROADBENT: He's studying to be a Surgical Registrar.

GRANNY SILK: Who's that?

MRS BROADBENT: Two months to go before his examination.

GRANNY SILK: How long's he been here?

MRS BROADBENT: Last year, June, July, nearly ten months. I don't see much of him. He has a little chat now and then. I try to encourage him to – he's shy. Yes. He's shy. Try to take his mind away from his studies a little now and then when I can. He studies all the time.

GRANNY SILK: Like our Kevin. There's too much of this swotting. No good for you too much of it, is it, Kevin lad.

MRS BROADBENT: It's for everyone else's good and benefit in the long run. Leave that now, Kevin.

KEVIN: But I haven't –

MRS BROADBENT: Books away for tonight, darling. Up to bed now. I'll wake you early in the morning and you can finish them then.

KEVIN: But you said I could watch television Mummy.

MRS BROADBENT: It distracts you from your work, come along.

GRANNY SILK: Let him watch it for a bit if he wants to.

MRS BROADBENT: You can read your book in bed.

GRANNY SILK: It'll do him no harm, na' you either.

KEVIN: Can I, Mummy?

MRS BROADBENT: Not tonight. Off you go. Say Good night to Grandma.

KEVIN: Mum.

MRS BROADBENT: Kevin.

GRANNY SILK: Now do as your mother says, Kevin.

KEVIN: Good night, Grandma. (*He kisses her.*)

MRS BROADBENT: Brush your teeth. And say your prayers.

KEVIN: Alright.

MRS BROADBENT: Good night, darling.

GRANNY SILK: Dearie me, y'aven't sugared it. I'll miss that ten to.

MRS BROADBENT: You have ten minutes. Here you are.
(*She adds the sugar.*)

GRANNY SILK: I'm not rushing for nobody.

MRS BROADBENT: Catch the next one. It doesn't matter
now there's no one here to listen to you.

GRANNY SILK: Why be so uppity with him for? He'd
done nothing. Sending him off like that.

MRS BROADBENT: I don't like him in the room when
you are, mother.

GRANNY SILK: Meaning?

MRS BROADBENT: I mean you can stay as long you like
– care to now that Kevin isn't in the room to hear you
deliberately distorting –

GRANNY SILK: Distorting! Me?

MRS BROADBENT: You undo all the good I try to do.

GRANNY SILK: What good's that?

MRS BROADBENT: Encouraging him to disobey me.
I know he never would, but it doesn't make it any easier
for me you –

GRANNY SILK: When have I –

MRS BROADBENT: I can't afford elocution lessons as
well and if he continues to listen to you he'll need
them. I spend all my money sending him to a private
school as Roger wanted so he'll grow up to be the kind
of man he would have been proud to call his son and
you speak to him as though he were a common boy
with council house origins and no more ambitions than
they have.

GRANNY SILK: John Ormes's lad's going –

MRS BROADBENT: Kevin's no son of John Ormes. He's
Roger Broadbent's son and he's going to be something.

GRANNY SILK: Yes. Stuck up. A young prig you can't do
owt with if you go on. Marster K Broadbent, three-ho-
fayve, Morlborough Terris.

MRS BROADBENT: He's going to be somebody and not
in this town. Mr Pond has high hopes. He says he's a
'sensitive child, artistically inclined and very susceptible
to outside influences.'

GRANNY SILK: Like me.

MRS BROADBENT He has 'great personal charm for a
    boy of his age.'

GRANNY SILK: What's his lucky number?

MRS BROADBENT: He can be anything he wants to be,
    like Roger could.

GRANNY SILK: Well, if he wants to be a playboy I hope
    I'm alive to say I told you so. Pass us my coat quick.
    You're mad for me to miss this bus.
    (*Silence.*)
    I'd better not come again, then, is that it?

MRS BROADBENT: I never said that.

GRANNY SILK: All t'same if you had, I shouldn't have
    taken any notice. Somebody's got to roughen him out a
    bit or he'll grow up to be a pansy. We don't want that.
    Neither would Roger. Don't be so silly, Gabby love, let
    him behave like a normal lad now and then.

MRS BROADBENT: I know what I'm doing. I'm his
    mother, not you. You were my mother and you made a
    mess of it. I'm what I am now in spite of you, not
    because. You've nothing to be proud of as a parent. Aunt
    Mabel brought me up and paid for me to go to boarding
    school. Don't you want your tea?

GRANNY SILK: No, I don't.

MRS BROADBENT: See you next Tuesday, then.

GRANNY SILK: Yes, you will.
    (*MRS BROADBENT answers a knocking on the kitchen door.*)

MRS BROADBENT: Hello, Lena dear.

LENA: Hello. I haven't got a shilling, have you?

MRS BROADBENT: Stay there.

GRANNY SILK: How are you, love?

LENA: Oh, I'm alright. Look a mess, don't I?

GRANNY SILK: You look alright, love, very well. When is it?

LENA: Next week but I don't know.

GRANNY SILK: You ought to lay down. Keep your
    strength up.

MRS BROADBENT: You're strong enough, aren't you, Mrs
    Watts? I'm going to study you when the baby's born to
    see if I can't pick up a few tips on motherhood and

parenting. You have a lot to offer the future generation of our country, I'm sure. One shilling.

LENA: Thank you. That's not a shilling change. I'm tuppence short –

MRS BROADBENT: Of a shilling as the saying goes. Yes, you are.

LENA: I'll see you get it.

MRS BROADBENT: So will I.

LENA: Tomorrow. (*She goes.*)

MRS BROADBENT: Good night.

GRANNY SILK: Goodbye then, love. Don't take no notice of me, I'm naughty, take no notice. Just see me to t'door. I mun hurry up. I said I wouldn't rush, didn't I. Right. Night. Thank you.

(*She toddles off waving to her daughter, who is standing on the porch before going back inside, pouring a whisky and staring at her reflection. WATTS is slumped in his chair, reading.*)

KENDRICK: Poor Granny Silk. She missed the ten to bus by a good four yards but managed to hit a motor cycle coming in the opposite direction head on. There goes the bus now – and here comes the bike. If the fool had dipped his headlamp she might have stood a chance – (*The accident is heard, the headlamps' beam comes to rest along the pavement.*) but I suppose it would have been more painful for her if he had. As it is, she's one less to care about. One less to drain our sympathy. They brought her to Emergency in the ambulance. She died on the way. What makes you sick to death at accidents is the ordinary man and woman in the street who have a little get-together, a sort of whip-round to gather a group to look at the blood. The sounding horn, the screeching brakes, the fragile scream had made a few people stop and stare. Alert for once, concerned, frightened, even compassionate – but only because they'd seen an accident. For a flickering moment they're aware of the acute existence of life. Mrs Broadbent wasn't with her Scotch and mirror image. Kevin had dropped off to sleep with the light on reading Biggles.

And in another part of the house on that evening two months ago, Mister Watts was reading too, the erotic bits in a novel by Erskine Caldwell. God, those phrases. How they teased him. He read them over and over, squirming into his chair. Sometimes he'd take an optimistic glance across the room at his pregnant wife, then turn back frustrated to the easy painful pleasure of the printed porn. Poor Eric Watts.

LENA: We owe her tuppence.

WATTS: 'Tight and easy, like putting a nail in a plank. Fit like a nail in a plank.'

LENA: You what? You're not going to start hammering at this time, Eric? Kid's in bed.

WATTS: No.

LENA: That's alright then. You don't want your supper yet, do you?

WATTS: No.

LENA: I think I've got a headache, have you?

WATTS: No.

LENA: It's this gas fire, you know. Fumes. Shall I turn it off?

WATTS: No.

LENA: But it's giving me a headache.

WATTS: I'm glad.

LENA: Now there's no need to talk like that, Eric. I can't help having a headache coming on, can I?

WATTS: I suppose not.

LENA: Course I can't. What is it you're reading?

WATTS: It's a book about sex.

LENA: I wish I could read.

WATTS: Would it make any difference? If it would I'd teach you.

LENA: There's no need to talk like that. I can't help –

WATTS: No, you can't help.

LENA: It's not my fault is it?

WATTS: No.

LENA: Well don't shout at me Eric. It's not my fault, not my fault –

WATTS: I didn't say it was, it's my fault, it'll be my fault if the brat isn't fed and clothed and sent to school and given pocket money and brought up in a happy home with a happy bed-sitting family background.

LENA: We can afford it, Eric.

WATTS: We?

LENA: I can still go to the school canteen.

WATTS: I can't afford it. I can't afford to spend all I've saved for the last six years on prams, nappies, orange juice, schoolbags –

LENA: You sound as though I'm going to have twins.

WATTS: I can't afford it. (*He throws his book away.*)

LENA: You'd only have spent the money on something foolish.

WATTS: What could be more foolish than you as a mother?

LENA: I'll do my best, Eric. I'm sorry, Eric. I'll stop smoking and going to the pictures.

WATTS: And where are we going to live? We can't stay on here. It's not fair on Mrs Broadbent, like she says.

(*MRS BROADBENT knocks on their door.*)

MRS BROADBENT: Could I see you a moment Mister Watts please.

LENA: Were we making a noise?

MRS BROADBENT: It's alright, Mrs Watts. I won't keep him a minute.

(*WATTS leaves the room and joins MRS BROADBENT in the hall. LENA picks up the book and turns the pages as though reading it – upside down.*)

Was she being difficult again?

WATTS: She was.

MRS BROADBENT: I thought she must be when I heard you raising your voice.

WATTS: I was sitting in there quietly reading a good book when she –

MRS BROADBENT: What were you reading?

WATTS: A book on engineering – from work.

MRS BROADBENT: You'd think Lena would have the sense to leave you in peace when you're studying. You ought to have a room apart from her.

WATTS: A hundred miles.

MRS BROADBENT: Aha-ha. You are terrible.

WATTS: Do you think so?

MRS BROADBENT: I know what it must be like for you, night after night. An intelligent man like you with no one to talk sensibly to. I try to help. Perhaps I interfere too much sometimes…

WATTS: Oh no, never think that. I'm always glad to see you. You came in at the right moment just now, I should have hit her if she'd gone on much longer.

MRS BROADBENT: I should have waited. I'd like to see you hit someone. I don't think you ever would.

WATTS: I felt like hitting her.

MRS BROADBENT: You're worried about her, aren't you, Mister Watts.

WATTS: A bit.

MRS BROADBENT: I'm sorry to add to your troubles but you do understand I can't have you staying here when the baby arrives. The other tenants. And Kevin, he is so sensitive. Babies, cry don't they. I shall be sorry to see you go. Have you managed to find a place?

WATTS: No, not yet.

MRS BROADBENT: I found this little jacket this afternoon. It used to be Kevin's. Do have it.

WATTS: That's very thoughtful. Thank you, Mrs Broadbent.

MRS BROADBENT: Have you got a pram?

WATTS: No, not yet.

MRS BROADBENT: Well, a friend of mine has one. I've spoken to her and she says you can have it.

WATTS: That's very good. One thing less.

MRS BROADBENT: For five pounds. Very reasonable, isn't it?

WATTS: Yes.

MRS BROADBENT: I told her I felt sure you'd have it. She wheeled it over this afternoon. It's in the cellar.

WATTS: Very kind of her and you.

MRS BROADBENT: Only too pleased to be able to help you, Mister Watts, you know that. Would you like to see it?

WATTS: Of course.

MRS BROADBENT: I'll lead the way. The steps are narrow and tricky and the light's at the bottom. It's coffee-coloured with a nigger-brown hood.
(*Noises in the dark before they appear in the cellar. MRS BROADBENT, torch in hand, pulls the pram close to the hanging bulb.*)
It's in very good condition, don't you think?

WATTS: It is. Very good indeed. It's worth five pounds.
I could paint the framework up a bit.

MRS BROADBENT: I think I have some beigey-tan paint over here somewhere.

WATTS: I can get brushes from work.

MRS BROADBENT: I have a few but they're not very –
you could soak them in sugar soap.

WATTS: Don't bother – I'll get some from work.

MRS BROADBENT: What are you hoping for, boy or girl, Mister Watts?

WATTS: I haven't given it much thought. I suppose I hope it's a girl – no – I think a boy. If it's a girl it might be like Lena.

MRS BROADBENT: And if it's a boy he'll be like you.

WATTS: He wouldn't be very handsome.

MRS BROADBENT: Oh, you're too modest. You're not at all bad-looking in this light.

WATTS: It's the light makes you say so.

MRS BROADBENT: You've nothing to worry about. Who would you like the baby to look like if it were a girl?

WATTS: If it's a girl?

MRS BROADBENT: Some film star, I suppose.

WATTS: I don't put much faith in a woman's looks. What they are is more important to a man if he's any sort of a man at all.

MRS BROADBENT: You know you sounded like my – like Roger then.

WATTS: A voice from the dead, you mean?

MRS BROADBENT: No... Ah, here's the beigey-cream.

WATTS: Good, that'll be alright. If she's as kind and nice as you when she grows up, she won't go far wrong.

MRS BROADBENT: Nice of you to say so. But I thought you hoped she would be a boy?

WATTS: I do, did, either way, doesn't worry me.

MRS BROADBENT: I'm glad.

WATTS: I expect it'll have a skin on top.

MRS BROADBENT: I wanted a girl and a boy, but there wasn't time. Roger died so suddenly. He just lived to see Kevin christened at...before he...

WATTS: Hey now, come on, you mustn't cry about a thing like that after all this time. (*He takes MRS BROADBENT to him.*)

MRS BROADBENT: Not really crying. I'm as hard as nails.

WATTS: You're soft and sweet, my dear...

MRS BROADBENT: Don't talk like that or I shall cry. No need to tell lies. I'm alright now. Let's get the lid off. Here's a screw driver.

WATTS: It's been on a long time. I wasn't telling lies you know.

MRS BROADBENT: Then you'd no business to talk like that at all if you weren't lying.

WATTS: Yes, you're quite right. Yes, it has got a skin on it.

MRS BROADBENT: No, it was my fault. I shouldn't have been so silly in the first place. I've been in a bad mood all day today, you'll be going and I have so many rooms vacant. I had an argument with Mother tonight and she'd done nothing really. Come along, you might as well leave that down here.

WATTS: You're the boss.

MRS BROADBENT: I'm not. I don't want to be. I don't know what I'd do without you, all of you about the place sometimes, you're all a great nuisance.

WATTS: You do too much.

MRS BROADBENT: Not enough. You go first. I know my way in the dark.

(*ANNE is at the foot of the stairs, her hair in pins. WATTS and MRS BROADBENT reappear. WATTS says good night to MRS BROADBENT at the door of her kitchen, nods to ANNE and goes to his room.*)

ANNE: Good evening, have you seen – oh, there you are. Have you got a shilling for two sixpences, please, for the meter?

MRS BROADBENT: Afraid not, Mrs Clegg. Mrs Watts took the only one I had earlier this evening.

ANNE: Oh dear. I want to dry my hair. 'Spect I'll have to go out. I put one in tonight already. I thought that'd be enough.

MRS BROADBENT: You won't have to go out. I can open the meter. Ask Mister Tubbs first, though – he might have one to spare. Tap on his door.

ANNE: Right. Thank you.

(*She goes to TUBBS' door, and knocks. MRS BROADBENT goes back into her kitchen. WATTS has entered his room.*)

LENA: You've been a long time. Was she annoyed?

WATTS: No, no, she's been showing me a pram. I've bought it. It's in the cellar.

LENA: Ooh, Eric, is it a big one?

WATTS: Medium. Independent sprung carriage.

LENA: Was it a lot of money?

WATTS: Ten pounds.

LENA: Ooh, I say, Eric.

WATTS: Are you pleased?

LENA: Ooh, yes I am, right pleased.

WATTS: Let's hope the baby likes it. She gave me this too.

LENA: Aah, a little jacket.

WATTS: He'll need more than one. (*He looks at LENA knitting, five ounces of dropped stitches.*) Did you finish the little bootees?

LENA: This is the little bootees. I had a lot more wool left over, so I thought I'd make, like, little leggings, you know – stockings.

WATTS: We'd better go and buy a few bits of things on Saturday.

LENA: Ooh yes, Eric.

(*TUBBS has had to get out of bed. His TV adds to the noise. MRS BROADBENT comes out of her kitchen.*)

MRS BROADBENT: Did you knock hard enough dear? I'm sure he's in.

ANNE: I think he must have heard.

MRS BROADBENT: (*Knocking hard and calling.*) Are you there, Mister Tubbs?

TUBBS: (*Stubbing his toe.*) Owookristphughcoughshite.

MRS BROADBENT: He's in.

TUBBS: Alright, yes, I'm coming. I was in bed.

MRS BROADBENT: Mister Tubbs, please, you shouldn't come out into the hall in your pyjamas.

TUBBS: Nay, Missus.

MRS BROADBENT: I thought you knew better.

TUBBS: I'm sorry Mrs B, but –

MRS BROADBENT: Put something on if you must argue out here.

TUBBS: I said I'm sorry, but –

MRS BROADBENT: What sort of house do you think we'd have if everyone paraded around and about in their pyjamas?

(*The front doorbell rings.*)

Into your room, please.

(*TUBBS obeys; ANNE follows. MRS BROADBENT opens the front door.*)

Oh, it's you, doctor. Left your keys at the hospital?

KENDRICK: I'm afraid –

MRS BROADBENT: You'll leave them in a patient one day. Have they given you the night off? What is it?

KENDRICK: Your mother. Your mother was knocked down by a motor cycle this evening. She suffered severe injuries to the skull and spine. She had gas in the ambulance to numb the pain but she was dead on arrival. I signed the certificate.

ANNE: (*Calling.*) It's alright, Mrs Broadbent – he had one. Thank you very much.

MRS BROADBENT: (*To ANNE.*) Don't bother. I'll attend to it. (*To herself.*) Oh. So, Mother's dead.

ANNE: Anything wrong?

MRS BROADBENT: No. Good night, Mrs Clegg.

(*ANNE goes. KENDRICK pours brandy from a flask into the cap.*)

KENDRICK: Swig of brandy.

MRS BROADBENT: Thank you. Unpleasant job for you to do.

KENDRICK: I'm glad I was there.

MRS BROADBENT: How long before she –

KENDRICK: Three, four minutes at the most. The morphia.

MRS BROADBENT: Four minutes isn't long to die.

KENDRICK: Long enough.

MRS BROADBENT: You must have seen a lot more suffering than that.

KENDRICK: At the hospital. At least people are more alive when they're suffering. They can't help noticing it. Life, I mean. A patient walks in, is wheeled or carried in. They might have cut a finger off or burnt their foot or they might have cancer but whatever the reason for being under a hospital roof they're aware of their surroundings and other people. They read all the notices on the corridor walls – Orthopaedic Fracture Clinic Urgent Blood X-Ray Isolation Ward No Smoking Please Return Your Crutches Here Others Need Them – and they look at the faces of the other patients, of the nurses and the doctors and the cleaners and the porters and they see them, they're in touch with their thoughts and feelings in a way that makes them rare. When friends and relations visit, their presence is noticed and yet, in a street, on a train, in a cinema, theatre or shop or on your own front doorstep, people don't care about each other at all. They're alive but they're oblivious to it. How do you achieve this apathy towards the universe, Mrs Broadbent? I wish I could learn.

MRS BROADBENT: What were you saying?

KENDRICK: I was saying – thinking – You take your mother's death very calmly.

MRS BROADBENT: Thank you. Your sympathy's a great help.

KENDRICK: Don't upset yourself.

MRS BROADBENT: I'll do my best.

KENDRICK: She's one less to care about.

MRS BROADBENT: One less to love me. *Skol.* I'll get my coat. (*She goes inside.*)

KENDRICK: Cheers. (*He screws the top back on the flask, steps forward and looks up into the night sky.*) She said it might rain.

(MRS BROADBENT returns. KENDRICK opens her umbrella and holds it over her. She links her arm in his as they walk off into the darkness. The house joins the shadows as the light filters away into the rain.)

End of Act One.

ACT TWO

A church bell clangs to rally a congregation for ten o'clock. The coffee-coloured pram stands on the daisied lawn, the baby in it is softly crying. The sun shines. KENDRICK comes through the front door, checks the baby in the pram and goes off to buy the Sunday papers. MR TUBBS opens his curtains, puts his coat on over his pyjamas before going to collect his News of the World *and half pint of milk from the front doorstep. A mop appears from the CLEGGS' window. ANNE is at the other end shaking it. She wears an apron over her undies. She leans out and picks off the pieces of fluff that remain, letting them fall on to the lawn below. JOHN, apparently naked, attacks her from behind. ANNE cries out in fond protest but she can't let go of the mop to fight him off – and now it's too late for she can feel the warm unshaven skin about his lips on her throat. He reaches out and takes the mop handle, slamming the window down onto it causing it to stick out at right angles, rigid like a flagpole. ANNE pulls his hair with one hand and closes the curtains jealously. They get back into bed. MRS BROADBENT is heard calling for KEVIN inside the house. The front door opens and KEVIN appears in his Sunday School best. He carries a bible and wears a black band round his sleeve. MRS BROADBENT wears a black jersey suit. She stands on the top step.*

MRS BROADBENT: Don't lose your collection.
KEVIN: No, Mummy.
MRS BROADBENT: Come straight home.
KEVIN: Yes, Mummy.
MRS BROADBENT: Be careful crossing the road.
KEVIN: Look right, look left, look right again.
    (*He looks in the pram as he passes. The baby cries louder. MRS BROADBENT goes inside and knocks on the WATTS' door. KEVIN puts his glasses on as though they would double up for earplugs.*)
LENA: (*Inside the room.*) Yes, hullo?
MRS BROADBENT: Only me – Mrs Watts.
LENA: Who is it? Come in.
WATTS: OPEN IT!

LENA: Oh. (*She opens the door.*)
MRS BROADBENT: Gwendolyn's crying again, Mrs Watts.
LENA: I thought she were. She never stops, does she?
WATTS: I'll go.
LENA: Give her a dummy.
MRS BROADBENT: Lovely day, Mister Watts.
WATTS: Yes.
(*KENDRICK returns, reading a Sunday paper.*)
KENDRICK: Good morning, Kevin.
KEVIN: Hello.
KENDRICK: Sunday School?
KEVIN: Yes.
(*WATTS comes out with a baby's dummy.*)
WATTS: Morning.
KENDRICK: How are you getting on?
WATTS: Mustn't grumble. (*He goes to the pram.*)
KENDRICK: Why not?
WATTS: Eh?
KENDRICK: Why not grumble? Complain. It's not illegal.
    Well, have you?
WATTS: Oh, yes. (*He silences the baby with the dummy.*)
KENDRICK: Well, have you?
WATTS: What?
KENDRICK: Got something to grumble about?
WATTS: Plenty. (*He rocks the pram.*)
KENDRICK: What?
WATTS: My feet for one thing. I must have walked down
    every street in this town in the last two weeks, I have,
    looking for another place.
KENDRICK: I didn't know you were moving.
WATTS: Have to. With the baby you see. Should have
    moved before she was born you see really like, quite
    understandable, but couldn't find a place. Mrs Broadbent's
    given us another week. Plenty of rooms, lots of places
    vacant, but not with the girl, they won't have a baby in
    the house, they won't let them with kids. There was one
    place that took couples with kids but they only took
    Buddhists and non-Europeans, so what can you do?
KENDRICK: No Irish.

WATTS: Too white. (*To the baby.*) We're too white, aren't we? Yes you are, too pink and lovely. Looks as though we'll have to sell you to the highest bidder, put you in an auction and knock you down. Looks as though we'll have to buy a place. But I don't want to spend my money, I don't want to, I don't. I don't want. I want to keep it. Keep it for when she's older, when she's growing up, that's when she'll need it... Awh...he doesn't want to hear my grumbles, does he? No he doesn't – a-boo-boo-bo –

KENDRICK: No, you're right. Tell them to Gwendolyn.

WATTS: Hoh, she never stops grumbling herself, do you?

KENDRICK: Who wouldn't. Forced to lie on her back all day. You can walk, sit down, stand up, hop, jump or skip and run whenever you want.

WATTS: Oh yes. Lovely day, isn't it.

KENDRICK: Yes. You can't help noticing it.

WATTS: Roses chuck out a smell, don't they?

KENDRICK: They do.

WATTS: Privet's a bit wild, though. Could do with a short back and sides.

KENDRICK: And thinning out on top.

WATTS: Like me.

KENDRICK: Why don't you have a go?

WATTS: Mrs Broadbent likes to keep them tall. Says it stops passers-by from being inquisitive.

KENDRICK: Doesn't say much for their curiosity.

WATTS: Years since this garden was touched. I mow the lawn in summer but that's all. I planted this lawn you know, dug it all up, set seed. Made a good job of it. Lovely lawn first year. Seven or eight years ago I did it.

LENA: (*Calling from the window.*) Eric, would you go to Wyatts for a pint of milk, love.

WATTS: Another?

LENA: Ah well, it's just boiled over, I've boiled it over, a panful over on t' stove, ooh and it has made a mess. Don't come in look, stay there. Here's your coat, I'm passing it. Have you got some money?

WATTS: Unless you've emptied the pockets.

LENA: Oow, saying things like that, I haven't touched –

WATTS: Anything else?

LENA: No, that's all. Get me ten Woodbines. Five then.

(WATTS goes and KENDRICK enters the house. He knocks on the kitchen door. MRS BROADBENT is preparing vegetables and wears a large apron over her mourning garb, plastic cuffs round her forearms and gloves.)

MRS BROADBENT: Oh, good morning doctor. Isn't it a lovely morning?

KENDRICK: You've noticed it too.

MRS BROADBENT: Come in. Excuse the mess. Everything alright? Aren't you studying today?

KENDRICK: I thought I'd give it a rest.

MRS BROADBENT: Doesn't do any harm to relax now and then. When is it, the examination?

KENDRICK: Four weeks.

MRS BROADBENT: Close. Goodness. Perhaps you'd better study after all. I'm always tell – was always telling Mother how much time you spent locked away in your room studying. I get quite concerned about you sometimes, wondering whether you're having enough to eat. Still, you've got to keep at it to get anywhere these days. That's what I tell Kevin. He takes his exams next week. I tell him the same. He must study and do his homework if he's to get through. Cup of coffee as you're taking the day off from your books?

KENDRICK: I haven't had breakfast yet.

MRS BROADBENT: I knew you didn't have regular meals. Have a bacon sandwich.

KENDRICK: No –

MRS BROADBENT: Toast. Alright? I've put it on now so you can't refuse. Black?

KENDRICK: Toast?

MRS BROADBENT: Coffee.

KENDRICK: White.

(MRS BROADBENT puts milk on to heat.)

MRS BROADBENT: Won't take a minute. It's soluble.

KENDRICK: No grounds for complaint, then.

MRS BROADBENT: O-ha-ah. What are you planning to do instead of your studies?

KENDRICK: I thought I might work in the garden if you don't mind.

MRS BROADBENT: Mind? Goodness no. It hasn't been touched for years. Mister Watts turned the soil over and planted lawn seed the first year he was here. He didn't do a very good job, it took ages to grow green all over and the seed we planted was the...

KENDRICK: I wasn't thinking of anything as strenuous as digging. I thought I might do some pruning. Got any shears?

MRS BROADBENT: Oh yes, in the cellar. I don't know what they're like, they haven't been used for –

KENDRICK: I thought I'd trim the hedge.

MRS BROADBENT: Yes. I don't think they're very sharp... You mean the privets at the front?

KENDRICK: Yes. They've taken over. They need cutting down to size.

MRS BROADBENT: You know, I let them grow on purpose.

KENDRICK: Why?

MRS BROADBENT: To stop people looking in.

KENDRICK: Let them have a stare if they want. Why frustrate them?

MRS BROADBENT: Privet's for privacy.

KENDRICK: What happens in the winter when the leaves blow down the road? People can see in then.

MRS BROADBENT: They don't – blow down the road. It's evergreen, *ligustrum ovalifolium,* better than *vulgare sempivirens* or *italicum.* It's from Japan.

KENDRICK: If anyone was really curious all they need do is sit upstairs on a thirty-four bus and ride past the gate. Get the full picture for the price of a ticket. Anyway, from this side you can't see what's going on either, any more than they can from theirs. You're cutting off your view to spite your curiosity and mind your own business. So if I trim them down a bit everybody should get a look in, and you can keep a look out. Satisfaction all round.

MRS BROADBENT: Aha, well really, less privet less privacy, no, I don't think. If they're cut now, you know, they have flowers, lovely big white sweet-smelling cones like lilac called erect panicles that blossom soon. Pity to stop them flowering when they're just about to come out.

KENDRICK: Okay. I just felt a bit of horticulture might put me in touch with nature and hayfever –

MRS BROADBENT: If you want to clip the hedge, you shall. I'll fetch the shears this minute. One proviso. Mind you make a good job of it.

(*She goes down to the cellar. The milk boils over. KENDRICK pours the remainder into the cups. One must be topped up with water from the kettle. He wipes the stove. The toast burns. He scrapes the charred surface. MRS BROADBENT returns.*)

I heard you making the toast. The butter's in the butter dish.

KENDRICK: How eccentric.

MRS BROADBENT: Aha – ho. Here they are. Very rusty.

KENDRICK: Drop of oil, they'll be alright.

MRS BROADBENT: You've made the coffee too, splendid. (*She takes the watered cup.*) Sit here and eat your – I have some oil, keep it for the sewing machine – here – and – a newspaper to put it on.

KENDRICK: How does it feel to have a baby in the house again?

MRS BROADBENT: Gwendolyn.

KENDRICK: Yes. Not a name you'd think they'd choose. Did Mrs Watts – ?

MRS BROADBENT: Lena! Don't think she'd ever heard the name before. No. As a matter of fact Mister Watts asked me what I thought they should call the child. I suggested Gwendolyn. He liked the name and used it.

KENDRICK: I expect she'll get Gwen when she's older.

MRS BROADBENT: I hope not. Gwendolyn's so attractive. One of my mother's names. Gwendolyn Rose Silk. One dies, another's born. *Skol.* (*She drinks.*) I'm sure they water the milk these days.

KENDRICK: Why do you say *skol?* Tribute to Hitler?

MRS BROADBENT: I'll always say it.

KENDRICK: Why?

MRS BROADBENT: Roger said it. He'd travelled a lot.
He'd been to Germany in the war. I always say *skol*.

KENDRICK: You sound as though you're still in love.

MRS BROADBENT: Do I...?

KENDRICK: He's dead, you're alive.

MRS BROADBENT: Part of me died when he did.

KENDRICK: You're sharing his coffin?

MRS BROADBENT: I certainly don't do that. How unkind.
I think I'm very much alive. Anyway. Why should you
care – I'm very conscious, was from the first few days
after, very early on when he died – there was only me,
I had to carry on for both of us for Kevin. It wasn't easy
for him either, neither of us, being without a father, no
one to look up to, do things with. I do try to keep him
alive, his memory, the memory of him for both of us not
because I'm still in love with him, that would be silly,
I don't think I'm silly like that, people in books and
films and television pretending, so much as it's just the
memories of him and missing him and missing out on
what we might have done, would have done, together.
When I think about him now and I don't, try not to, but
I don't force myself not to but when and if I do I hardly
cry at all any more – when I remember everything about
him. I did the first year. Couldn't stop, couldn't go
anywhere, hardly talk in case I made, you know,
embarrassed, got upset and filled up, apologised and
bored friends on the phone and anywhere, in shops, the
library, getting books with just my tickets, not his, but
not now, not any more – (*She cries.*) What's it to you,
anyway.

KENDRICK: You're very tense.

MRS BROADBENT: Yes, I'm tense.

KENDRICK: Relax.

MRS BROADBENT: I will. I am. I do. I am tense. You
make me tense. I mean, you're an intense sort of man
and us all living together, not knowing what's going to
happen to us from one day to the next, makes you tense.

I am still in mourning. Bereaved. Not for Roger, though. Mother. Another part of me has gone. Just gone.

KENDRICK: Well – don't live in the past. Better to be here and now than there and then, eh?

MRS BROADBENT: Yes. Yes. I try to be here for you, all my tenants.

KENDRICK: Lodgers.

MRS BROADBENT: Lodgers. At this minute I feel I'm living in the present. Do I look like I'm here now to you?

KENDRICK: You look closer than you did.

MRS BROADBENT: Thanks to you.

KENDRICK: And caffeine.

MRS BROADBENT: You made it.

KENDRICK: Cheers.

MRS BROADBENT: Cheers.

KENDRICK: You've coped very well with your mother's death I'd say. Took it in your stride. I hoped you'd avoid the respectable weeks of gloom but I see you couldn't resist dressing up to encourage them to outstay their welcome.

MRS BROADBENT: You mean this?

KENDRICK: Yes, your mourning garb. You could afford to buy a new frock or two now. I'm sure she'd've wanted you to have a good time on her savings. Why don't you go to Blackpool for the weekend. Get lit up by the illuminations.

MRS BROADBENT: I can't bear Blackpool.

KENDRICK: Well – tour the cathedral towns, then.

MRS BROADBENT: Ho – really.

KENDRICK: Go to Spain. Why not. See a bit of life in the sun – bullfights, matadors, flamencos, be marvellous for you, just what you need, a good holiday. Have an adventure. Wake you up. If I were your doctor that's what I'd prescribe.

MRS BROADBENT: Would you, doctor?

KENDRICK: Douglas. Cost you more than a prescription charge, though.

MRS BROADBENT: I'm sure.

KENDRICK: How's Mister Watts settling down after his fling on the Isle of Wight?

MRS BROADBENT: Poor Eric. He'll never be content with Lena. What man could? I'm sure she's not sane sometimes. She's not the woman for him. He could have been so successful if he hadn't married her. He's a brilliant engineer. He can mend any appliance. He reads. He's intelligent, but Lena – never met such a noodle.

KENDRICK: He must have fancied her for some reason.

MRS BROADBENT: Vacant possession, no sitting tenant. She's simple-minded.

KENDRICK: Very endearing. I bet they'll be walking arm in arm, pushing the pram like two young lovers, like the Cleggs.

MRS BROADBENT: Young lovers! The Cleggs. Young animals, more like. You'd lose your bet. I'm glad to say they're leaving at the end of the week.

KENDRICK: The Cleggs?

MRS BROADBENT: The Watts first. The Cleggs next.

KENDRICK: You've asked them to leave?

MRS BROADBENT: They've been told and Mister Clegg will be at the end of the week. He's discharged on Saturday. It's not possible to have him here all the time. It's bad enough at the weekend as it is. The noise and behaviour. Tenants don't like that sort of thing.

KENDRICK: There won't be any when they've gone.

MRS BROADBENT: You and Mister Tubbs.

KENDRICK: Has he complained?

MRS BROADBENT: He doesn't approve.

KENDRICK: You mean you don't.

MRS BROADBENT: No, I don't. Do you?

KENDRICK: Of course. Eric's reproduced himself at last. With any luck the Cleggs might have one before the year's out. Get Tubbs married and pull off a hat trick. Get the house a reputation and get yourself a fan club of happy copulating couples. Lust in the dust of Marlborough Terrace. Turn the place into a nursery.

Prams all over the garden, babies everywhere, bawling their lungs out. Keep us all awake.

MRS BROADBENT: What about you and me. Would we be in this club? Having fun?

KENDRICK: I'd move. I can't stand babies. Count me out. I'm happy single.

MRS BROADBENT: You've given me an idea. No more couples. I always preferred letting to single professional men. No trouble. Peace and quiet and lots of men about the house for Kevin to look up to and do the odd job.

KENDRICK: I'd better get started, before I give you any more ideas.

(*He goes into the garden, hangs his jacket on the pram and attacks the hedge. WATTS returns, carrying a pint of milk and finishing an ice cream.*)

WATTS: What do you think you're doing?

KENDRICK: Gardening.

WATTS: She won't half be annoyed.

KENDRICK: She is.

WATTS: You'll cop it.

KENDRICK: She gave her consent. It's all yours. There's only one proviso: 'mind you make a good job of it.' (*He goes in and up to his room.*)

WATTS: I will. (*He clips the hedge.*)

LENA: (*At the window.*) Eh – Eric – what you doing, Eric?

WATTS: Gardening.

LENA: Looks like it. Did you get milk?

WATTS: Here you are – and ten Woodbines.

LENA: Ooh, you shouldn't have got ten.

WATTS: Five for you and five for me.

LENA: You don't smoke.

WATTS: I'm starting.

LENA: Ooh, heck. You were a long time.

WATTS: I had to queue.

LENA: Oh, I thought… (*She goes in.*)

TUBBS: (*From his window.*) Morning.

WATTS: Hello.

TUBBS: 'Ey, what you doing?

WATTS: Gardening.

TUBBS: Aye. Is it alright?

WATTS: Is what alright?

TUBBS: With Missus.

WATTS: She wants me to. Gave her consent.

TUBBS: That's alright, then. Think I'll sit out for a bit with the paper. Do you mind?

WATTS: Join us if you like. Be a bit noisy with the shears.

TUBBS: That's alright. Er – would you take this for me? Saves bringing it round. Ta.

(*WATTS takes a chair from him, puts it on the lawn and goes on clipping. TUBBS comes out with the* News of the World.)

Aw, I've left mi glasses. Nice day, isn't it?

WATTS: Sun's out.

TUBBS: Aye, for a bit...

(*He goes back into the hall, where MRS BROADBENT is knocking on the WATTS' door.*)

LENA: Hullo, yes?

MRS BROADBENT: Is your husband in?

LENA: Who is it? Come in.

MRS BROADBENT: Mrs Broadbent.

LENA: I'll open t' door.

MRS BROADBENT: Is he in? Mister Watts?

LENA: Oh. No. He isn't.

MRS BROADBENT: Will he be long?

LENA: No. He'll have to be in for his dinner soon.

MRS BROADBENT: When he comes back tell him I'd like to see him, please.

TUBBS: Did you want Eric?

MRS BROADBENT: He's out.

TUBBS: Aye, in t' garden.

LENA: Yes he is, out in t' garden. Shall I tell him?

(*MRS BROADBENT goes into the garden, TUBBS into his room.*)

MRS BROADBENT: Mister Watts, can I have a word.

WATTS: Young Kendrick said it was alright to –

MRS BROADBENT: Yes, it doesn't matter. It wasn't that I –

WATTS: I think it'll look a lot better when it's –

MRS BROADBENT: You can stay on here with the baby if you want to, Mister Watts. You've found another place?

WATTS: No. I haven't. Ooh, that's wonderful. That's very good of you. I wouldn't have liked to have left you after – you get used to –

MRS BROADBENT: I thought Doctor Kendrick was cutting the hedge?

WATTS: Oh, he was.

MRS BROADBENT: You've started smoking again.

WATTS: First for two years. Have one. They're only Woods.

MRS BROADBENT: Thank you.

(*WATTS lights her cigarette. She exhales graciously. He admires her style. TUBBS returns and eyes them over his spectacles.*)
Finished with the oil?

WATTS: Yes, they're well oiled now. They've eased up. Quite sharp, too.

MRS BROADBENT: I'll take it in.

WATTS: Sun's very hot, isn't it?

TUBBS: Aye, for a bit.

MRS BROADBENT: Yes. I think I'll go and change. This yours, Mister Watts?

WATTS: Catch me in a blazer. It's Kendrick's. Had quite a conversational talk with him just –

MRS BROADBENT: Did you.

WATTS: About garden and looking for another place and that, you know.

MRS BROADBENT: Yes. He doesn't have much time to chat and make friends. She's quiet now.

WATTS: She must have heard you telling me she could stay on. Very grateful, Mrs Broadbent. Very glad. Thank you.

MRS BROADBENT: I'll take this indoors. (*She goes.*)

TUBBS: She letting you three stay on?

WATTS: You heard.

TUBBS: Go on. I saw him using the shears before you.

WATTS: Who?

TUBBS: Kendrick.

WATTS: I let him have a go.

TUBBS: Notice how she speaks up for him, soft-pedals him.

WATTS: Queer feller, Kendrick.

TUBBS: Aye.

WATTS: Sometimes he hardly says hello, like you're not there, next minute he's asking how you are and all about you.

TUBBS: Must be the weather brings him out.

WATTS: Aye, like the little lady on the barometer.

TUBBS: That's him.

WATTS: Comes out when the sun shines, goes in when it rains.

TUBBS: That's just it.

WATTS: Never know where you are with his sort.

TUBBS: You can't make friends with him.

WATTS: I can make friends with anyone.

TUBBS: Ah well, you're married.

WATTS: Course, he's scholarly, we know that.

TUBBS: You can hold your own.

WATTS: I don't tolerate fools gladly. Mind you, I suffer Lena.

TUBBS: You're a man of the world, a father and an 'usband.

WATTS: I'd better tell her. (*He taps on the window.*)

LENA: What? I'm cooking.

WATTS: Come here.

LENA: What?

WATTS: She says we can stay on here.

LENA: Does she?

WATTS: I needn't have tramped about for the last two weeks.

LENA: I wondered what were up. She looked put out.

WATTS: It's only two weeks since her mother died.

LENA: Yes. Enjoying yourself?

WATTS: They're a bit blunt.

LENA: Drink of tea, both of you?

WATTS: Jack?

TUBBS: Ooh, very nice – er – very nice, thank you, Lena, lovely.

LENA: I'll bring it out when it's ready.

TUBBS: Lovely.

WATTS: She's improving.

(*MRS BROADBENT has changed into a summer dress and is on her way to KENDRICK's room. They meet on the stairs.*)

MRS BROADBENT: I was bringing your coat up, you left it hanging on –

KENDRICK: I was just going out. Thanks.

MRS BROADBENT: I'm sorry you thought I'd done the wrong thing asking the Watts to leave.

KENDRICK: Did I say it was wrong?

MRS BROADBENT: You were quite right. We should encourage them to make a go of it now there are three of them. I've said they can stay.

KENDRICK: Congratulations.

MRS BROADBENT: Pleased?

KENDRICK: Surprised and delighted. And the Cleggs, too?

MRS BROADBENT: I shan't tell them to go if you think –

KENDRICK: Now you deserve a medal.

MRS BROADBENT: From my fan club?

KENDRICK: When do I have to leave?

MRS BROADBENT: You can stay, too, if you behave.

KENDRICK: I'll go tomorrow. I'm off for a drink – want one?

MRS BROADBENT: In a public house?

KENDRICK: No, a horse trough. The Prince of Wales.

MRS BROADBENT: I can't. Must get the dinner ready. Kevin will be home any minute.

KENDRICK: I see you've changed your frock.

MRS BROADBENT: It's cooler.

(*KENDRICK goes outside.*)

WATTS: I see you got your jacket.

KENDRICK: Yes.

WATTS: 'Ey, come here a minute. She says we can stay here after all.

KENDRICK: What made her change her mind?

WATTS: It's my charm, you know, the way I look at her.

TUBBS: Eh? I said you what?

WATTS: I think she fancies me sometimes.

TUBBS: Fancies you?

WATTS: 'Specially now I've proved my worth, eh? You know, she cadged a cigarette off me just now, what do you think of that Jack? She's not bad for her age, not bad, nice pair of legs, nice pair of – good figure – I reckon she'd be a really good –

(*KEVIN returns from Sunday School. He stops to put his glasses on.*)

– real good friend.

KENDRICK: Your mother's waiting for you, Kevin. (*He goes in.*)

KEVIN: Does Mummy know you're cutting our privets?

TUBBS: Yes, Mummy knows, Kevin.

KEVIN: (*Looking in the pram.*) I don't think I like babies.

TUBBS: You were one once.

KEVIN: Yes, but I didn't have a turned-up nose.

(*He goes in. The baby starts to cry. WATTS replaces the dummy in its mouth. He looks at the baby, smiles, looks at the sky, goes back to the hedge.*)

MRS BROADBENT: Did you behave yourself in Sunday School?

KEVIN: Yes. You have to. You haven't got your black frock on for Granny. Can I take this off my arm?

MRS BROADBENT: Tomorrow.

KEVIN: Good. They call me lance-corporal at school.

MRS BROADBENT: That's very naughty.

KEVIN: Mummy – Teddy Ormes is going camping with his dad in the summer holidays.

MRS BROADBENT: Is he.

KEVIN: Yes, he is. He's asked me to go too.

MRS BROADBENT: Has he?

KEVIN: Can I go, Mum?

MRS BROADBENT: You haven't got a tent.

KEVIN: There's room for me in theirs. Mum?

MRS BROADBENT: No, you can't go.

KEVIN: Oh, Mum, please.

MRS BROADBENT: Mummy has a surprise for you, dear. She wasn't going to tell you until after your exam. But if you promise to do well I'll tell you now. Promise to do your best.

KEVIN: I'll do my best, promise. What's the surprise?

MRS BROADBENT: I'm taking you overseas on holiday this year.

KEVIN: Abroad. Where to – America?

MRS BROADBENT: No, not to America, darling, you
  don't want to go there, that's the same as it is here. We're
  going where it's warm.

KEVIN: Africa?

MRS BROADBENT: I'm not going to tell you where. You
  just tell Teddy Ormes to tell his dad you're going on the
  continent and not in a tent either.

KEVIN: Africa's a continent.

MRS BROADBENT: I'm not feeling very well, Kevin. I'm
  going out for a little walk and I want you to be a good
  boy and help Mummy. Finish laying the table and watch
  the things on the stove.

KEVIN: Can't I come with you?

MRS BROADBENT: You stay and look after everything.
  I won't be long.
  (*She sets off with her handbag, then doubles back for a shopping
  basket, composing herself in the hall before going back into the
  garden. KEVIN takes his glasses off and breaks a plate on purpose.*)

KEVIN: I bet it's Africa.

WATTS: How's it looking?

MRS BROADBENT: I'll tell you when it's finished. (*She
  notices the mop.*) Mrs Clegg! Mrs Clegg don't leave
  your…oh.
  (*She gives up and goes to the 'Prince of Wales'. WATTS and
  TUBBS look up. ANNE appears at the window undressed
  and calls after MRS BROADBENT.*)

ANNE: I was just shaking it.
  (*The mop disappears. WATTS and TUBBS think alike and
  exchange looks and nods.*)

JOHN: (*In bed.*) Two hours ago.

ANNE: Whose fault is it it's still stuck through t'window?

JOHN: Yours. You shouldn't have bent over tempting me.

ANNE: I hope you're satisfied love. I've had enough. (*She
  pulls her skirt on and throws clothes at JOHN.*) Come on,
  gerrup. Here you are.

JOHN: Temptress.

ANNE: And don't let me see you without your clothes on
  again today.

JOHN: Alright, love. What shall we do instead?

ANNE: It's smashing out.

JOHN: Where would you like to go?

ANNE: I've got dinner to start.

JOHN: We haven't had breakfast.

ANNE: No, and you're not going to, either. It's twelve o'clock. You had a cup of tea.

JOHN: Was that my breakfast?

ANNE: You had your breakfast in bed and you made a right meal of it. There won't be any lying in next week, love.

JOHN: I know, breakfast at seven every morning.

ANNE: Don't remind me.

JOHN: Where's my razor?

ANNE: Plugged in waiting.

JOHN: Be alright, though, won't it.

ANNE: Smashing. (*She puts her apron on.*)

JOHN: What you doing?

ANNE: What?

JOHN: Hurry up and get changed. (*He starts the shaver.*)

ANNE: I can't change before I've got dinner and –

JOHN: (*Turning the shaver off.*) You don't think I'd let my wife prepare Sunday dinner, do you? Take that apron off and get washed. We're going out to lunch. (*He turns the shaver back on.*)

ANNE: Aw, darling, can we afford it?

JOHN: You're paying.

ANNE: Oh yes. You can't get fish and chips on a Sunday.

JOHN: Where would you like to go?

ANNE: Are we really going out for lunch?

JOHN: It'll be teatime if you don't –

ANNE: What shall I put on? (*Taking her skirt off.*)

JOHN: Clothes. And don't let me see you without your clothes on again today either.

ANNE: I've got to change. You'll have to not look.

JOHN: We'll catch a bus to Loughrig, have some dinner and go to the Lido for a swim.

ANNE: Ooh, yes. It's ever so hot. Ey, I don't think we've got a clean towel.

71

JOHN: We can get towels there. Don't want to be laden down with things.

ANNE: Alright. When we come back we'll go to the pictures. I'll pay for that.

(*She begins to sing an improvised version of 'Sugar in the Morning'. JOHN joins in by the second verse, and they make an alternating duet of it. They fade as the light goes from them. TUBBS and WATTS strain their necks upwards.*)

TUBBS: They're off again. Right couple aren't they?

LENA: (*At the window.*) Sugar, Mister Tubbs?

TUBBS: Yes, please.

(*LENA ducks back in, then out again.*)

LENA: How many?

TUBBS: One and a half to two.

(*LENA ducks back. Thinks. Reappears.*)

LENA: Do you like milk, Mister Tubbs?

TUBBS: One and a half to two.

LENA: Eh! Pints?

TUBBS: Eh?

LENA: Milk, do you take it?

TUBBS: Oh yes, I do take it, yes, I take it.

LENA: Right. (*She ducks back in.*)

WATTS: She takes it alright up there, cream off the top, can't get enough.

TUBBS: I couldn't drink tea without milk.

WATTS: They'll soon learn.

TUBBS: Strikes me they've learnt already.

WATTS: I mean they won't be singing long.

TUBBS: Oh, I don't know, you know. She's a right belter is his missus. Ey, they've stopped already.

WATTS: Oh yes, she's a nice piece.

TUBBS: They must have heard you.

WATTS: He's a fine young feller too, makes me feel an old 'un.

TUBBS: You aren't old. You're a strapping chap. Plenty of meat in you yet. 'Ow old are you, Eric?

(*LENA joins them with two beakers of tea.*)

'Ow old is he, Mrs Watts?

WATTS: How old? How old do I look? You shut up.

LENA: I never spoke.

TUBBS: Well, it's hard to say.

WATTS: Go on, guess.

TUBBS: Thank you, Lena. Well. Let me see. Stand
   sideways. Er. Well.

WATTS: Well?

LENA: Your tea, Eric.

WATTS: Wait a minute.

TUBBS: Well, of course –

LENA: I have to feed t'baby.

WATTS: Hurry up, Jack.

TUBBS: You can't be much over forty.

WATTS: (*Taking tea.*) I'm not.

TUBBS: There, am I correct?

WATTS: I'm thirty-eight.

TUBBS: Well, you don't look it.

LENA: He hasn't got his suit on, have you? And he didn't
   shave this morning, did you? (*She rocks the pram.*)

WATTS: That doesn't make any difference. Over forty.

TUBBS: 'Ey, I wouldn't have said anything if I'd thought
   you'd take on.

WATTS: Don't I get a spoon?

TUBBS: You did ask me. Here, use mine.

LENA: Oh, didn't I give you one?

WATTS: I wouldn't have said I hadn't got one if I had,
   would I? 'No, you wouldn't.' So why ask? Why ask if you
   gave me one when you know, you knew, didn't you, that
   you hadn't, you couldn't have, because I said already
   you'd given him one, not me.

LENA: Have I to get you another?

WATTS: Another. I haven't had the first one yet.

TUBBS: 'Ey, look who's coming.

LENA: Who is it?

WATTS: Mrs Broadbent, that's all.

TUBBS: Look who's with her.

LENA: Who?

TUBBS: Kendrick. He's a sly operator.

WATTS: What do you mean? He's alright.

TUBBS: You didn't say so earlier on. You said he were a queer feller. Like a lady on a barometer.

LENA: What's he mean?

TUBBS: It isn't the warmth of the sun that brings him out Mrs Watts. It's the gold. You never know where you are with him, you said. Well, I've got a pretty good idea where he is and where he's coming from. Mrs Silk were worth a fair bit, you know. And she didn't leave it to you, did she?

LENA: He-hee, no she didn't. I wish she had a' done.

TUBBS: And she didn't leave it to me. She left it to her ladyship.

LENA: She left it to Mrs Broadbent.

TUBBS: Course she did. There. He's working his way in.

WATTS: He wouldn't do a thing like that.

(*LENA has the baby in her arms. She is taking her in to feed. The CLEGGS, togged for the Lido, come from the house.*)

ANNE: Hello, Mrs Watts.

JOHN: This your baby?

LENA: Yes.

WATTS: Ours.

ANNE: You haven't seen it yet, have you, darling?

(*KENDRICK and MRS BROADBENT return.*)

MRS BROADBENT: Quite a gathering.

TUBBS: Reception committee, she means.

MRS BROADBENT: Given up already, Mister Watts?

WATTS: Just resting.

JOHN: Warm work, eh?

ANNE: Afternoon, Mrs Broadbent.

MRS BROADBENT: Going out for the day?

ANNE: We're going out to lunch.

JOHN: Then for a swim. Want to join us?

MRS BROADBENT: I wouldn't let you see me in a swimsuit.

(*General laughter.*)

Is it so funny?

ANNE: Look at the baby, John. Hello, Gwendolyn.

JOHN: She's got sunburnt.

LENA: Eh?

JOHN: You should cover up her head.

LENA: What's wrong with her head?

JOHN: It's brown.

ANNE: Nothing, she's beautiful.

LENA: She's not sunburnt, is she? (*She backs away from them all up the steps to the house.*) She's not – she's not brown – she's alright...

(*KENDRICK goes to LENA to investigate. She appeals to him. He lifts the baby's palm with his index finger. LENA goes inside and to her room. KENDRICK looks at WATTS who goes to the window and looks in at LENA still fearfully clutching the baby. WATTS sits astride the window-sill a moment before going into the room. KEVIN is in the hall.*)

KENDRICK: It's clouding over.

TUBBS: Aye, I said it would.

(*The sun fades. It is dark by the time everybody has moved into the house. Only KENDRICK stays, listening to a steel band softly sounding as if across water.*)

KENDRICK: Gwendolyn was born off-white. Within seven days the Caribbean content in her blood pulsed from her heart to the surface of her dusty-pink skin, transforming it to an instant half-caste bronze.

(*The music swells as LENA flees from the house with the baby and a suitcase.*)

Lena, scared of the miracle and her husband and what he would do to her first-born, wrapped it in a blanket and went home to her father. He lived alone, was old and poor and suddenly a grandfather. And he reached out and hugged and kissed them both and they all three cried together happily ever after. Her father wasn't alone any more, but he was still old and poor.

(*The steel band fades. The light comes up on WATTS slumped in his armchair.*)

And Eric – Eric wasn't old, was better off financially, free again but alone.

(*'Domani', an Italian romantic and popular song, is heard in the darkness. A diesel taxi engine runs underneath. MRS*

BROADBENT and KEVIN, with WATTS helping them,
come from the house with holiday luggage which is put into
the taxi as though it were Phineas Fogg's balloon.)
And three weeks ago – Gabrielle, scared of the situation
and the questions her first-born was beginning to ask,
fled from the scandalous low life goings on under her
roof to what holiday leaflets promised would be the
romantic high life going on under the blue skies of the
Côte d'Azur, and Venice. Kevin had failed his exams and
was now to receive the prize. A package tour paid for by
the timely death of his granny. His show-off mummy had
taken him shopping in stores she'd never quite been able
to afford to shop in before, to buy herself boatnecks and
honeycombs, pleated skirts cut on the cross, smart shoes
and a stole, gloves to go with the hat and luggage to
match. A suit for the sea and a suit for the air and an
afternoon frock for San Marco square and the pigeons
and a cocktail dress for evenings spent in Grand Canal
gondolas with guitars and the stars and Kevin...and all
paid for from the proceeds of the policy taken out on the
life of the deceased, tax free courtesy of the Inland
Revenue and the solicitor in charge of administering the
estate for the sole beneficiary. Gabrielle. She sent sunny,
sighing, having-a-lovely-time postcards to Mister Watts
and Tubbs – and a black-and-white photograph of the
leaning tower of Pisa to the Cleggs, who thought it
looked familiar and pinned it to the wall above their bed.
And to me she sent, from Cannes, her kind regards, from
Nice her best wishes, from Monte Carlo her fond
thoughts and from Venice her deepest affection. 'We only
possess those we love when they're absent.' Mauriac.
(*The music, water lapping gondolas, pigeons, WATTS reading*
others' mail, TUBBS in the TV's glow, the CLEGGS
undressed, disperse and fade as MRS BROADBENT and
KEVIN return in a taxi. WATTS sees them, leers and comes
from the house when KENDRICK ambles off.)
Two weeks later she returned with a gondolier's hat –
a purchase not a conquest, a glass chandelier, wine,

gramophone records, a suntan and Kevin. Not to mention boatnecks, honeycombs, smart shoes and a stole, matching luggage and gloves…
(*His voice fades. The taxi drives away.*)

MRS BROADBENT: Thank you no, we can manage. Take the box, Kevin.

KEVIN: Yes, Mummy.

MRS BROADBENT: Glad to be home?

KEVIN: I suppose so.

WATTS: (*Joining them.*) You got back alright.

MRS BROADBENT: Hello Mister Watts, yes, so tired, travelling.

WATTS: I'll give you a hand.

MRS BROADBENT: Thank you so much.

WATTS: Didn't think you'd be back until tomorrow.

MRS BROADBENT: Ah, I know, but Kevin has to be at school on Monday, so I thought if I got back today it would give us a nice quiet day tomorrow to recuperate.

WATTS: You look very well. Caught the sun.

MRS BROADBENT: Do you think so?

WATTS: I wish I felt as you look. I've not been well all this week. Been off work.

MRS BROADBENT: Oh dear, I am sorry.

WATTS: Had a nice time, I expect.

MRS BROADBENT: Oh yes, it's been wonderful. I'll tell you all about it tomorrow. Just leave them in the hall for now. Thank you. You must excuse me, I'm dying to spend a penny. (*She goes upstairs.*) Have you managed alright?

WATTS: Oh yes, everything's alright.

MRS BROADBENT: Good.
(*KENDRICK comes from the bathroom minus shirt, a towel round his neck. MRS BROADBENT almost forgets why she went upstairs as they meet.*)
Douglas!

KENDRICK: Hello. Good to see you back.

MRS BROADBENT: It's good to be back. I missed you. How did the examination go?

KENDRICK: Very well.

MRS BROADBENT: Oh good, so glad for you. Now it's all over you'll be able to relax, come down more often. Whenever you feel like it. I'm always in and I'll play you my records. I brought a whole lot back with me.

KENDRICK: Thanks.

MRS BROADBENT: Come down for an hour this evening. Kevin's to have an early night after the journey.

KENDRICK: What time?

MRS BROADBENT: Say eight thirty?

KENDRICK: Half past eight. (*He goes up.*)

MRS BROADBENT: And I'll tell you all about the Côte d'Azure and Venice.

(*WATTS has been listening in the hall. Now he speaks to KEVIN.*)

WATTS: Had a good time did you?

KEVIN: Yes, thank you, Mister Watts.

WATTS: That's right. (*He goes to his room and slumps in his armchair as the light fades.*) Everything's alright, everything's alright. Alright.

(*The vivace lilt of a Neapolitan melody recorded in the heat of a Decca studio is heard coming from MRS BROADBENT's den. KENDRICK reads a record sleeve. A cocktail dress with MRS BROADBENT in it materialises.*)

MRS BROADBENT: Did you get the postcards I sent you?

KENDRICK: Yes, I did.

MRS BROADBENT: From Venice?

KENDRICK: 'With deepest affection' – thank you.

MRS BROADBENT: Did I say that…? Well. I'm so grateful you made me go. I bought you a present. (*She gives it.*) From Venice. In appreciation.

KENDRICK: A pair of earrings.

MRS BROADBENT: No – silly – cufflinks. Two gondolas and two little gondoliers punting. I didn't know what to get you.

KENDRICK: It's the thought that counts. Thank you.

MRS BROADBENT: Try some of this. I'm glad you came down –

KENDRICK: How could I –

MRS BROADBENT: Because I have a favour to –

KENDRICK: Your first night –

MRS BROADBENT: A little favour to ask you.

KENDRICK: Speak.

MRS BROADBENT: It doesn't matter now, but I wonder, when you've time, if you'd do a little job for me? I would ask Mister Watts but he's not feeling very well.

KENDRICK: If I can.

MRS BROADBENT: Well, I know you could do it. I'd pay you, of course. I mean, I'd have to pay an outsider if you didn't do it, so we might as well keep the money in the family. That is, if you say you'll do it.

KENDRICK: You don't have to pay me.

MRS BROADBENT: No, we must be fair. If I ask you to do a job for me, I must pay you for doing it. Oh yes. Besides, I'd rather you did it. I'd know it was well done then and I know you wouldn't make a mess. I'd be frightened, expecting it to fall on me, if a stranger did it.

KENDRICK: What is it you want me to do?

MRS BROADBENT: Well. I bought a chandelier in Venice. Fifteen thousand lire, for my little den. I can't fix it, of course, I'm so helpless – at that sort of thing. I can just about mend a fuse.

KENDRICK: *Skol.*

MRS BROADBENT: Cheers. Would you like me to show it to you?

KENDRICK: I'll let you know –

MRS BROADBENT: Now.

KENDRICK: When I've seen it.

(*MRS BROADBENT positions stepladders and starts to unpack the chandelier.*)

MRS BROADBENT: It's very fragile. We'll have to be very careful when we're putting it together. It's a beautiful thing. They escorted me round the factory where they make them – fascinating – a whole shed full of chandeliers, all shapes and sizes dangling from the roof.

KENDRICK: Glass.

MRS BROADBENT: Yes, all glass, even the bulbs. Venetian glass. You must have heard of Venetian glass.

KENDRICK: Yes.

MRS BROADBENT: Some beautiful things they make with it don't they. *Salute. (She clinks glasses.)* It is amazing how they do it. That's one of the arms. They're so clever. That's the centre-piece.

KENDRICK: I see.

MRS BROADBENT: It holds these pretty twisted arms. They had them from five thousand lire – there's a ball – but I chose this one at fifteen thousand. It has such a pretty pink tint in the leaves, to give a softer light, I thought. The leaves sit in here. The guide who showed me round, behind the Prado Mani this factory was, this shed, was called Dino. He was so courteous and well informed – number six – we stopped and watched them, the men, blowing wine goblets – I do hope nothing's broken – four and two. It's already wired. Dino got the men to do it for me while I was there.

KENDRICK: Did you watch them?

MRS BROADBENT: Oh no, not wiring it up, just the blowing. They must have very strong lungs to blow as they do. They have this very long pole, you see, and turn it and that makes the shape as they blow and pull and lift and turn. Their cheeks come right out – they hold it over a little furnace, hot and intense it is, and just as you think they can't go on without collapsing or bursting or dropping off they take it away at just the right moment when they're satisfied – oh, they are clever. *(She pours more wine.)* It's not easy. These poles they blow through are quite heavy to lift. They let me try. I was afraid I might break something. The men wear long leather aprons, shiny like the glass, and the chandeliers all around you and above you tinkling as they turn about in the heat. It's very strong and heat-resisting.

KENDRICK: The leather?

MRS BROADBENT: No, the glass they blow. It was so hot inside I had to go outside for some air with Dino while we waited for them to wire it. We sat outside in the Prado Mani and had a long cool Dubonnet instead of a

Martini. It tasted so quenching. The climate's so hot and
the Italians are so, well, they're not reserved like we are.
I mean for instance, whilst we were sitting there cooling
off two young women walked by on the pavement and a
young Italian sitting at the table next to ours got up and
walked after them. He'd only gone a few yards when
they turned round and he started to talk to them. They
came back to the table beside us and he bought drinks
for the two of them. They all wore open sandals and
I could see their feet, touching under the table. He was
kissing her hand and resting his fingers on her neck in a
few minutes, it was terrible. And I'd thought before, what
a nice young man you look, as he was sitting there alone.
Not unlike yourself about the eyes. We turned away and
went to look in a canal. It was obvious what they were
leading up to.

KENDRICK: A threesome.

MRS BROADBENT: Well – yes. An orgy. They have no
morals, the Italians.

KENDRICK: The Borgias had them.

MRS BROADBENT: Not morals.

KENDRICK: Orgies.

MRS BROADBENT: That's right, Roman Catholics, that's
where it all started, in Rome. Decadence. Before they
built the Coliseum and the Roman Empire. Julius
Caesar. Nero. They'd do anything to enjoy themselves.
They tried to spread it here. Roman Britain. Centurions
marching up and down our Roman roads from one
garrison to the next, setting up their orgies on the way
and when they got there. It's what they're famous for. Ice
cream and Roman orgies.

KENDRICK: Roman architecture, Roman alphabet, Roman
baths.

MRS BROADBENT: Yes, I know, but they didn't succeed
because we're not like that. They're not like us. I mean,
these two young women who walked off with this young
man who'd bought them a coffee – there was no question
of them being in love. They'd obviously just met for the

first time. It's different when you've known someone a long time, isn't it?

KENDRICK: What?

MRS BROADBENT: Going with them.

KENDRICK: No.

MRS BROADBENT: Oh, I think it is.

KENDRICK: You either want to or you don't, simple as that.

MRS BROADBENT: Isn't it pretty?

KENDRICK: I'll plug it in. Where's the two-pin point?

MRS BROADBENT: There isn't one. (*She pours more wine into KENDRICK's glass and her own.*)

KENDRICK: I've got an adaptor. I'll fetch it.

MRS BROADBENT: Don't be long. I hope we don't fuse anything.

KENDRICK: That's alright. You can mend a fuse.
(*He opens the door. WATTS stands outside.*)

WATTS: I just wanted to say I've taken the big case upstairs. It's on the landing. Mind you don't trip up.
(*KENDRICK goes upstairs.*)

MRS BROADBENT: That is good of you. How are you feeling?

WATTS: I have a bit of a headache. Must be the fumes from the gas fire.

MRS BROADBENT: Oh, I am sorry. Perhaps a little Italian Wine. (*She gives him KENDRICK's glass.*)

WATTS: Just a minute, I'll put my jacket on.

MRS BROADBENT: You're alright as you are. Come and see my chandelier. Isn't it lovely, don't you think?

WATTS: Very nice.

MRS BROADBENT: Douglas has gone for a plug.

WATTS: Don't need a plug. Here, stick these two wires in with a match.
(*He does so, pulling out the plug that connects the record-player. The turntable slows down and the music drones into silence. In its place the CLEGG's turntable revolves playing 'Little Things Mean a Lot'; lights change to the CLEGG's room.*)

ANNE: Aw no, darling, you've not to take it.

JOHN: I've a good mind to. I'm fed up driving a bread van round all the back streets.

ANNE: You haven't given it a chance yet.

JOHN: It depresses me.

ANNE: Well, you can get another job here. There's no need to go off all over the country driving a lorry. Besides, it's dangerous, them big lorries.

JOHN: Ah, it's no more dangerous than driving in back streets with cats and dogs and children and age-old pensioners running under your front wheels all t'time.

ANNE: Pensioners can't run under your wheels, you know.

JOHN: No, they stand in the middle of the road and gape at t'bonnet as though they'd never seen a car before.

ANNE: Well.

JOHN: Yes, well.

ANNE: Well, it's no reason for you to go off on long-distance lorry drives. I'd never see you.

JOHN: You'd see just as much of me then as you did before I was demobbed.

ANNE: Aw, darling. I don't want you to go off again and be stuck here by myself again all week.

JOHN: You didn't complain before.

ANNE: No, well, you had to be away then.

JOHN: I can earn a lot more on long-distance drives. They need chaps like me that's had experience with big army stuff.

ANNE: Look, with what I get waiting on at the grocer's we can save up just as much. If you were away you'd have to spend more, it'd be like having two homes going.

JOHN: No it wouldn't. You get your expenses paid. I can probably make on my expenses. They allow you fifteen bob a day and I could sleep in the truck and keep it. Course, I might only be trailer mating at first but it'll be much better.

ANNE: Yes, and you'd come home at t'weekend dog-tired.

JOHN: Must you play that bloody soppy record?

ANNE: Yes I must.

JOHN: Put summat else on.

ANNE: I will if you promise not to be a long-distance lorry driver.

JOHN: I'm only trailer mate to begin with.

ANNE: Well, trailer mate –

JOHN: Look, I'm going. I've told them I'm leaving and I've told Hamilton's I'll start there in a fortnight and so that's that. (*He snatches the disc from the turntable.*)

ANNE: No, lerrit play on, love.

JOHN: No, lerrit play on, love.

ANNE: Now look what you've done.

JOHN: It's alright,

ANNE: It's not, it's got a crack right across – Aw, love, you did that on purpose.

JOHN: No I didn't, honest.

ANNE: You meant to break it.

JOHN: No. I'm sorry.

ANNE: Too late to be sorry now –

JOHN: I'll get you another –

ANNE: Now it's done.

JOHN: Next week.

ANNE: It wouldn't have happened if you'd let it play on till –

JOHN: Oh, for God's sake don't go on about it. I've said I'll get you another bloody record next week.

ANNE: Don't start bloody swearing at me, then.

JOHN: I'm not swearing at you, I said it was a bloody awful record.

ANNE: No you didn't. I know what you meant.

JOHN: It's only a record.

ANNE: How would you like me to smash one of your favourite records?
(*JOHN turns away.*)
No, you wouldn't like it, would you.
(*JOHN turns back. She takes his record from his hands and breaks it.*)

JOHN: What did you go and do that for? I only cracked yours.

ANNE: Well.

JOHN: Very clever.

ANNE: Aw, love.

JOHN: Very funny.

ANNE: I'll get you another next week.

JOHN: Aw, gerroff, kid.

(*There is a knock at their door.*)

ANNE: Mrs Broadbent, see.

JOHN: Well, go open it.

ANNE: I shan't ope –

JOHN: (*Opening the door.*) Yes Mrs –

TUBBS: I'm not complaining, like, but could you shut up for a bit 'cos there's a boxing match on in five minutes and I can't hear very well. I don't want to turn it up loud 'cos Eric's not too well, you know, like, you don't when they're –

JOHN: We shan't say another word.

TUBBS: Aw, I don't mean you to sit quiet, like, just so's I can hear, you know.

JOHN: Yes. Alright.

TUBBS: It's Dai Gower and er – someone else. A big fight.

JOHN: Ben Scott, isn't it?

TUBBS: I believe so. Would you like to see it?

JOHN: I'd like to, yes.

TUBBS: And your missus?

JOHN: She doesn't like boxing. Keep her quiet for a bit, anyway.

TUBBS: Come on then.

(*JOHN and TUBBS go. ANNE puts her record on and tearfully drifts into the past as the needle skids across the cracked groove and plays 'Give me your shoulder to cry on-ryon-ryon'. The sound fades with the light as the chandelier is lit and the turntable revolves again, restoring the strains of 'Domani'.*)

WATTS: There. Gives you some idea how it'll look.

MRS BROADBENT: Oh isn't it lovely?

WATTS: It's a bit bright with this other bulb on. I'll take it out. (*He climbs the ladder and takes the bulb from the hanging light.*)

MRS BROADBENT: Yes, I shan't be needing that in here any more.

WATTS: See how it looks.

MRS BROADBENT: That's better. (*She turns slowly in the pink light. Anna Neagle in Technicolor.*)

WATTS: You've got the frock to go with it too.

MRS BROADBENT: This is a cocktail dress. I wore it for the carnival on the Grand Canal. Fireworks, stars, music, oh it was so beautiful and warm and the bridges were all lit up and reflected so prettily in the water with the lamps swinging from the gondolas. (*She is turning.*) On the last night our party went to a dance. They played this and I loved it so they played it again for me – but I had no one to dance with there. They all danced...
(*WATTS rescues the glass from her hand.*)
round and round...

WATTS: I wish I'd been there with you. I'd have danced you round and round.

MRS BROADBENT: Would you? That would have been nice. Can you dance?
(*WATTS takes her to him.*)
You can – ha-haa, so you can.

WATTS: I could have gone with you, too, if I'd known in time about Lena.

MRS BROADBENT: Oh yes. Where has she taken it?

WATTS: To her father.

MRS BROADBENT: Won't he throw her out when he sees what she's brought home?

WATTS: He won't know the difference. He's blind.

MRS BROADBENT: Poor Eric.

WATTS: She's better out of the way – isn't she.

MRS BROADBENT: Yes, much better out of the way.

WATTS: Both of 'em.

MRS BROADBENT: Da da da da – da de da de *domani. Uno bello domani. Domani.* Do you know what that means *Señor? Domani?* Tomorrow. *Oona bellasima domani.*

WATTS: I'd like to have gone.

MRS BROADBENT: You must go – next year, *señor,* he-haa, next month – go *domani.*

WATTS: I could almost believe I were there now, with the wine and the chandelier and the music and us dancing

MRS BROADBENT: Ha-haa, here, you're a gondolier.
(*She scoops up the gondolier's hat and puts it on WATT's head.*) Row me to the bridge of sighs.

(*WATTS is too close and sensual.*)
You've had too much to drink, Mister Watts. What are
you trying to do?

WATTS: I always knew you weren't the restrained type.
Once you let yourself go a bit you're alright.

MRS BROADBENT: I'm dizzy.

WATTS: I've had it in mind to hold you like this for years.
Pressed up against you close, whispering in your ear,
breathing –

MRS BROADBENT: Let go ughmm!

WATTS: I've got you.

MRS BROADBENT: Let go of –

WATTS: You let go, just hold on, let yourself go.

MRS BROADBENT: Take your hands –

WATTS: Relax a bit. (*He now has MRS BROADBENT's
breasts in his palms and presses her nipples against his
thumbs.*) Come on, I'll fix you up.

MRS BROADBENT: Your coarse engineering hands off –

WATTS: Take you in hand.

MRS BROADBENT: Don't speak – (*She breaks free and
almost falls over.*)

WATTS: You like me, don't you?

MRS BROADBENT: Hmmm.

WATTS: Pretend I'm a gondolier, then.

MRS BROADBENT: That's enough, Mister Watts.

WATTS: Punting you down to the canals.

MRS BROADBENT: You're making a fool of yourself.

WATTS: With the lamps swinging.

MRS BROADBENT: You have already.

WATTS: And the fireworks.

MRS BROADBENT: How's your headache?

WATTS: Bursting above us.

MRS BROADBENT: Very much better by the –

WATTS: Or pretend I'm –

MRS BROADBENT: Sound of you.

WATTS: Doctor Kendrick. Yes. That should please you,
alright. Pretend I'm Doctor Douglas, eh? Alright? Oh,
I've noticed. I'm not silly and so has Mister Tubbs.

He saw it before I did, the postcard – 'from Venice yours deepest affectionate'. We shouldn't have read it but it were lying there the whole day, he didn't come back until teatime.

MRS BROADBENT: If you're trying to, to upset to to and provoke me and and by inventing and –

WATTS: No. No. Nay. No. I don't want to do that. Why would I want to do that? I'm on your side, your side. I've met his sort before, do anything for their egos, that's all they are, all they have is egos, couldn't care less about you. You know I've been fond of you for years and I could do nothing about it before this but when Lena packed off and I saw I was rid of her for good an'all I thought we'd get together and make the best of things and instead you let Kendrick play you up. You'd let Doctor Douglas turn your den into a consulting room, I bet, wouldn't you, medical examination on the sheepskin rug eh?

MRS BROADBENT: I've never shown any more interest in the doctor than I have in any of my other tenants. I never encouraged you in any way. I tried to help. I saw you were unhappy with Lena, that's all, and that's the only reason I concerned myself with your affairs. Now that she's gone there's no need for me to go on sympathizsing with you any more at all.

WATTS: You've shown me more than your sympathy with the way you look at me in these six years past, you turned me on, you put perfume on, you –

MRS BROADBENT: Don't insinuate yourself to me.

WATTS: I used to think you were stuck up at first, then I felt sorry for you. I could tell you were just frustrated, your refined airs and your false front weren't the real you, I knew that, knew I was in with a chance… So did you.

MRS BROADBENT: I wish you'd go, Eric.

WATTS: Yes, I will.

MRS BROADBENT: And I hope you'll have the sense to leave by the end of the week.

WATTS: You make me want to go. I didn't need you that bad or your money either. I suppose I just felt a bit

randy, like, now that Lena's taken her hook. Lena never
knew what it was about half the time, poor girl. I liked
her most when she was like that, when she didn't know
what we were at.

(*KENDRICK appears.*)

You know what you're at, though, and you're scared
aren't you? You know what you're at, too, don't you?
And you're not scared. Do you know? He's after your
mother's money, that's what. That's all you or any
woman's got that he wants. Money. Night, Douglas.

(*He goes to his room. KENDRICK backs away during what
follows and retreats to his room to pack his case. MRS
BROADBENT follows him.*)

MRS BROADBENT: Douglas – oh Douglas, hold me and
tell me it isn't true – tell me he's lying. You love me, you
do, you must love me. He's listening now, tell him, he
can hear us, don't let him. I'm so glad you came back
when you did. You rescued me just in time – it was
terrible – what he tried to – he made advances, made
love to me... I didn't let him, I couldn't, I thought of
you and I couldn't. He said he'd fix it, push the wires in
and light up my chandelier, he drank some wine, he took
hold of me and danced. He made me dance with him.
He tried to kiss me. I fought him off, I struggled and he
tore my dress – he's stronger than I am and he – it isn't
money you want, it's me, isn't it, me you're fond of – it's
not the money. Tell me he's lying.

KENDRICK: He's lying.

MRS BROADBENT: Oh, I knew – forgive me for –

KENDRICK: So are you.

MRS BROADBENT: I'm not, he –

KENDRICK: I don't want you either.

MRS BROADBENT: Douglas –

KENDRICK: I want you to be real, face reality.

MRS BROADBENT: Yes, I know –

KENDRICK: Be yourself. That's all. Live in the present.

MRS BROADBENT: I am.

KENDRICK: No.

MRS BROADBENT: I need you, love you.

KENDRICK: I'll have to come back for the books.

MRS BROADBENT: It's real, I'm real.

KENDRICK: Spell it.

MRS BROADBENT: You need me.

KENDRICK: I need to move out. You need a week's rent in notice. (*He gives MRS BROADBENT money.*)

MRS BROADBENT: Pretend I'm young.

KENDRICK: It wouldn't help.

MRS BROADBENT: And sober.

KENDRICK: You're sick.

MRS BROADBENT: Or pretend –

KENDRICK: I'm off.

MRS BROADBENT: I'm a patient. That's all I ever was to you, isn't it, a patient.

KENDRICK: Yes.

MRS BROADBENT: Am I very ill, doctor?

KENDRICK: It's not terminal. You'll recover.

MRS BROADBENT: Take care of me.

KENDRICK: I'm not available.

MRS BROADBENT: Don't leave me.

KENDRICK: You'll survive.

MRS BROADBENT: Not on my own.

KENDRICK: You have Kevin. Worry about him, he's the one needs looking after. You should be teaching him to live in the real world.

MRS BROADBENT: I am, I do.

KENDRICK: And your chandelier?

MRS BROADBENT: It's mine and it's real.

KENDRICK: It's out of place. You don't live in a ballroom or the tea lounge at the Ritz.

MRS BROADBENT: I like it.

KENDRICK: It's phoney.

MRS BROADBENT: It's pink.

KENDRICK: If you don't change, Kevin'll grow up a snob with the opinions of a genteel pre-war Sunday school teacher.

MRS BROADBENT: Don't you love this song... 'Why don't you change your name to mine, *domani...*' I don't want to change you... (*She puts her arms round KENDRICK.*)

KENDRICK: Yes you do. You would. You're drunk.

MRS BROADBENT: I know I am, I know how to spell, dee – ar – yoo – en – kay and I'm really thirty-eight and not the right shape not clever – frustrated, in love with you because you're young and very mean to me and want me to be real and not have a chandelier in my little den with music in the background playing from the Mediterranean – and you think I'm making a fool of myself in front of everybody, Mister Watts is listening, are you listening Mister Watts and Mister Tubbs?

(*JOHN comes from TUBBS' room.*)

– oh and Mister Clegg too, what are you doing down here?

JOHN: Boxing.

MRS BROADBENT: Not Mister Tubbs, punching Mister Tubbs?

TUBBS: (*Coming out.*) What's going on?

(*ANNE also comes down to investigate.*)

MRS BROADBENT: I'm living in the present. It makes life worth living. 'Specially if you mean what you say and say what you mean. Eh? Try it, all of you. Douglas is leaving us.

KENDRICK: Goodbye.

(*He nods and leaves with his case. Awkward silence. MRS BROADBENT, in distress, goes to the front door.*)

MRS BROADBENT: I'll post your books on to you at the infirmary – doctor.

(*KENDRICK stays by the gate. MRS BROADBENT goes in, numbed. ANNE, JOHN and TUBBS stare at her. Silence. WATTS opens his door and takes in the scene.*)

WATTS: Everything alright?

(*Silence.*)

JOHN: Hope you don't mind my saying it, Mrs Broadbent, but you must try and be a bit quieter around the house.

TUBBS: Aye. We wondered what all t'noise was.

JOHN: Disturbing us tenants.

MRS BROADBENT: Does it. Oh. Yes. Oh, Mister Clegg, would you like to finish off the rest of this wine?

JOHN: Oh, yeah. Thanks.

MRS BROADBENT: Chianti.

ANNE: Never had that before.

MRS BROADBENT: You'll like it.

TUBBS: Nice bottle. You could hang it up with that raffia.

MRS BROADBENT: Put a candle in it and have candlelit
    suppers in your room. No. Don't. Throw it away. Good
    night. Sorry about the noise.

JOHN: Only joking.

MRS BROADBENT: Good night, everybody. (*She goes to
    her room.*)

TUBBS: Night, Mrs Broadbent.

JOHN: Thanks for letting us watch television.

TUBBS: Any time. Night, then. (*He goes into his room.*)

ANNE: Was it alright?

(*JOHN and ANNE go upstairs, arms on each other's shoulders.
TUBBS undresses for bed watching his set. MRS BROADBENT
takes off her earrings, picks up the light bulb and starts to
climb the stepladder as though about to replace the bulb. She
rests her forehead on the top step. KEVIN appears on the
landing in pyjamas, listening. WATTS, alone in the hall,
moves to the doorway of MRS BROADBENT's room and
stays there, looking in. KENDRICK is facing the house as
the slow moving figures fade into its dark silhouette. A figure
stands behind him in the shadows. KENDRICK turns away.
The man stands in his way. It is GENTLES.*)

KENDRICK: Sorry.

GENTLES: I was right. Douglas. I don't forget you, see.

KENDRICK: Yes, wait – Winston.

GENTLES: Clement.

KENDRICK: Clement. I knew it was a prime minister.

GENTLES: This where you live?

KENDRICK: Not any more. I just moved out.

GENTLES: I saw you leave, I jus' passing and I saw you
    come out, jump out from the door. Like the place on fire
    or what?

KENDRICK No.

GENTLES: Something wrong?

KENDRICK: No.

GENTLES: So why you movin' house so fast in the moonlight for?

KENDRICK: I'm not moving in anywhere, just moving out.

GENTLES Oh Gawd, you move out with no place to go. Now I know why I come for a walk. Is fate so we meet up again Dee. You stay over my place.

KENDRICK: Your bed's a bit small for staying overnight.

GENTLES: I got a new one since last time you come. I save up. King-size firm mattress now man, all comfort to lie back and stretch yourself on. Clean sheets, pillows, I'll fix you so good you won't want to get up all weekend. Gimme that. (*He takes the case.*) Anybody passing'll think you gimme a tip to carry it for you. We don't want people to get the right idea.

(KENDRICK and GENTLES hold a look of amused sensual anticipation. They slap each others palms and walk off along the pavement, speaking as they go.)

KENDRICK: I forget where you said you were born.

GENTLES: Where you think?

KENDRICK: Trinidad?

GENTLES: Slaves on plantations.

KENDRICK: Jamaica?

GENTLES: Sugar plantations.

KENDRICK: Cuba.

GENTLES: Brown sugar.

KENDRICK: Barbados.

GENTLES: Right.

KENDRICK: Brown sugar has more taste, but white's more refined.

GENTLES: Oh yes? You think so. We'll see. We'll see. (*Blackout.*)

The End.

ALL GOOD CHILDREN

Characters

ANNA BOWERS
aged 31, single

MAURICE BOWERS
aged 35, her brother, a merchant seaman

CISSY BOWERS
aged 60, their mother

ELIZABETH MATTHEWS
aged 56, a friend of the family

CLIFFORD BOWERS
aged 33, second son, a biochemist

FRANK BOWERS
in his late 50s, Jacob's brother

REV JACOB BOWERS
aged 65

All Good Children was commisioned by George Devine and first performed at the Bromley Little Theatre in 1959, with the following cast:

ANNA BOWERS, Prunella Scales

MAURICE BOWERS, Jeremy Brett

CISSY BOWERS, Betty Pinchard

ELIZABETH MATTHEWS, Constance Lorne

CLIFFORD BOWERS, David Korda

FRANK BOWERS, Clifford Parrish

REV JACOB BOWERS, Robert Eddison

Director, Vladek Sheybal

The play was subsequently performed at the Hampstead Theatre on 30 April 1964, with the following cast:

ANNA BOWERS, Frances Cuka

MAURICE BOWERS, Garry Watson

CISSY BOWERS, Marion Spencer

ELIZABETH MATTHEWS, Nora Swinburne

CLIFFORD BOWERS, Gilbert Wynne

FRANK BOWERS, Trevor Reid

REV JACOB BOWERS, Mervyn Johns

Director, Donald Howarth

Designer, Kenneth Mellor

A note about staging. A door into a tiled hall leads to the kitchen and the front door. The staircase starts where the hall ends. The door to the bathroom is on a landing halfway up the stairs which continue to a passage to the bedrooms. There is a cupboard under the stairs, coat hooks and a mirror. The living-room looks out on to the garden. A door with glass panes leads to it. A heavy curtain can be drawn across the door. A fireplace with fender boxes, a sofa, a drop-leaf dining-table set for tea, a sideboard and an upright piano.

ACT ONE

Scene 1

The living-room of Donisthorpe Manse, a converted farmhouse, in South Yorkshire. Five o'clock on the last Saturday afternoon in August. The doors into the room are open.

ANNA BOWERS waits. Past caring, she sits at the table, her head on her arm. An aster hangs limply from her hand. CISSY, her mother, and LIZ MATHEWS are in the garden, chatting about flowers. MAURICE, her brother, stops whistling and comes from the bathroom. He wears a navy-blue vest revealing a suntan and tattoos. He is rugged and good-looking. He towels his hair dry, leans over the banister, listens, then whispers loudly.

MAURICE: Anna. Anna.
   (*ANNA goes into the hall.*)
   Sssssh!
ANNA: What?
MAURICE: Is Haughty Culture still with us?
ANNA: In the garden.
MAURICE: She's not staying, is she?
ANNA: She hasn't said so.
MAURICE: Well don't let her.
ANNA: I won't.
MAURICE: Good girl.
   (*He goes upstairs. ANNA pulls a petal off the aster and goes back into the living-room. The hall clock chimes five. She puts the aster in a vase on the table as she goes to the garden door.*)
ANNA: Are you staying for tea, Miss Mathews?
LIZ: (*Off.*) Am I what dear?
ANNA: You must stay for tea.
LIZ: (*Off.*) Oh, tea – no, no, dear child, thank you.
   (*CISSY and LIZ appear. CISSY is sixty years old, soft and always agreeable. LIZ is fifty-six, false and gay.*)
CISSY: Yes you will. Lay a place, love.
LIZ: I must get back, really I should.

CISSY: You can stay for half an hour, just to see Clifford.
    (*She puts her gardening gloves on the mantelpiece. They fall off.*)
LIZ: I'll see him tomorrow. He's not flying all the way from
    Africa to see me, you'll want to be alone with him. How
    long is it since he was home?
ANNA: Two years.
CISSY: Yes it is, two years.
    (*ANNA moves the vase of asters.*)
LIZ: Don't bother, Anna, I won't stay, your mother's
    insistent but I mustn't.
ANNA: There's plenty of everything.
LIZ: Yes, and I'll be one too many. Now I'm quite firm.
    (*She puts her gloves, handbag and wrapped cuttings on the
    piano stool.*) I'll just slip upstairs if I may.
CISSY: Has Maurice finished in the bathroom, dear?
    (*She takes up her needlework.*)
ANNA: Yes.
LIZ: The garden's looking so pretty isn't it Anna – a real
    picture, Cissy – what a shame, such a pity you have to
    leave it all after so many years. You do keep it nice.
    I don't know how you find the time.
CISSY: The doctor says I don't have to work too much in
    the house. Anna manages wonderfully by herself.
ANNA: I'd rather do it myself.
CISSY: I'm pushed into the garden whenever it's fine.
LIZ: Best place for you – oh, I wanted to ask, can I move
    lupins now or should I wait till January?
CISSY: Yes, you can move lupins now, any of those perennials.
ANNA: Apart from Michaelmas daisies.
CISSY: Yes.
LIZ: I have lashings of them now, the daisies.
CISSY: So have we. Little Gethsemane's overgrown with
    them, Anna.
ANNA: I know.
LIZ: Gethsemane –
ANNA: Maurice christened it that when we played betrayals.
LIZ: Oh yes, oh I know, I remember. Clifford was always Jesus.
ANNA: And Maurice Judas.

CISSY: That's right, he was, yes.

ANNA: I prayed in the tool shed while he earned his thirty
  pieces of silver. Sometimes he'd be Simon Peter and I'd
  ask him to deny he was a disciple from Galilee. Clifford
  made the hens squawk every time he said no.

CISSY: They stopped laying for weeks. Jacob was very
  cross with them all when he found out.

ANNA: He was even crosser when he came home and
  found we'd changed Gethsemane into Eden for a day and
  used cabbage leaves to dress up as Adam and Eve.

CISSY: Ooh, yes.

LIZ: You were very naughty.

ANNA: Maurice was the serpent hanging naked upside
  down from the apple tree trying to tempt me.

CISSY: Maurice was always the wicked one.

ANNA: Twenty years makes a difference.

LIZ: Are these the asters that Vernon gave you?

ANNA: Yes.

LIZ: They're lovely. I hear he's engaged, by the way. His
  mother was telling me. To the girl who works in her
  wool shop.

CISSY: Judy Pollard – she's a pretty girl, he's lucky.

LIZ: (*Handing CISSY the vase.*) You can put them back now,
  Anna, I'm not staying, you can't persuade me. (*She goes
  into the hall. Her mood changes, she relaxes. She looks up the
  staircase, waits, then calls back.*) Has Jacob gone into town?

ANNA: No.

CISSY: He's gone over to Rosebank.

ANNA: (*Going into the hall.*) With Uncle Frank as usual, for
  a round of golf.

LIZ: (*Going upstairs.*) That means two.

ANNA: (*Watching LIZ.*) They're going on to the station
  afterwards to meet Clifford.

CISSY: (*Calling.*) He said they'd just time for one game round.
  (*LIZ has reached the small landing.*)

ANNA: They shouldn't be long now. (*Confidential and
  unpleasant.*) If you hurry you'll miss them.

(*LIZ smiles and goes into the bathroom. ANNA returns to the living-room and opens the fender box for CISSY's slippers. She kneels and removes CISSY's gardening shoes.*)

CISSY: Should we lay a place for Frank, do you think?

ANNA: It's done.

CISSY: I hope we won't need it. I want it to be nice and quiet for Clifford on his first few hours back home. (*ANNA dumps the shoes in the fender box and bangs the lid violently. CISSY pretends not to notice. ANNA reverts.*)

ANNA: Did you bud the chrysanths?

CISSY: (*Handing ANNA a needle and a length of wool to thread.*) Yes, I've done that. There 're ever so many tiny little buds again this year. Liz leaves hers on and gets a lot of small flowers. Ours wouldn't come out at all if I did that. Anyway, I like a bigger flower. Nip off the tiddlers and have one or two really big blooms. Look at her chrysanths last year, they were like your Michaelmas daisies when they finally came out. (*She waits.*) I wish Jacob would take some interest in the garden, there's so much weeding to be done.

ANNA: It's too late now.

CISSY: You've let your patch get very untidy too, Anna. I'll spend an hour on it after tea – Oh no – well, tomorrow or some time early next week. I'll put some seedlings in.

ANNA: (*Going to the garden door.*) I like it as it is. It's natural. Please don't touch it.

CISSY: You used to keep it ever so nice. Clifford'll be surprised and disappointed too when he sees how you've let it go. You kept it nicer when you played in it. (*MAURICE comes along the landing as LIZ comes from the bathroom. They talk as they go down the stairs.*)

MAURICE: Good afternoon, Elizabeth.

LIZ: Oh hello, Maurice. Elizabeth!

MAURICE: Are you staying for tea?

LIZ: Your mother's just been trying to persuade me.

MAURICE: Did she?

LIZ: They both have but I'm not to be tempted.

MAURICE: No?

LIZ: (*Picking up her handbag and gloves.*) I must be on my way. You're looking very smart.

CISSY: That your new suit, Maurice?

LIZ: Oh, a new suit.

CISSY: Won't you stay, dear?

LIZ: Ha-ha-ha no-no-no.

ANNA: (*Picking up the cuttings.*) I'm sure you would if Maurice asked.

LIZ: Master Maurice never did what I asked him to, so why should I? You never practised your piano lessons when you were young.

ANNA: I'm sure Father would want you to stay.

LIZ: I'd stay like a shot if Clifford asked me.

ANNA: Clifford isn't here.

MAURICE: Yet.

CISSY: They are late.

LIZ: Clifford never missed a lesson.

ANNA: Neither did I. (*She discards the cuttings.*)

LIZ: I used to think he'd be a pianist one day.

CISSY: Don't forget your cuttings.

LIZ: No. Aren't they lovely, those little orangey French marigold type in the bathroom?

ANNA: Has she given you some of those?

CISSY: Some of which, love?

MAURICE: The French types in the bathroom.

CISSY: (*Passing the cuttings to ANNA.*) Oh, the little – yes, yes there is a root there, Liz.

LIZ: Lovely, thank you.

MAURICE: Not at all.

CISSY: You might as well have them.

LIZ: I'll look forward to those.

ANNA: (*Giving LIZ the cuttings.*) They won't survive. They're annuals.

LIZ: Well, I *will* be off. And I'll see you tomorrow all of you, at the service.

CISSY: We must be there tomorrow.

MAURICE: Mustn't miss the last judgement –

ANNA: See you tomorrow.

LIZ: Give my love to Clifford. Tell him I'll be round for a duet.

CISSY: I will.

MAURICE: He'll look forward to that.

ANNA: Yes, he'll like that.

CISSY: We all will.

LIZ: Goodbye children.

CISSY: Come through the garden.

LIZ: Love to. (*She turns and goes to the other door.*)

MAURICE: *Au revoir.*

ANNA: Afternoon, Miss Mathews. (*She follows LIZ.*)

LIZ: Liz. Miss Mathews. (*She hops up into the vestibule, takes a chiffon scarf from her pocket and waves it at them.*) Sing up tomorrow.

ANNA: We will.

    (*LIZ and CISSY go.*)

MAURICE: Jesus wept.

ANNA: Maurice.

MAURICE: Thank Christ for that.

ANNA: Don't.

MAURICE: Well, she gets on my New Testament.

ANNA: They'll hear you.

MAURICE: How'd you like to travel to Damascus with her?

ANNA: You're not likely to.

MAURICE: Hallelujah.

ANNA: You shouldn't swear.

MAURICE: What did I say, for Christ's sake?

ANNA: You shouldn't blaspheme.

MAURICE: I didn't swear.

ANNA: Not in this house.

MAURICE: God's house. Christ's not swearing. He'd have sympathised. He'd have understood.

ANNA: God wouldn't.

MAURICE: God's not at home.

ANNA: He will be any minute.

MAURICE: Angels like you should be seen not heard.

ANNA: Guardian angels have to speak sometimes.

MAURICE: I listen to my conscience.

ANNA: Tell it to speak up.

MAURICE: What did you say?

ANNA: It's lost its voice.

MAURICE: Pardon?

ANNA: Fool –

MAURICE: Can't hear.

ANNA: Deaf fool.

(*They laugh. ANNA half hits and half pushes MAURICE away.*)

CISSY: (*Calling off.*) Anna, I'm just walking part way down the lane with Liz. I shan't be long.

ANNA: Fasten your cardigan.

LIZ: (*Off.*) I've told her not to bother.

CISSY: (*Off.*) Yes, I will.

MAURICE: Well – poor Liz, she's going to have a lonely time of it when Father leaves.

ANNA: Spare some of your sympathy for me. I have to go with them.

MAURICE: Poor Anna.

ANNA: I'll retire with them to the outer darkness of outer Hockton and never be heard of again.

MAURICE: Except in the obituary column of the local paper.

ANNA: Pleasant prospect.

MAURICE: You should have run away at fifteen as I did.

ANNA: You should have taken me with you, I missed you.

MAURICE: You were under age.

ANNA: And under-privileged.

MAURICE: You were a girl.

ANNA: A good girl.

MAURICE: That would really have finished Mother, if we'd both gone. Father blames me for her collapse, when I left home the shock nearly killed her, he says.

ANNA: (*Picking up CISSY's gardening gloves and shoes from the hearth.*) She's been weak ever since I was born; in giving me life she gave too much of her own –

MAURICE/ANNA: – he says.

ANNA: Don't tell me I should have run away, I didn't have the opportunity.

MAURICE: Would you have taken it?

ANNA: I'd take it now.

MAURICE: Elope? Who with? Vernon?

ANNA: Vernon's engaged. Liz just told us.

MAURICE: I'm sorry.

ANNA: I'm not, he's too fond of asters to make a good husband. (*She thrusts the gardening gloves and shoes at MAURICE.*) Here – put these under the stairs and stay with them.

MAURICE: I've just changed.

ANNA: Never mind.

MAURICE: Like this suit?

ANNA: No.

MAURICE: Good, that means she will.

ANNA: Who?

MAURICE: Bernadette Grindley. We're going dancing. My last night here, my last chance.

ANNA: You can't go out tonight, Maurice.
  (*CISSY enters.*)

CISSY: Anna, pass my gloves, dear. I want to pick a slug off the path.

ANNA: Maurice.

MAURICE: Hello.

ANNA: Gloves please.

MAURICE: Boots?

ANNA: Just gloves.

MAURICE: Just gloves.

CISSY: Only one.

MAURICE: Only one.
  (*ANNA takes a glove from MAURICE.*)

ANNA: Here you are.

CISSY: Thank you, Maurice.

MAURICE: Pleasure.

CISSY: (*To herself.*) I'd forgotten I had my slippers on.
  (*She goes. MAURICE puts the boots and the one glove away in the hall cupboard. The clock chimes five thirty. ANNA goes up on to the vestibule and looks into the garden. MAURICE comes back.*)

ANNA: (*Turning to MAURICE.*) I do like your suit really, Maurice.

MAURICE: You do?

ANNA: Yes.

CISSY: (*Off.*) Beastly horrid thing.

MAURICE: Suits me?

(*ANNA nods.*)

Swear it?

ANNA: God's honour.

MAURICE: Cross your heart and wonder why.

ANNA: Wonder why.

MAURICE: Cross your fingers and hope to lie.

ANNA: Hope to lie.

MAURICE: Cross your eyes and try to cry.

ANNA: Try to cry.

MAURICE: (*Holding his tie out.*) And this?

ANNA: I like it.

MAURICE: You've got your eyes shut.

ANNA: I saw it before I closed them.

MAURICE: Goes well?

ANNA: Very well.

MAURICE: You're just saying that.

ANNA: Yes, I was.

CISSY: Just saying what?

ANNA: That I ought to go and look at my weeds. (*She opens her eyes. She is crying.*)

CISSY: Not before tea, Anna.

ANNA: (*Looking out into the garden to hide her face.*) Just look at them.

CISSY: You always pick the wrong time to do things. Fancy gardening just before tea.

(*She puts her glove on the mantelpiece. It falls off. FRANK BOWERS comes in from the garden carrying golf clubs.*)

FRANK: Hello dearie.

ANNA: Hello Uncle Frank.

CISSY: Frank –

ANNA: Miss Mathews –

LIZ: (*Entering.*) Yes, I'm back again.

CISSY: Liz.

FRANK: Hello, Cissy. Hello, Maurice. I called in to see you last night but you'd just gone out.

CISSY: Where are they, Frank?

FRANK: You mean to say they're not here yet?

LIZ: I told him they wouldn't be.

FRANK: I left Jack at the station. I didn't think he'd want me on the platform when Cliff steps off the train and then they can talk on the way home in the taxi.

CISSY: Yes.

FRANK: I've walked.

LIZ: He insisted I be here to say hello.

CISSY: I am glad. We laid a place for her but she wouldn't stay.

MAURICE: Elizabeth can have my place, Anna.

FRANK: You're not leaving us, Maurice?

MAURICE: It's Saturday. (*He helps to take CISSY's cardigan off.*)

CISSY: You're not going out again tonight, dear. You haven't seen Clifford for longer than any of us.

MAURICE: I kept him in mind.

CISSY: I know you think about us all when you're off on the boat –

MAURICE: Ship.

CISSY: Ship – he'll want to know where you've been –

MAURICE: And what I've been doing.

LIZ: Yes, and how you're getting on.

CISSY: We must all be here for your father's sake.

FRANK: Aye, it's a reunion.

MAURICE: I'm going to a dance at the Co-op Hall.

ANNA: With Bernadette Grindley.

CISSY: What time does it start?

MAURICE: Eight till twelve.

FRANK: You'll wait till they get here, though.

CISSY: Yes, he will. You'll be able to talk for an hour or two before you go.

MAURICE: We're catching the six o'clock.

ANNA: Must you?

MAURICE: Promised.

CISSY: Yes, there is one at six.

LIZ: They run every hour.

CISSY: I haven't been to a proper dance for as long as I can remember.

FRANK: You're not married yet, then?

MAURICE: Not yet.

FRANK: No, you wouldn't look like you do if you were –
    hahergh – well, it's about time one of you got married.
    How's Anna's little romance getting on? Vernon
    Athrington.

ANNA: I don't see much of him.

FRANK: Not much of him to see is there, eh?

CISSY: He's a nice boy.

FRANK: Oh, he's alright, Vernon, well off, little gold mine
    that wool shop of his mother's.
    (*A kettle begins to whistle in the kitchen. LIZ puts the cuttings
    and her handbag down and sits.*)

ANNA: We're not engaged, we just see each other.

CISSY: At Sunday School.

ANNA: Every Tuesday evening at the Christian Endeavour
    classes.

CISSY: Vernon takes the Senior and Anna the Junior
    and on –

MAURICE: Let me take your clubs, Frank.
    (*ANNA goes into the kitchen.*)

FRANK: Thanks.

CISSY: How was the golf, Frank?

FRANK: How was the golf – hah! How was the golf? I won.
    I did. I beat him proper.

CISSY: That is unusual.

FRANK: (*To LIZ.*) First time I've won a round in four years.
    You should have seen your father's face when I got a
    birdie, when he was bunkered in the pit, spraying sand
    up on to the green as though he was shovelling a trench.
    He got real hot under the collar – hah! dog collar. Glad
    I won the last round.
    (*MAURICE puts the clubs in the hall.*)

CISSY: Let me take your coat, Liz, Anna must have forgot.
    (*ANNA comes from the kitchen.*)

ANNA: Would you fetch a tray please, Maurice.

CISSY: What time is it?

FRANK: Turned half five.

CISSY: Yes, I'll go and wash my hands and just look to see if they're coming through the bathroom window.

FRANK: Bound to be, I should think, unless the train was late in.

(*CISSY hangs the coat in the hall. MAURICE gets a tray from the living-room.*)

CISSY: I'm going upstairs to watch from the window, Anna. I do hope they get here before Maurice goes.

ANNA: I'll speak to him.

CISSY: Don't upset him. (*She goes.*)

MAURICE: You're not married yet then?

FRANK: Not yet.

MAURICE: No, you wouldn't look like you do if you were. Both of you.

(*LIZ smiles. MAURICE closes the door of the room and goes into the kitchen with ANNA. FRANK looks at LIZ who turns away wearily.*)

LIZ: No, Frank. (*She folds her gloves.*)

FRANK: I wasn't going to say anything.

LIZ: I knew I shouldn't have come back with you.

FRANK: I wasn't going to ask you, I swore I'd never ask you again years ago. Well...I'm not asking you now. I'm saying nothing.

LIZ: Good.

FRANK: Anyway, we're neither of us so young any more like that, are we?

LIZ: No.

FRANK: I shall be giving up the business soon. I did just think that with Jacob going now, perhaps you might reconsider – I mean, I feel the same you know.

LIZ: Thank you, Frank. You needn't say any more. (*She puts CISSY's needlework in the sewing bag.*) You're taking the furniture down to Hockton for them, aren't you?

FRANK: Yes, I am. On Wednesday, taking the pantechnicon. I've only got two vans now. Course, I'm not charging them.

(*CISSY comes from the bathroom and goes up the stairs.*)

LIZ: Of course not. How long will it take you?

FRANK: About six hours, a day's work. It's my going-away present to them.

LIZ: Will you miss them very much?

FRANK: I shan't have a golf mate on Saturdays. Will you miss him very much?

LIZ: Perhaps – on Sundays.

(*A taxi is heard approaching. It stops. Car doors bang. JACOB and CLIFFORD BOWERS are heard. ANNA comes from the kitchen pushing a loaded tea-trolley. MAURICE helps her.*)

ANNA: Perfect timing. They're here.

LIZ: Oh good.

FRANK: Here we go, come on.

ANNA: Call Mother.

MAURICE: I'll take the trolley.

ANNA: No, you go and unload.

CISSY: (*Calling off.*) He's here... Frank, Maurice.

FRANK: (*Calling.*) We know. You're too late.

(*FRANK goes out. CISSY appears at the top of the stairs. LIZ goes to the foot of the stairs.*)

CISSY: (*Coming down.*) I'd just got to the window in the front bedroom when I heard them.

(*ANNA goes to the vestibule, blocking the way.*)

LIZ: Come along, hurry up, you must be on the doorstep.

JACOB: (*Off.*) I'll take that, Clifford.

(*MAURICE faces ANNA.*)

ANNA: Maurice –

MAURICE: If I don't go now I'll miss the train.

ANNA: Just for one minute.

MAURICE: You can explain.

FRANK: (*Calling off.*) Cissy.

CISSY: I'm coming. (*She joins LIZ at the foot of the stairs.*)

ANNA: Hold the taxi for five minutes, you'll be on time.

MAURICE: And you'll pay?

ANNA: I'll pay.

MAURICE: Hah!

ANNA: I can.

MAURICE: I wouldn't take money from the char.

ANNA: From your sister then.

MAURICE: From any woman. (*He pushes past ANNA.*)
ANNA: Stay.
MAURICE: I couldn't.
ANNA: You won't. (*She holds on to MAURICE's upper arms.*)
MAURICE: I can't. (*He takes hold of ANNA's upper arms.*)
ANNA: You don't care.
MAURICE: That's right.
ANNA: Genesis, Exodus –
MAURICE: Leviticus, Numbers –
ANNA: Judas –
MAURICE: Iscariot –
ANNA: Peter –
MAURICE: Caiaphas –
ANNA: Samson –
MAURICE: Delilah –
ANNA: Goliath.
　　(*MAURICE breaks free.*)
MAURICE: Martyr.
ANNA: Snake.
MAURICE: Virgin.
ANNA: Coward.
MAURICE: Saint.
ANNA: Maurice –
MAURICE: Anna –
CISSY: Clifford –
　　(*CLIFFORD comes in. JACOB follows carrying a suitcase.
　　CLIFFORD is thirty-three, JACOB sixty-five.*)
MAURICE: You win.
　　(*He sits. ANNA closes the garden door.*)
CLIFFORD: Hello, Mother.
CISSY: We thought you were never coming.
LIZ: Was the train late in?
CLIFFORD: Hello, Elizabeth.
JACOB: No, very punctual; we had to wait for the
　　Donisthorpe taxi.
FRANK: (*Coming in.*) No call for taxis in Donisthorpe. How
　　are you, Clifford? Welcome home.
CLIFFORD: Very well, Frank.

FRANK: You look very well.
(*They shake hands.*)
Where's your other luggage?
CISSY: He's only here for three days.
JACOB: Where's Maurice?
MAURICE: (*Getting up.*) I was combing my hair.
CLIFFORD: Well, well. Hello, Maurice.
MAURICE: Well, well. Hello, Clifford.
(*They shake hands.*)
CLIFFORD: He's browner than I am.
CISSY: Yes, you're both looking very well.
JACOB: Take your coat off, son.
CISSY: Yes, take your coat off, Clifford. (*She helps him.*)
MAURICE: We're in the nursery together.
LIZ: No pillow fighting, either.
CISSY: No.
LIZ: Remember, I'd no sooner have tucked them in than
they'd be at it, feathers all over the room.
CLIFFORD: I'm a pacifist now.
JACOB: I hope you always were. (*He takes CLIFFORD's coat
from CISSY and hangs it in the hall.*)
FRANK: Shall I take that case upstairs?
JACOB: Leave it in the hall until we've had tea.
ANNA: It's all ready. Hello, Clifford.
CLIFFORD: I wondered where you were hiding. (*He kisses
ANNA on the cheek.*)
ANNA: You're right, you're not as brown as Maurice.
Doesn't the sun shine in Africa either?
CLIFFORD: I spend most of my time under the laboratory
roof, no time for the sun.
JACOB: Where are we all going to sit, Anna?
ANNA: I thought you at the end.
JACOB: Clifford and Elizabeth this side, then. You've
changed the position of the table.
ANNA: To face the sun.
FRANK: Good idea.
JACOB: Frank.
(*ANNA picks up the piano stool and takes it to the bottom
end of the table.*)

CISSY: I'll stay here, Anna, and you can bring it to me.

ANNA: Alright.

CISSY: If you don't mind.

ANNA: Why should I?

JACOB: For what has gone before is now and yet to come our grateful thanks to thee we give O Lord.

LIZ/ANNA/CISSY: Amen.

(*MAURICE coughs. An approaching train is heard in the distance.*)

CISSY: Help yourself, everybody.

ANNA: Pass things round.

CISSY: Shall you pour the tea Anna, or shall I?

ANNA: (*From the trolley.*) I'll do it.

(*Food is passed, tea poured and distributed, sugar spooned, salt sprinkled and celery bitten but nobody speaks. The clock chimes six.*)

MAURICE: What's on the wireless?

CISSY: You don't want to listen to the wireless. I'm sure we all want to hear from Clifford how he's getting on with his researching.

FRANK: Aye, of course.

JACOB: No no, not yet, don't answer them yet, Clifford. I want to speak first.

(*The train leaves the station. ANNA gives a plate of salad, a napkin and a knife and fork to CISSY.*)

LIZ: Must we be quiet?

MAURICE: As church mice.

JACOB: I'm not going to preach, Maurice, I just want to say how happy I am to see us all together under this roof again after so long. I wish you could be here all the time, (*Looking at LIZ.*) every one of you.

FRANK: Aye.

CISSY: Yes.

LIZ: Yes.

JACOB: So come along, Clifford, tell them how your experiments are progressing.

CISSY: Yes, are you still trying to cure malaria, Clifford?

CLIFFORD: We never were trying to cure malaria, Mother. The antibiotic drugs are very efficient these days.

MAURICE: (*Explaining.*) Quinine, you know.

CLIFFORD: Not any more, Maurice. When the supply of quinine stopped during the war, other drugs had to replace it. Mepacrine and Paludrine.

JACOB: Yes, I remember how proud we all were at home to learn that you were involved in the new discoveries.

FRANK: It was in the church magazine, Maurice.

JACOB: I have the copy upstairs, many lives were saved as a result.

MAURICE: Of the church magazine?

LIZ: Oh, Maurice!

MAURICE: Well, so alright so you're not trying to cure malaria. What do you do?

CLIFFORD: Well, you see, malaria typhoid leprosy et cetera destroy enzymes in the organic medium.

MAURICE: Oh.

FRANK: What's that?

CLIFFORD: The blood, fluids, lymph –

LIZ: Lymph?

CLIFFORD: Or plasma. The leukocytes –

MAURICE: Luke O' who?

CLIFFORD: A type of cell. Everyone has something like fifty billion leukocytes suspended in the plasma.

CISSY: Fifty billion –

CLIFFORD: They mass together in the plasma to defend diseased tissues. It's one of our natural processes.

MAURICE: Oh, I see.

CISSY: You could learn a lot from Clifford, Maurice.

MAURICE: About leukocytes.

CLIFFORD: Although they're suspended in the plasma they are in fact cells of the blood. Don't forget the blood is a tissue.

MAURICE: I hadn't remembered.

CLIFFORD: No.

ANNA: (*Offering it.*) Liver sausage, Uncle Frank?

FRANK: Er – no thanks.

CISSY: Your grandfather died from a haemorrhage.

MAURICE: A bell-boy on our ship had piles, but I didn't tell the captain.

CISSY: It just occurred to me.

MAURICE: Well, don't let it occur again.

JACOB: I shouldn't have to remind you how to behave at table at your age Maurice.

MAURICE: Sorry, I get used to the mess talk on board.

JACOB: And you should be more respectful to your mother.

MAURICE: Respectful – she loves it, don't you? Look, she's laughing. Grandfather had a haemorrhage. Terrific.

CISSY: You interrupt too much, Maurice, it's harder to follow what Clifford's saying when you interrupt him.

MAURICE: Sorry sorry, it's my leukocytes, they mass together spontaneously to defend my diseased moral conscience.

ANNA: Don't listen to him, Clifford. (*She takes the cake-stand from the trolley and offers them round.*)

CLIFFORD: I'll be more explicit.

MAURICE: Good.

CLIFFORD: A certain type of cell which determines the intensity of our organic life is destroyed by malaria. For six years we've been trying to discover how and why because our health and well-being depends upon the proper functioning of the enzymes.

MAURICE: Except in your case.

CLIFFORD: (*Dryly.*) Shall we change the subject before I get emotional?

MAURICE: Yes, cheer us up, Father. Give us a synopsis of tomorrow's sermon.

JACOB: As a matter of fact I was just thinking about it… The text is very appropriate, the parable of the talents – which I suppose you've forgotten, Maurice.

MAURICE: Matthew –

ANNA: Twenty-five –

MAURICE: Verse ten –

ANNA: Fourteen.

JACOB: (*Taking a cake.*) Remarkable.

MAURICE: For the kingdom of heaven is –

ANNA: As a man travelling into a far country –

JACOB: Who called his servants about him and delivered unto them his goods.

CISSY: Oh, that's one of my favourites. (*She takes a cake.*)

MAURICE: To one he gave five talents.

JACOB: To another two –

ANNA: (*Putting the cake-stand back.*) And to another, one.

JACOB: Each according to his ability.

FRANK: Very good.

JACOB: I have three children, to one I gave a good education and you responded to it, Clifford. I've always had faith in your talent and it has given me great joy to see you making headway over the years, benefiting humanity as you followed the career of your choice.

CLIFFORD: I've done what I can. I didn't choose to become a biochemist, you set me off, beginning with the missionary stories about the lack of tropical medicine supplies in the Archipelago. (*To JACOB.*) I'm a biochemist alright. I've done what I can.

MAURICE: Pass the bread, Anna.

CLIFFORD: But I know nothing about life like you, Maurice.

MAURICE: I'd have thought your absorption with chemical reactions would have stimulated your sex –

ANNA: Bread, Maur –

MAURICE: Your sensitivity towards women. Thank you.

JACOB: You forget your brother's nature's fortunately always been free from the licentious kind of practices and – and lewdness which you seem to have developed during your journeyings at sea so much that it infects the rest of your character.

MAURICE: I've done what I can.

JACOB: I'm sure you have.

FRANK: Cheese and chalk, Maurice and Clifford, always were.

CISSY: Yes.

JACOB: Yes, Maurice was always a wilder boy than
    Clifford. It would have been unwise of me to have
    curbed your natural good spirits unduly.

MAURICE: Good spirits! I was licentious a moment ago.

JACOB: I knew you'd take it as a compliment if I said it
    twice. Anyway, licentious or good-spirited, I believe in
    no uncertain manner that the life you've chosen at sea is
    exactly suited to your temperament.

MAURICE: I ran away, I had to work somewhere. I enjoy it
    alright, shore leave's alright you know. New Guinea, New
    Mexico, New York, all those heathen places.

ANNA: Havana.

MAURICE: Yes, and old Habana.

JACOB: You've seen the world, anyway, and just as Clifford's
    intellect has led him to discover allergies where no one
    knew they existed – I am right?
    (*CLIFFORD nods.*)
    – similarly as you voyage through life you will make
    discoveries of your own, though I doubt if they will in
    any way benefit your country or mankind.

FRANK: We can't all be alike.

CISSY: No.

FRANK: The world would be a dull place if we were.

CISSY: Yes.

FRANK: And we can't all talk like you, Jack.

MAURICE: A dull place the world would be if we did.

CISSY: Maurice, you're very late. If you're going to Little
    Town you'll have to hurry up.

JACOB: Little Town?

FRANK: You've had the six o'clock.

CISSY: Maurice has promised to go there this evening Jacob.

JACOB: You planned to go out on the first evening your
    brother spends under the same roof with you for years?

MAURICE: How could I?

JACOB: I'm asking you.

MAURICE: I changed my mind.

JACOB: Your mother said quite distinctly that you promised
    to go.

CISSY: I *thought*. I thought you were, Maurice. He must
   have meant tomorrow.

JACOB: Sunday.

CISSY: No, Jacob.

ANNA: You're very quiet, Clifford.

CLIFFORD: I'm listening.

JACOB: What attraction is there in Little Town strong
   enough to persuade you to disappoint Clifford and the
   rest of us by your absence?

ANNA: Bernadette Grindley.

FRANK: There's a dance at the Co-op Hall.

MAURICE: Would my absence have disappointed you,
   Clifford?

CLIFFORD: (*Goading him.*) Yes, Maurice, it would.

MAURICE: That's why I couldn't go. How could anybody
   disappoint Clifford?

CLIFFORD: Life is full of disappointments, Maurice.
   By not going to the dance tonight I'm sure you're
   disappointing Bernadette. I had to disappoint my
   employers last month by handing in my resignation.

JACOB: Your resignation!

CISSY: Why, Clifford!

FRANK: You've left, then.

CISSY: Does that mean you don't have to go away again so
   soon?

JACOB: They didn't accept it, of course.

CLIFFORD: They had no choice – I've been offered
   another post.

FRANK: Oh well, if you've been promoted.

CISSY: That's wonderful. I'm very pleased for you, Clifford.
   Are you going to cure a new disease?

CLIFFORD: Yes.

CISSY: Fancy! When do you start?

CLIFFORD: They'll be contacting me by letter.

CISSY: Wonderful.

ANNA: Why didn't you tell us before?

JACOB: Clifford's modesty's a natural asset.

CISSY: Yes.

MAURICE: Must take after you.

ANNA: Have you all had enough?

MAURICE: Quite enough.

CISSY: More tea, anyone – Liz?

FRANK: Not for me, thank you.

CISSY: It's getting dark in here.

ANNA: I'll put the light on and clear away.

FRANK: Nights are drawing in fast now.

CISSY: It's getting colder too. I noticed it in the garden this afternoon.

JACOB: You shouldn't stay out in the garden when it's cold. Anna should have made you come in.

ANNA: The doctor said –

JACOB: That she needs fresh air, that's true, but her heart – if she should catch a chill it might have repercussions. Prevention is better than cure.

CISSY: I wasn't cold.

ANNA: (*Wheeling the trolley.*) Maurice, open the door please. (*ANNA exits into the kitchen.*)

FRANK: You'll miss the old home, eh?

CISSY: Well, you get used to a house after twenty-eight years. Of course, we've been very lucky to have been able to stay in the same place for so long.

JACOB: That's an unfortunate phrase to use, Cissy. It's needed more than luck to keep us here for more than a quarter of a century.

(*MAURICE picks up a bible and perches on the keyboard lid, turning the pages.*)

CISSY: I meant –

JACOB: Before I finally became Superintendent Minister of the circuit six years ago I'd been considered for no less than five other churches –

CISSY: Yes –

JACOB: In circuits in the more industrial areas. There the work required of me would have been rigorous and demanding and therefore more rewarding. If I hadn't emphasised the risk involved in forcing you to live in districts where the atmosphere is polluted with the grime and soot of industry, we would not be here now in this comparatively rural environment.

MAURICE: For which you are truly thankful.

JACOB: So you see, 'very lucky' is not the phrase to use in connection with our twenty-eight years at Donisthorpe Manse.

CISSY: No – er – yes, Jacob. I don't know why I said –

JACOB: If you don't know why you said it, dear, it's time you thought before you spoke.

MAURICE: (*Closing the bible.*) And you practised what you preached.

(*ANNA returns.*)

JACOB: If you had ever been to one of my sermons since you passed – at least the *age* of adolescence, Maurice, I might consider your remark before I made a reply. But as you so arrogantly pride yourself on your agnosticism, you can hardly expect me to take any moral observation you might make seriously.

MAURICE: And vice versa.

CISSY: Don't start fighting.

ANNA: Bring the plates, Maurice. (*She replaces the piano stool.*)

FRANK: Thank you for the tea, Anna, it was lovely, very nice.

(*MAURICE takes a pile of plates with cutlery stacked on top of them from the downstage end of the table. He moves towards the door.*)

LIZ: And now that's all over, I've got a little speech to make. I'm not as good as you, Jacob, but here we are.

(*The clock chimes six thirty.*)

How quiet it is. I don't know how to say it with you all listening.

MAURICE: Would you rather we left the room?

LIZ: Now don't laugh at me. Frank and I are engaged. He's going to be made a respectable man at last.

(*MAURICE lets the cutlery slide off the plates on to the floor.*)

CISSY: (*Moving to pick up the cutlery.*) Ooh, dear! You are clumsy, Maurice.

ANNA: Congratulations. I'll take them.

MAURICE: Yes, congratulations, Frank.

(*ANNA goes with the plates.*)

CLIFFORD: Wonderful news.

CISSY: I'm so glad, very happy for you both.

FRANK: I'd have been happier if she'd said yes twenty-five years ago.

CISSY: We all would.

JACOB: When will you be getting married. Frank?

FRANK: Well – I – thought we'd – er...

LIZ: The first week in October, all being well.

FRANK: Yes. Before the cold weather sets in.

CISSY: At chapel – church?

FRANK: Er – yes, yes...

LIZ: They'll be calling the banns a week next Sunday.
(*ANNA returns.*)

CISSY: I always want to say chapel, I'll never get out of the habit. Father's always telling me it's old-fashioned to say chapel these days, I never remember.

FRANK: Chapel, church, makes no difference.

CISSY: (*Picking up her cardigan.*) Your grandfather would always say his chapel and my brother – Uncle Stanley, did too before he went to the war. (*She turns in the doorway, smiling.*) It's hard to change something you learnt automatically like that – when you were younger. (*She takes the cutlery into the kitchen.*)

ANNA: (*Folding the tablecloth.*) How was the golf this afternoon, Father?

JACOB: Golf? I didn't play golf this afternoon.

FRANK: Course we did.

JACOB: Oh. I went round the course for the exercise but my mind was on other things, naturally.
(*ANNA goes into the kitchen with the rest of the tea things. MAURICE puts his feet up on the table.*)

LIZ: Yes.

JACOB: Have you noticed, Frank, that before we leave the clubhouse I always pause on the top step of the verandah and look out –

FRANK: No, I can't say as I –

JACOB: Oh – only for a brief second or two.

FRANK: Aye?

JACOB: I do.

FRANK: And I never noticed.

JACOB: Look out over the wide green acres. Sometimes
I feel the whole of the land of Canaan's there before me,
a fertile plain too perfect to be peopled. And it occurs to
me as we begin the game that its pattern is the pattern of
our lives. Each green is unexpected – and different from
the one before and each has its snares to trap us.
(*CISSY comes from the kitchen followed by ANNA. CISSY
moves very slowly down the hall to the stairs and climbs them.
ANNA watches her from the shadows.*)
We must choose the right attitude of mind – as well as
the right club from the bag – for once a stroke has been
made and the ball has curved away from us, we must go
on, we must follow: each stroke, each flight is a
continuation of the one before, we must always keep to
the pattern laid out and the rules set down. If we don't
we are pillars of salt...pillars of salt.

FRANK: Well – you didn't play your best today, Jack.

JACOB: No – I – I didn't have my mind on the game, as
I said. Maurice home and Clifford and tomorrow – the
last green on the course for me tomorrow. The end of
my game.
(*ANNA appears in the doorway.*)

MAURICE: (*Rising suddenly.*) Well, then, why don't we all go
into Little Town, make a party of it to celebrate father's
retirement? Clifford's home, I'm home, Frank's engaged.
Coming, Cliff? Might find you a good woman.
(*ANNA goes into the hall and takes CLIFFORD's, MAURICE's
and LIZ's coats from the hooks.*)

LIZ: What a lovely idea, I feel like a party.

FRANK: Yes, I'm all for that. It's darts night for me anyway.

LIZ: Can't we go to the dance?

FRANK: You can come with me, watch me throw the
feathers. Coming, Jack?
(*ANNA comes back with the coats.*)

JACOB: Where's Cissy?

ANNA: She went to bed.

JACOB: Was she not feeling very well?

ANNA: I sent her. In case she has a chill.

FRANK: (*Taking LIZ's coat.*) Yes, wisest thing.

(*JACOB goes to the foot of the stairs.*)

LIZ: You'll come too, Anna?

ANNA: No really, I'd rather stay and clear up and there's mother's hot-water bottle. Your coat, Cliff. If you hurry you'll just make the seven o'clock.

MAURICE: Martyr.

ANNA: (*Throwing MAURICE his coat.*) Go out the back way – through Gethsemane.

CLIFFORD: You still call it that?

ANNA: Yes. (*She folds down the leaves of the table.*)

MAURICE: And the toolshed the Sepulchre of the Virgin?

ANNA: What else?

MAURICE: Of course.

ANNA: Have a good time.

MAURICE: We will. Come on, you two.

CLIFFORD: Aren't you coming with us, Father?

JACOB: Good night, boys. See you tomorrow.

(*CLIFFORD goes to the vestibule. FRANK and ANNA move the table.*)

MAURICE: See you tomorrow. Right, Cliff? Got some money?

CLIFFORD: Yes.

MAURICE: Good boy.

(*ANNA goes into the kitchen. MAURICE and CLIFFORD go into the garden. LIZ is about to follow them but the door is closed in her face.*)

LIZ: We'll go the front way. I can't manage the lane in the dark.

JACOB: It's just as quick.

(*LIZ faces JACOB. She indicates her gloves on the sofa. He misunderstands her gesture at first, thinking she wishes to shake his hand. He puts out his hand to take hers but she withdraws, embarrassed. He corrects his mistake and hands her the gloves. She takes them gratefully and swings them gaily in front of him.*)

LIZ: Good night, Jacob. (*She goes into the hall.*)

JACOB: Good night. See you tomorrow.

LIZ: (*Fastening a chiffon scarf round her head.*) Tomorrow.

FRANK: What was to stop you from going out with the boys now? You would've done forty years ago when we were in the army – or even after the war we had good times.

JACOB: I must work on tomorrow's sermon.

FRANK: Aye, I thought. Good idea. Last round up, eh?

LIZ: (*Calling.*) Ready, Frank?

FRANK: Good night then Jack. (*He goes into the hall.*) You weren't having me on were you? You meant it alright. (*LIZ is too unhappy to say anything. She looks at FRANK and gives him the parcel of cuttings. ANNA comes from the kitchen with a hot-water bottle.*)

ANNA: Good night, Frank. See you tomorrow.

FRANK: Good night. And say good night to your mother for me.

ANNA: Yes.

LIZ: And thank her for the tea. (*FRANK and LIZ go. ANNA closes the door firmly.*)

JACOB: Good night Frank.

ANNA: They've gone.

JACOB: Oh.

ANNA: (*Dragging the sofa into position.*) He said good night. (*She goes to the vestibule, hugging the hot-water bottle.*)

JACOB: (*Taking his bible from the top of the piano.*) Good night, Anna.

ANNA: I'm not going to bed yet. It's only seven o'clock.

JACOB: Of course, yes. (*ANNA opens the door and looks out across the garden. JACOB switches on the light on the mantelpiece.*) Anna. (*Sharply.*) Ann. (*ANNA turns to him.*) Please close the door. There's a fair wind blowing through.

ANNA: The north. It's good for the winter jasmine. It grows all along the back wall. Facing north.

JACOB: Yes, it's lovely in the winter.

ANNA: The flowers come before the leaves begin to grow. (*She closes the door and pulls the curtain across.*)

JACOB: We won't be here to see them this year.

ANNA: No. (*She switches a light off.*) Light enough?

(JACOB nods. ANNA takes a chair out into the hall. A train can be heard arriving in the distance. ANNA goes to the foot of the stairs. She takes CLIFFORD's case and carries it up as JACOB reads.)

JACOB: '...each according to his several ability... He that had received five went and traded and made another five, and his Lord said well done...enter thou into the joy of thy Lord... Likewise he that had two...

(ANNA comes down the stairs. The train is heard leaving the station.)

...but he that had received one went and digged in the earth – and hid.'

ANNA: *(In the doorway to the room.)* I'll be in the kitchen if you need me. *(She goes.)*

JACOB: '...unto everyone that hath shall be given and he shall have abundance, but from him that hath not shall be taken away – even that which he hath...' *(He looks up and stares in front of him. The sound of the train recedes into the dark silence.)*

Scene 2

Four hours later. The clock starts to chime eleven during the silence. The light returns on the eighth stroke of eleven. There is a small tray with a beaker on it. ANNA's bible and some papers are spread out on the table. JACOB is sitting on the sofa with his bible and some papers beside him. He is nearly asleep. ANNA is standing by him with his beaker.

ANNA: Have you had enough, Father?
JACOB: Mm?
ANNA: Another cup?
JACOB: No, no thank you. I'm very tired.
ANNA: *(Putting the beaker on the tray and picking up a bunch of airmail letters from the table.)* You should be in bed.
JACOB: You won't mind if I leave you?
ANNA: I won't mind.
JACOB: What time is it?

ANNA: Eleven.

JACOB: You won't wait up for the boys? They'll be some time yet.

ANNA: An hour and a half.

JACOB: Perhaps longer.

ANNA: Father.

JACOB: What is it?

ANNA: What would you say if I said I didn't want to retire with you to Hockton?

JACOB: Not come with us?

ANNA: Would you care much?

JACOB: Who would look after your mother?

ANNA: You, Father.

JACOB: Yes. I suppose so.

ANNA: And you wouldn't like that.

JACOB: Duty has nothing to do with liking. Duty is sacrificing one's own desires for the benefit of others.

ANNA: That doesn't seem a fair exchange, duty for desire. It isn't right to deny our natural feelings – it's immoral. We should always respond to the true feelings inside us.

JACOB: Who says so?

ANNA: Maurice.

JACOB: He'd say anything to justify his own loose way of living.

ANNA: Yes, you're right, you always are. But isn't it also your duty to convince him that our natural feelings aren't worth anything without a love for God?

JACOB: Are those Maurice's letters you've been reading?

ANNA: Yes, yes they are.

JACOB: I haven't asked you to show them to me before.

ANNA: They're wonderful letters.

JACOB: May I see them?

ANNA: (*Sitting beside JACOB.*) Oh yes – yes, here.

JACOB: The stamps are attractive. Bad handwriting.

ANNA: He describes everything he sees, both on board and when they're at a port o' call.

JACOB: 'Give my love to our father dot dot dot dot.' What do the dots mean?

ANNA: To our father which-art-in-heaven. You know – the game.

JACOB: I didn't know you still played it.

ANNA: It's hard to change something you learnt automatically like that when you were younger, it becomes part of you. Maurice calls it Do It Yourself Theology.

JACOB: Does he? 'Landed at Port-au-Prince today.'

ANNA: (*With a French accent.*) Port-au-Prince, it's French – in Haiti – patois. Those are the best ones. The Caribbean ones.

JACOB: 'The brothels here aren't as good as the ones in Cuba dot dot dot.' Is that all in the game too?

ANNA: No, that's punctuation.

JACOB: 'But they're still an improvement on anything we've got at home. Every row of buildings in the native quarter has its ever-open door, very hygienic, very international and quite satisfying if you like that sort of thing.' I wish you'd shown them to me before, Anna.

ANNA: You never showed any interest before. I'd like you to read them properly.

JACOB: (*Rising and turning to the fireplace.*) Would you like me to put them on the fire?

ANNA: (*Rising abruptly.*) Not before you've read them. I know them by heart.

JACOB: (*Putting the letters on the mantelpiece.*) I'm going to bed. You're not coming yet?

ANNA: I – I want to do some final work on tomorrow's lesson too. (*She picks up her bible.*)

JACOB: (*Picking up his bible and papers from the sofa.*) What is your text this week?

ANNA: I've chosen one independently of the Union Curriculum. It's the last time I'll be taking my class.

JACOB: Of course, good idea.

ANNA: Solomon.

JACOB: Solomon for Sunday School –

ANNA: Four-sixteen.

JACOB: (*Opening his bible.*) It's not an easy book for children, Anna. When I was a probationer I could never reconcile myself to reading it as an allegory of the church's love unto Christ. (*Finding the place.*) Where are we? Four. Here now. (*Reading.*) 'A garden enclosed is my sister, my spouse, a spring shut up, a fountain sealed...'

ANNA: (*Correcting JACOB and pretending to read the text which she knows by heart.*) Sixteen. 'Awake, O North wind and come thou South; blow upon my garden that the spices thereof may flow out. Let my beloved come into his garden and eat his pleasant fruits.'

JACOB: Very difficult text, Anna. I think you should find something else.

ANNA: It's really very right for a farewell text Father. The allegorical paraphrase is (*Reading.*) 'the church prayeth to be made fit for his presence'. It tells the children to prepare for their new minister and teacher.

JACOB: There are some things you will never understand, Anna. You have a simple nature, your mother was the same when she was a girl.

ANNA: Is that why you married her?

JACOB: You're very alike in many ways.

ANNA: She's an invalid, she's married and she has three children. I don't think we're alike at all. I think I'm more like you, Father, alone with God and bound to him – by duty. Repressed. I'm sorry you're tired. I'm keeping you up.

JACOB: I'll go up. (*He switches the light on and goes to the stairs.*)

ANNA: Good night. (*She picks up the letters and calls.*) You've left Maurice's letters.

JACOB: If you'd like me to read them they can't be very interesting. (*He starts to climb the stairs.*) Leave the door open for the boys.

ANNA: I will.

JACOB: Good night, Anna. (*He goes into the bathroom.*)

ANNA: (*To herself.*) I said good night. (*She calls.*) Sleep sound. (*She notices CISSY's gardening glove in the hearth, replaces the letters and puts the glove on. She takes a torch and a pair of scissors and goes into the garden. MAURICE enters the hall, drunk. He looks into the living-room, sees it's empty*

*and is about to climb the stairs when he hears JACOB cough
in the bathroom. He scrambles quickly into the cupboard under
the stairs. JACOB comes from the bathroom, leans over the
banister and looks down the hall. ANNA comes back carrying
a bunch of Michaelmas daisies and assorted weeds. JACOB
goes upstairs, switching the lights off as he goes. ANNA replaces
the asters in the vase with the daisies. She puts the asters into
the fire. MAURICE comes cautiously from the cupboard. ANNA
hears then sees him and is suddenly excited. She looks around,
wondering what to do. She sees her bible, picks it up and
stands on a chair behind the door. MAURICE hears her and
goes into the room. As he enters ANNA brings the bible down
on his head. He falls like a stone. She giggles delightedly.)*
Judges. Hehhaah... Shshshshshs!

MAURICE: *(Kneeling behind the sofa.)* Psalms! Hoohu!
(ANNA shakes her head.)
Kings?

ANNA: Samuel.

MAURICE: Book One. Hoohu!

ANNA: *(Closing the door.)* Sshshshshhs –

MAURICE: How can I shshs –

ANNA: Ssh –

MAURICE: *(Whispering.)* How can I sshshsh when you
bring down the Wrath of God on my head?

ANNA: But very gently. *(Her fingers soothe MAURICE's scalp.)*

MAURICE: Why aren't you in bed?

ANNA: I was waiting for you.

MAURICE: Eh?

ANNA: I thought you'd be hours yet. *(She starts to take
MAURICE's coat off.)*

MAURICE: We went for a drink.

ANNA: *How* many?

MAURICE: We went for *two* drinks.

ANNA: And Clifford?

MAURICE: Clifford went for two drinks too, so did
Elizabeth and Frank.

ANNA: You didn't go to the dance?

MAURICE: Nope.

ANNA: Then where is Clifford?

MAURICE: (*Rising and pointing to the garden.*) Sshusha! In the tool shed, the Sepulchre of the Virgin. I came to see if the coast was clear. (*He sees the tray.*) Any coffee?

ANNA: I'll make some.

> (*She takes the tray into the kitchen. MAURICE belches and goes into the garden. CLIFFORD enters the hall. He is quite drunk. He carries a garden syringe and totters into the living-room. He sees the vase and sprays the flowers, giggling. MAURICE re-enters from the garden. He wears CLIFFORD's raincoat and a garden hat which he picked up in the tool shed.*)

MAURICE: (*Whispering.*) Cliff…

CLIFFORD: (*Pointing.*) That's my coat, you have my coat on you.

MAURICE: (*Pointing.*) You weren't in the tool shed.

CLIFFORD: Take it off.

MAURICE: Come on.

CLIFFORD: (*Loudly.*) My coat.

MAURICE: Quiet.

CLIFFORD: Hnun?

MAURICE: Sshsh. You'll wake the captain.

CLIFFORD: Hello.

MAURICE: (*Referring to the spray.*) Give that here.

CLIFFORD: No – it's my coat…

> (*He sprays MAURICE as MAURICE grabs the spray. CLIFFORD giggles. MAURICE is about to spray him back when CLIFFORD holds his hands up.*)

Stop, stop, give in, give in…

> (*MAURICE drops the syringe and prepares to pick CLIFFORD up in a fireman's lift.*)

MAURICE: Come on, then. (*He puts the hat on CLIFFORD's head.*)

CLIFFORD: Where?

MAURICE: Sofa.

CLIFFORD: (*Not wishing to be lifted in a fireman's lift.*) Piggy-back.

> (*MAURICE gives CLIFFORD a ride around the room, speaking as they go.*)

Maurice –

MAURICE: Cliffy – ?

CLIFFORD: I wish, I wish I could be like you –

MAURICE: Eh?

CLIFFORD: Like you, Maurice. A merchant seaman flogging the oceans in a great boat –

MAURICE: Ship.

CLIFFORD: Eh?

MAURICE: In a great ship.

CLIFFORD: In a great ship like a young Conrad. I bet you have a good time on your ship.

MAURICE: (*Crashing on the sofa.*) Boat – on the boat, a very good time.

CLIFFORD: With those rich lady tourists – as a cabin steward I bet you have a good time.

MAURICE: It's the wine stewards who have it easy.

CLIFFORD: Is it?

MAURICE: (*Sliding down to the floor between CLIFFORD's legs, using them as arm rests.*) When they're serving up drinks at dinner they get the eye from rich lady passengers –

CLIFFORD: Do they?

MAURICE: Some ladies are more forward than others.

CLIFFORD: Are they?

MAURICE: Depends how many cruises they've been on before. The novices leave little notes on the table-mats with their room number on. And a special time. And a big tip. But the old hands, they'll order a bottle of something and ask the steward to bring it round to their cabins any time after dinner. Any time, you see. Because they know he'll be on duty till late. Oh, they've got it all worked out – real cunning.

CLIFFORD: You can't blame the stewards, can you?

MAURICE: Not at all.

CLIFFORD: Can't you?

MAURICE: Of course not.

CLIFFORD: It's very easy, then, is it?

MAURICE: Very easy.

CLIFFORD: (*Incredulous.*) Is it?

MAURICE: The warmer the sun, the easier it is.

CLIFFORD: It is, is it?

MAURICE: The nearer the equator you get, the busier you are.

CLIFFORD: The heat you mean, you mean the heat, because it's hot?

(*MAURICE nods professionally.*)

I see. Well, they've nothing else to do, nothing else to think about. If I weren't a chemist, if I were different, I'd like to try, out of interest.

(*ANNA brings a tray with two black coffees on it.*)

I wondered where you were.

MAURICE: (*Hauling himself up next to CLIFFORD.*) Marvellous.

CLIFFORD: What do cabin stewards do?

(*ANNA puts the beakers into their hands.*)

MAURICE: I'm not a cabin steward not any more. I'm a kitchen steward, a porter –

ANNA: Like me.

MAURICE: I was demoted two cruises back.

CLIFFORD: Why?

(*ANNA behind MAURICE, starts to take his coat off.*)

MAURICE: I'd been to the purser's office one night and as I was going back to crew quarters a woman came up right in front of me and asked me where hers was.

CLIFFORD: She didn't know? Where hers was? Where was it?

MAURICE: Hers?

CLIFFORD: Her what?

MAURICE: Cabin.

(*ANNA wanders to the vestibule with the coat. She bolts the door, draws the curtain and stands in the shadows listening.*)

CLIFFORD: How did she think you'd know?

MAURICE: She was drunk.

CLIFFORD: Was she?

MAURICE: I asked her which deck she was on. She wore a sort of maroon sort of cocktail dress and walked along the corridors in front of me. When we got there she asked me in for a drink.

CLIFFORD: Did you go in?

MAURICE: I was thirsty.

CLIFFORD: So you did go in? (*He lies down.*)

MAURICE: I go in. She pours me a drink. I have it in my
hand. I was just putting it to my lips to have a sip, when
there's a knock on the door.

CLIFFORD: No.

MAURICE: Yes.

CLIFFORD: No.

MAURICE: A knock at the door.

CLIFFORD: What did you do?

MAURICE: Got dressed in a flash. A flaming wine steward
had seen me go in and reported me. Poaching on his
preserves.

ANNA: What happened?

MAURICE: (*Going to ANNA.*) I was put on the pool. Once
you've been on the pool and made a mess of your book
they send you out to China on the P and O or to the Far
East. To get to Haiti – Puerto Rico – Tobago – you must
get a cruise. You must go to these places, mustn't you –
you must go. When you get back – you – you can say
you've *been.*

(*The clock in the hall chimes eleven thirty.*)

ANNA: I've never been. What's it like, Maurice?

MAURICE: Most of the time off is at night and you don't
see a lot, though the moon hangs low and white enough.
Most of the boys don't go on shore to see the sights
anyway. Bars, pin-tables and sassy high-heeled tarts is as
much local colour as most of them ask for. But I like to
go in the day. See cathedrals. Forts. (*He stands on the sofa,
and poses.*) The monuments and museums and the old
colonial buildings. That gets me. You know. That's what
gets me. (*He sinks to his knees facing CLIFFORD.*)

CLIFFORD: You're English, that's why.

MAURICE: I'm uneducated, that's why.

ANNA: Don't be silly.

MAURICE: Ever hear Clifford talk of monuments, museums
and old forts? Ever hear him talk of anything? No. And
why? Because he's educated. Did Elizabeth talk to me or

you tonight? No. She talked to Clifford. And why?
Because he's educated.

CLIFFORD: I hardly spoke to her.

MAURICE: Because you're educated. He's clever.

ANNA: He went to college.

MAURICE: Yes, on what would have been *my* school fees.

ANNA: You ran away.

MAURICE: (*To CLIFFORD.*) I paid for your education.
He wouldn't be where he is now if it weren't for me.

ANNA: (*Spreading the coat over CLIFFORD.*) Laid out on
the sofa?

MAURICE: Yes, he's too shrivelled up to take a drink.
Poor Cliffy.

CLIFFORD: What else do you do beside look at forts?

MAURICE: Get drunk. It's cheap enough, so's the other.
Get tattooed.

CLIFFORD: Have *you* been tattooed as well?

MAURICE: You can do anything when you're drunk.

ANNA: Have you had another?

MAURICE: Yes.

ANNA: On your last trip?

MAURICE: Yip.

ANNA: Why didn't you tell me?

MAURICE: Shy.

CLIFFORD: Where did you have it done?

MAURICE: Rainbow City.

CLIFFORD: Where's that?

MAURICE: Panama.

CLIFFORD: Let's have a look.

ANNA: Where, Maurice?

MAURICE: Panama.

ANNA: But where?

MAURICE: Shoulder blade.

CLIFFORD: Let's have a look.

ANNA: (*Taking MAURICE's jacket off.*) Which one?

MAURICE: Right.

ANNA: What is it?

CLIFFORD: They hurt, don't they?

ANNA: Give me your jacket.

MAURICE: A spider.

ANNA: Ugh!

CLIFFORD: Father's tattooed too.

(*They look at him.*)

Frank told me in the lavatory at the 'Prince of Wales'.

ANNA: Father –

MAURICE: Tattooed?

CLIFFORD: In Paris, in the army, nineteen sixteen before he was taken prisoner. Tattooed on his thigh.

MAURICE: A fig leaf?

CLIFFORD: A reptile of some kind, he said – or was it a bird?

MAURICE: (*Showing his upper arm.*) Like this?

CLIFFORD: That's nice.

MAURICE: Albatross.

CLIFFORD: Where's the spider?

MAURICE: (*Hauling his unbuttoned shirt off his shoulders.*) See it?

CLIFFORD: (*Leaning forward.*) I'd rather have the bird.

MAURICE: (*To ANNA.*) Suits me?

ANNA: Most things do.

MAURICE: Except a halo.

ANNA: Except a halo.

CLIFFORD: I never knew you were tattooed.

MAURICE: I never knew father was.

ANNA: Nor I.

CLIFFORD: Frank said not to say anything.

MAURICE: It wouldn't do for the parishioners to know.

CLIFFORD: Frank said they had good times in the war. He liked a drink and girls and they liked him, like you before he reformed – before he married... (*He mumbles himself to sleep.*) Like you. Like you Maurice...

ANNA: Are you all right?

CLIFFORD: I'm in a dream sleeping.

(*ANNA adjusts the raincoat over CLIFFORD.*)

ANNA: Revelations.

MAURICE: (*Sliding on to the floor in front of the sofa.*) Apocrypha. What's he done? He's ready enough to tell us what we've done with our lives, but what's he done? He liked the drink, he liked the girls, why did he have to spoil everything? He was getting along fine until he started to improve himself. What a waste.

ANNA: (*Hugging a cushion.*) He doesn't think so. He thinks there's nothing nobler than sacrificing your desires for the benefit of others.

MAURICE: He'd say anything to justify his own hypocrisy.

ANNA: (*Moving down with MAURICE.*) Yes, you're right. You always were – always.

MAURICE: How I hate coming here. Why can't everywhere be like the islands?

ANNA: (*Putting the cushion on the floor and sitting on it.*) Surrounded by water.

MAURICE: Like Cuba.

ANNA: (*Drowsily.*) Cuba.

MAURICE: Barbados.

ANNA: Cuba.

MAURICE: Havana.

ANNA: Yes – Habana, where the noise at Carnival fills the ears of hundreds of ribboned Cubans – who watch –

MAURICE: – and scowl –

ANNA: – and laugh –

MAURICE: – and listen and sleep –

ANNA: – in leafy colonial squares –

MAURICE: – where mauve orchids steam –

ANNA: – and coloured fountains dance to drums –

MAURICE: – trumpets –

ANNA: – maracas and –

MAURICE/ANNA: – shells.

(*They laugh together softly.*)

MAURICE: Havana, hah! (*He looks at ANNA.*) And here we have Donisthorpe. Havana's all right. But it's not enough any more, just to see it all, and take it all in. Just to be there. Just to be there's not enough when you know that it's night on the other side of the world and probably raining. Yet what can one person do to delight the world when it's so disenchanted? Where does one begin? Christ knows. Oh. He did too. For a bit.

ANNA: (*Touching her face.*) Am I very ugly, Maurice?

MAURICE: You're beautiful sis –

137

ANNA: (*Rising, to the mantelpiece.*) Don't call me that, that's her
    name, Cicely. Oh, Maurice, if you knew what it's been like
    for me here, year after monotonous sanctimonious year.

MAURICE: I do know.

ANNA: You don't know at all.

MAURICE: I had it for fifteen years.

ANNA: (*Taking a flower.*) You were a boy, and now you
    come home for a week and stay away fifty. You don't
    know. I wait for you to come home. When you're here
    I can breathe again for a little, when you're away I think
    only of the last time you were here, of what you said and
    how you looked, or else I look forward to the time when
    you'll come again. I read your letters over and over until
    I don't need to look at the words to know what you've
    written. At night I lay awake and imagine I'm with you,
    floating over the oceans with the great sky drifting
    away from us, away above us – like a million years of
    cloudless freedom. Then, when I wake in the morning
    the trains go by and Donisthorpe Manse is my prison
    again, and Cissy is there and Jacob and so am I. And
    after grace we have to eat, we have to thank God before
    breakfast dinner and tea, and after, we thank Anna for
    getting it ready and clearing it away.

MAURICE: She can't help being an invalid.

ANNA: (*Twisting the flower.*) If she could she wouldn't. I'm
    thirty-one years old. She's lasted them out, she'll last as
    long again.

MAURICE: I hope so.

ANNA: So do I.

MAURICE: Do you?

ANNA: (*Kneeling close to MAURICE.*) Of course. But I want
    to get away, Maurice, all the same. I could work anywhere
    as a companion or a maid.

MAURICE: Or a receptionist at a temperance hotel.

ANNA: I've had enough experience.

MAURICE: Perhaps father would give you a reference.

ANNA: And I'd meet people, new, interesting people who do
    things they shouldn't. I'm tired of being virtuous, it's its
    own reward and it's not enough. Take me with you when

you leave tomorrow. I'll see you to the station and get on the train with you. Take me to London, Maurice, I daren't go on my own.

MAURICE: You can't leave them to move house by themselves. You'll have more time to yourself in Hockton when father's retired. You'll meet new people there. Things will change for you automatically.

ANNA: You think either of them will change? I want to go with you. We've shared everything in the past. We never kept anything from each other before.

MAURICE: You didn't tell me you knew my letters by heart.

ANNA: I wanted to surprise you.

MAURICE: You did.

ANNA: You didn't tell me you'd been tattooed again.

MAURICE: I wanted to surprise you.

ANNA: You did. But you told Clifford as well. You let him see it first.

MAURICE: (*Turning on to his side and resting his head on the sofa.*) I didn't think Miss Muffet would approve of a spider.

ANNA: I've killed plenty in the garden.

MAURICE: Very unlucky.

ANNA: Let me see it now – properly. Your shirt bunched up before and I only saw its legs.

MAURICE: (*Closing his eyes, sleepily.*) I wonder what father had done on his thigh.

ANNA: That's mother's secret. (*She takes hold of MAURICE's shirt and tries to lift it away from him.*)

MAURICE: Dare you to ask her.

ANNA: Is it this shoulder?

MAURICE: Watch the collar. I'm wearing this tomorrow.
(*ANNA unrolls the shirt, exposing MAURICE's shoulders and the tattoo. The clock chimes the hour. Twelve.*)

ANNA: You're wearing it today.

MAURICE: What's that?

ANNA: Twelve o'clock.

MAURICE: Midnight. The bewitching Sabbath.
(*He sings softly. ANNA joins in harmony on the third line, still looking at the tattoo.*)

'The day thou gavest, Lord, is ended,
The darkness falls at thy behest;
To thee our morning hymns ascended,
Thy praise shall sanctify our rest.'
(*He doesn't know any more of the words but hums the tune.*)
Bed time.

ANNA: Yes.

(*She kisses the spider that sleeps beneath the freckled skin on MAURICE's shoulder. He inclines his head towards her. She kisses him on the mouth. He recoils and she sits back on her heels. He rolls over and crawls away. He stands up, then looks over his shoulder at her and whispers fiercely.*)

MAURICE: Judas. Judas.

ANNA: Maurice.

MAURICE: Good night.

(*He goes into the hall. ANNA puts CLIFFORD's beaker on the tray and takes it into the hall. MAURICE moves to the foot of the stairs, leaning heavily on the banisters. ANNA stops.*)

ANNA: You left your jacket.

(*She goes into the kitchen. MAURICE goes back, puts his jacket on and decides to take CLIFFORD upstairs. He gets him on to his shoulder in a fireman's lift. ANNA comes back. MAURICE carries CLIFFORD to the foot of the stairs. The light from the moon is sufficient to light the hall and stairs.*)

ANNA: Good night.

MAURICE: I said good night.

ANNA: Sleep sound.

(*JACOB appears in his dressing-gown. MAURICE passes him on the small landing.*)

MAURICE: He's drunk.

JACOB: Clifford –

MAURICE: (*Going upstairs.*) Go to bed.

(*ANNA comes forward from the shadows in the hall.*)

ANNA: Yes, go to bed, Father. Everyone else has. Go to bed.

(*She stares at JACOB. He goes. She stays in the dark silence.*)

End of Act One.

ACT TWO

Four o'clock the following afternoon. The garden door is open. CISSY and CLIFFORD are chatting outside. MAURICE is at the foot of the stairs with a golf club. He taps a golf ball up the hall and follows it. CISSY and CLIFFORD come in. He carries a cardboard box, she wears her gardening gloves and boots.

CISSY: I mustn't be out here when Jacob gets back. He gets upset so easily. (*She puts her gloves on the mantelpiece.*)

CLIFFORD: He thinks a great deal of you, that's why. He's concerned about your health.

CISSY: Yes... I think we've done everything we can. I'm so glad we managed to clear away Anna's Michaelmas daisies – like a forest. She likes them to grow up tall like that, but they push everything else out so. I hope the seedlings take.

CLIFFORD: The daisies have certainly impoverished the top soil over the years. It takes some time to recover.

CISSY: I gave them plenty to drink.

CLIFFORD: (*Taking CISSY's slippers from the fender box.*) I wonder if the new minister's an enthusiastic gardener?

CISSY: Oh, I'm sure he will be. I hope so and thank you for digging it over.

CLIFFORD: (*Kneeling and changing her shoes.*) When does he arrive?

CISSY: Jacob? No, the minister, Mr Roach he's called. I'd like to have seen them and showed them round, he and his wife. They haven't any children but they have a little boy. They adopted him from an orphanage just outside Hockton – father was telling me.

(*MAURICE hits the golf ball into the living-room and follows it.*)

MAURICE: Two o'clock, Frank said, and it's after four.

CISSY: You won't get a game in now, the course is busy on a Sunday.

MAURICE: I think it's going to rain anyway.

CISSY: Ooh, do you think so – We needn't have watered the seedlings so much.

MAURICE: Headache gone, Cliffy?

CLIFFORD: Improved.

CISSY: It's the sudden change in the climate, Clifford.
You'll feel better tomorrow. Maurice is the same when he
first comes home.

MAURICE: It's the smell of the hymn books that turns my
stomach. (*He picks up the Sunday newspaper.*)

CISSY: Yes, they do get a bit musty. You should have helped
me in the garden and got some fresh air like Clifford.
It's not like Frank to be late; I hope he isn't late on
Wednesday.

CLIFFORD: What time will you be leaving?

CISSY: Well, Frank sets off early on Wednesday morning
with the furniture. I hope the weather's fine for them.
We're going to stay with your Aunt Milly at Liversedge
just for Tuesday night and then we'll be catching a train
down on Wednesday morning, down to Hockton. We
should arrive about the same time, Frank says.

CLIFFORD: Would you like me to come with you? I could –
(*He hesitates before lying.*) telephone and explain that I won't
be back until later in the week.

(*He looks at MAURICE. MAURICE looks at him.*)

CISSY: Oh, no, no. Your researches are more important than
our little upheaval. The house is all ready for us to move
into… Oh, it is a lovely little house, Clifford, you'll fall in
love with it when you see it, Maurice. You must come and
see it as soon as you can. It's at the end of a lane with
trees all round on either side, like a long green tunnel in
the summer months, and when you get to the end of it
there it is all on its own with a garden all the way round
it. Of course, it's not very big, but we'll be alright.

CLIFFORD: I'll come as soon as I can.

CISSY: Yes.

MAURICE: I shan't be able to come for at least six months.

CISSY: (*To CLIFFORD.*) His boat sails tomorrow – no, his –

MAURICE: Tug.

CISSY: No.

MAURICE: Barge?

CISSY: No, not barge –

MAURICE: Canoe?

CISSY: Ooh, stop it, Maurice.

MAURICE: Galleon.

CISSY: I can't think when –

MAURICE: Punt.

CISSY: He always makes fun of me –

CLIFFORD: Ship.

CISSY: I know it's not a punt – ship, his ship sails tomorrow.

MAURICE: Not until the evening.

CISSY: But he has to report early in the morning and be on
    board so he has to leave after tea. A long eastern cruise
    isn't it, Maurice?

MAURICE: The Orient, India and Japan.

CISSY: That's right. I could be wrapping up some of the
    china, there's so much to pack. We've been saving up the
    papers for the last six months. Every one. (*She goes to the
    cupboard under the stairs.*)

CLIFFORD: Thank you for putting me to bed last night.

MAURICE: My brother's keeper.

CLIFFORD: You needed to be last night.

MAURICE: Was it really the first time you'd been drunk?

CLIFFORD: (*Opening the keyboard lid.*) And the last. I haven't
    got your constitution. It's bad for the liver, you know.

CISSY: (*Returning with an armful of papers.*) We shall use all
    these, I'm sure. Oh, are you going to play something,
    love? Yes, do.

CLIFFORD: It's – it's a long time since I lifted a keyboard lid.

CISSY: Is it dusty?

CLIFFORD: So long since I had the opportunity.

CISSY: Mr Whatmuff the tuner usually leaves it very clean.

CLIFFORD: It isn't dusty.

CISSY: You played it when you were here last.
    (*She takes a china dog from the piano and wraps it.
    CLIFFORD plays the piano. Purcell's exercise, 'Ground'.*)

CISSY: You're the only one who plays it now. Liz sometimes
    plays for Jacob – for us – when she calls, but she doesn't
    come round as much as she used to.

CLIFFORD: She was a very good teacher.

CISSY: But now you play better than her and she plays all the time. Of course, her hands are getting old and stiff at the knuckles – but she manages wonderfully. (*She doesn't know what to do with the wrapped ornament so she puts it back on top of the piano.*)

CLIFFORD: She played the introit very well this morning.

CISSY: Oh yes, she'd been practising for the occasion. She knew you'd be there listening. (*She wraps the small ornaments on the mantelpiece.*)

MAURICE: What's that called, Cliff?

CLIFFORD: A Purcell exercise.

MAURICE: Who wrote it?

CLIFFORD: Beethoven.

MAURICE: Any words?

CLIFFORD: Not yet.

CISSY: You should have been a pianist.

CLIFFORD: No. I shouldn't. I don't play with feeling. A concert pianist plays with feeling. (*He plays two bars with feeling.*) Maurice has feelings. He could have been a pianist. Couldn't you, Maurice?

MAURICE: Honky tonk.

CISSY: Maurice wouldn't practise.

CLIFFORD: Maurice indulged his emotions.

MAURICE: Maurice was a bad lot.

(*FRANK enters from the garden. CLIFFORD stops playing.*)

FRANK: There you are! Where've you been?

CISSY. Ooh Frank

MAURICE: I gave you up an hour ago.

CISSY: We thought you weren't coming. (*She puts some wrapped ornaments on a small armchair.*)

MAURICE: You're too late for golf.

FRANK: Aye, well, you see I thought it looked as if we were in for a spot of rain when I set off anyway, so –

MAURICE: So I can't win back the old man's reputation – On the golf-links of course.

CISSY: Well, I hope you won't be late on Wednesday, there's a lot to be done.

FRANK: You've started, I see.

CISSY: Yes. There's a little job you could be doing, Frank, if you don't mind. The carpets in the bedrooms are all tacked down –

FRANK: (*Taking his coat off.*) Where's the hammer?

CISSY: In the cupboard.

CLIFFORD: I'll give you a hand.

(*FRANK hangs his jacket and coat up in the hall.*)

CISSY: Yes – and I think you'll need the screwdriver as well to prise them out with – the tacks.

(*FRANK goes into the cupboard under the stairs, CLIFFORD into the hall.*)

FRANK: They'll be rusted in, I shouldn't wonder.

CISSY: (*From the doorway.*) But do be careful you don't tear the edges.

FRANK: Never fear.

(*CISSY closes the door, pleased to be alone with MAURICE. She takes some of the newspapers from the sofa to the sideboard. CLIFFORD starts to go upstairs. FRANK comes from the cupboard with a hammer and a screwdriver.*)

How are you after last night? Have you recovered?

CLIFFORD: No.

FRANK: I knew it wasn't Liz playing the piano. I could tell.

(*CLIFFORD and FRANK go upstairs. MAURICE plays the first few notes of 'The Day Thou Gavest' with one finger. He gets some of the notes wrong. CISSY takes a plate from the back of the sideboard.*)

CISSY: This is a lovely plate, isn't it, Maurice?

MAURICE: Grandmother's?

CISSY: Yes. It's very old. She had it given to her for a wedding present. She was married when she was nineteen just like I was.

MAURICE: How old was father?

CISSY: He was twenty-five when we were married.

MAURICE: Mum…

CISSY: Yes, love?

MAURICE: How did you meet father?

CISSY: (*Putting the plate down.*) Ooh, that was a long time ago.

MAURICE: Have you forgotten?

CISSY: Oh, no, I remember. (*She goes for the cardboard box and puts it on the floor.*)

MAURICE: Well, how – how did it come to pass?

CISSY: He came to our house.

MAURICE: In Huntingdon –

CISSY: Yes. After the war, to tell us about how your Uncle Stanley had been killed. Uncle was a padre in their regiment. (*She tries to open the sideboard doors but the dining-chair is in the way.*) He must have been a very brave man.

MAURICE: (*Moving the chair in front of the cardboard box.*) Stanley?

CISSY: Jacob. You see, Stanley was wounded very badly by a piece of shrapnel – and – your father – ooh, it must have been awful for them, I hate to think about it. (*She wraps the plate in newspaper.*)

MAURICE: Don't upset yourself. We'll talk of something else.

CISSY: Yes.

MAURICE: Grandmother must have been quite a girl to marry so young.

CISSY: Yes. Grandfather used to cycle twenty miles on a penny-farthing just to see her. He thought a lot of her. Jacob was wounded by a piece of shrapnel, too, as he was trying to carry Stanley back to his trench. Stanley died before they got there. (*Indicating a small ebony cross that hangs at her waist.*) This cross was his, I wear it every Sunday. When Jacob came to see us he brought it with him.

(*She gives MAURICE the plate. He puts it in the box on the floor.*)

Anyway, that's how I came to meet your father. Daddy looked on him as a second son and he'd ask him to stay with us some weekends. (*She takes a teapot and two other pieces of china from the sideboard cupboard and puts them on the chair.*) Jacob used to travel down from Goldthorpe and we'd go out to a dance or to the pictures or even just for walks together. (*She starts to wrap a piece of china.*)

I'd never had a young man before, and Jacob was so very charming and manly and very handsome – not like his brothers at all. He had a lot of brothers working in Goldthorpe colliery.

(*She gives the wrapped ornaments to MAURICE, who puts them in the box.*)

Most of them died in a terrible fall underground, you wouldn't remember. Yes, Jacob was quite different from the rest of his family – he wanted something better than coal mining. That's why he came to Huntingdon and started work on a farm.

MAURICE: What made him decide to go into the ministry?

CISSY: Ooh, well – in Paris. (*She takes the lid off the teapot. She keeps hold of the teapot and turns to MAURICE.*) Maurice.

MAURICE: Yes.

CISSY: I'm going to tell you something. I've wanted to before but I didn't think I ought until you were grown up and then when you were grown up I didn't know how to.

MAURICE: What is it?

CISSY: Well, when Jacob came to work on a farm in Huntingdon he didn't only come just to get away from Goldthorpe pits.

MAURICE: He came because you lived there.

CISSY: Yes he did. And we used to go out every Saturday. Sometimes we went on long bus rides and we'd arrive back late for supper, after ten o'clock sometimes. He always came in and had his supper. Well, one weekend Daddy had to go away on a convention, I'll always remember, and I'd forgotten to tell Jacob. He called for me as usual on Saturday afternoon and when I told him that we'd have the house to ourselves he suggested that we went off to London for the day. It was such an adventure, I'd never been in all my life. We pretended it was our own house we were leaving and I left a note on the door saying 'gone out for the day, back later'. I always remember. We caught the excursion train and arrived nicely in time for tea. We didn't go into a café, we bought some cakes and bananas and ate them in the

park. We rode on motor-buses, on top of them so that we
could see everything, and Jacob showed me all the
wonderful buildings and we looked in all the shops
though we didn't buy anything. In the evening we
queued at Prince Albert's Hall where they promenade
to the music and oh, they played Tchaikovsky's
symphony. Jacob always loved music, and we sat on
the floor. I'd never heard or seen anything like it ever,
Maurice, and the applause… But we didn't go back after
the interval, the floor was hard to sit on for a long time,
we motor-bussed through to the middle of London and
saw the lights. I remember so well. We got off at Nelson's
square and you should have heard the birds on the roofs
of the buildings, it was noisy with traffic and the water in
the fountains splashed but you could still hear all those
hundreds of birds singing – and pigeons! Hoh…one sat
on my hat, they wouldn't leave us, they seemed glad we
were there. Like birds of peace. But we couldn't stay with
them for long. We had to get back to King's Cross
station. Jacob knew the way, he said, he said it wasn't far,
so we took our time. We walked along by the river
Thames, past Downing Street where the Prime Minister
lives and into King James's Park. I always remember, it
was called Birdcage Walk, because of the birds in
Nelson's square – ooh, it isn't called that, not Nelson's
square – I can't remember for the minute.

MAURICE: Trafalgar?

CISSY: Trafalgar Square – that was it. Well, we weren't sure
of the time so we asked a policeman outside Buckingham
Palace. It was nearly a quarter to eleven and our train
left at eleven. We knew we'd have to hurry up, we half
ran and got to the station with five minutes to spare,
only to find that we'd come to Queen Victoria's station
instead, not King's Cross at all. Jacob had got it all
confused. Well we were so out of breath by then that we
could do nothing but sit down in the station – I remember
it so plainly, the first thing we did when we got our
second wind was to laugh, we did, we just sat there

looking first at the board that had the train destinations on and then at each other, and laughed. Trains went everywhere it seemed but to Huntingdon. Brighton, Worthing and Newhaven –

MAURICE: Dorking.

CISSY: Yes.

MAURICE: Epsom and Eastbourne –

CISSY: Oh, everywhere. Then Big Ben struck eleven o'clock. I can hear it now. It was getting colder in the station, so we had a cup of tea in the refreshment room and tried to think what to do. We thought we'd wait in the waiting room, but they didn't allow you, we even thought of going to the police station – Scotland Yard – but we didn't dare. Jacob wouldn't think of me staying out all night – I'd never been out so late before, not even when we went on bus rides, except on New Year's Eve.

MAURICE: Had you any money?

CISSY: I had a little and Jacob had.

MAURICE: Enough to stay in a hotel?

CISSY: Well, there was a big hotel outside the station. We were both tired. We hadn't enough money for two single rooms. We had to get tickets for the return journey as we'd missed the excursion return. (*She remembers.*) Jacob asked me. I'll always remember, he said if we were married would I share a bedroom suite with him in Queen Victoria's Hotel – 'But we're not married' I said and he said but would I if we were. 'We aren't even engaged officially yet' I said. 'You haven't even proposed' – oh – and we talked on and on, till finally we got officially engaged in the entrance to the station and to make it legal Jacob wrote our names over an announcement in the to-be-married columns of an evening paper. He read the banns as we crossed the road and we were married outside the hotel, all before half past eleven. He had a signet ring on his little finger and I put it on back to front – here it is, and we walked into the hotel as husband and wife. Jacob signed the book as Mr and Mrs Metcalf.

MAURICE: Why?

CISSY: Well, we were both afraid we'd be caught or questioned or asked to prove that we were married. I only had a handbag. Jacob said our luggage was in the station as we were going to Newhaven the next day for our honeymoon. Oh, Maurice, we were so excited. It was really romantic – really, Maurice... I wish you'd been there. We were so happy. We were taken up in a lift to our room, I always remember, number sixty-two it was – oh – we were so excited – and – when we were inside, so happy. I always remember Jacob as he was that night, laughing and kind, so different. We were both different then, both young and very silly. You wouldn't have been born if we hadn't been. Haha – Queen Victoria's Hotel, ten minutes from the Palace and King James's Park. I wonder what they'd have thought of us? What would you have thought of us, Maurice?

MAURICE: I'd have thought you were very lucky to get a room.

CISSY: It was a cancellation, the man said.

MAURICE: You got back to Huntingdon alright? (*He gives CISSY a sheet of newspaper.*)

CISSY: (*Wrapping the teapot.*) Yes, we caught the first train on the Sunday morning.
   (*MAURICE takes the china from the armchair and sits in it.*)
   The note I'd left on the door had disappeared. Daddy had come home unexpectedly the night before. I told him everything that had happened and he was so angry. He cried. He went very quiet for days. He wouldn't understand, he couldn't because he'd been brought up in a different generation and, being a minister, found it hard to believe that his daughter could do a thing like that. He thought it was a great sin. But we'd only behaved quite naturally. (*She puts the teapot into the box.*) Poor Daddy. (*She gets more newspaper.*) The worry was too much for him. He had a brainstorm.

MAURICE: (*Giving CISSY the teapot lid, smiling.*) Same old haemorrhage.

CISSY: (*Taking the lid, smiling back at MAURICE.*) Yes.

MAURICE: How soon after were you married?

CISSY: (*Wrapping the lid.*) Seven weeks, it was – seven or eight weeks, that's all. Jacob said we should sell the house and everything in it, so we did. Then we went away to Paris for our second honeymoon, really official. (*She gives him the lid.*) It was there that Jacob decided to be a minister. We went to the Unknown Warrior's grave – it could have been my brother Stanley – we lit candles there every day and your father decided that he would carry on Stanley's career as a minister where he'd had to leave it off. I remember so plainly. 'How would you like to be a minister's wife?' he said, in a voice so unlike himself. I'd been a minister's daughter and sister to a padre – a minister's wife couldn't have had a better training. There was no need for Jacob to make such a decision. But he felt it was his duty, serving others, our duty, to make amends for the wrong we'd both done. I've never regretted it for a moment. Such a good life. Although, sometimes – I can't help my feelings, I can't help myself – sometimes – I wish we hadn't gone – to Paris...

(*The clock chimes five o'clock. MAURICE puts the lid in the box and kisses CISSY lightly on the forehead. As the chimes fade the sound of hammering is heard coming from upstairs. CISSY goes out into the hall.*)

Ooh, dear – what are they doing?

MAURICE: I'll go.

CISSY: Clifford. What are – Clifford, what...?

MAURICE: Frank!

(*The hammering stops. FRANK comes down to the small landing. CLIFFORD follows.*)

CISSY: What are you banging?

FRANK: Nails.

CLIFFORD: We're knocking them in.

CISSY: I thought you were taking them out.

FRANK: Some of them have been in too long.

CISSY: Perhaps you'd better not do any more today.

(*MAURICE is standing in the doorway of the living-room when ANNA comes in from the garden followed by LIZ. MAURICE and LIZ stare at each other across the room. LIZ puts her music case down.*)

Most of the heavy furniture belongs here, but I'll sort it out with you on Tuesday, Anna knows – she'll go through it all with you.

ANNA: Mother.

CISSY: Is that you Anna?

(*MAURICE goes into the kitchen.*)

ANNA: And Liz…

(*FRANK goes up the stairs. CLIFFORD starts to go down.*)

CISSY: (*Entering the living-room.*) Liz.

LIZ: Is Clifford home?

CISSY: He's been waiting for you, he's played for us already.

ANNA: Looks as though someone's been busy.

CISSY: I wrapped a few things from the sideboard, that's all.

ANNA: Where am I going to put them?

CISSY: There are some empty chests upstairs still.

ANNA: I see you've cleared Gethsemane.

CISSY: Ooh yes, love.

(*CLIFFORD sits on the fender box.*)

ANNA: Nothing stays in its natural state for long in this house. Let me take your coat, Miss Mathews.

CISSY: Frank's upstairs.

LIZ: (*To CISSY.*) Thank you, dear.

CISSY: They're untacking the carpets for me.

(*MAURICE comes from the kitchen.*)

ANNA: (*Going to the hall with the coats.*) I'll ask Frank to bring a tea-chest. (*Calling.*) Frank –

MAURICE: (*Going up.*) I'll tell him.

CISSY: Would you like Anna to get you a cup of tea?

LIZ: Kind thought.

MAURICE: Were the children attentive this afternoon?

ANNA: (*Hanging the coats.*) No more than their elders.

(*MAURICE goes.*)

CISSY: We'll wait until Jacob comes home.

LIZ: He won't be very long.

ANNA: The Sunday School gave Jacob a present.

CISSY: Ooh, he'd be very pleased. What was it?

LIZ: A heavenly book with over thirty coloured prints of the most lovely photographs.

ANNA: It's a gardening book.

CISSY: And did you choose it, Liz?

LIZ: Well, yes.

(*FRANK comes down the stairs with a tea-chest.*)

MAURICE: (*Off.*) Can you manage, Frank?

FRANK: (*On the small landing.*) Course I can manage.

(*He misses the next step and drops the tea-chest. MAURICE appears at the top of the stairs, laughing. He has a hammer in his hand. ANNA goes to the foot of the stairs.*)

Blasted nail in it.

ANNA: I'll give you a hand. Maurice won't. (*She puts the tea-chest in the hall.*)

FRANK: Get the hammer, Maurice, and give that bastard a bash. (*To ANNA.*) This your idea, was it?

(*MAURICE starts to go downstairs.*)

ANNA: Mother's.

CISSY: (*Going into the hall.*) Have you hurt yourself, Frank?

(*LIZ follows CISSY.*)

FRANK: No.

ANNA: He's caught his finger on a nail.

CISSY: Ooh, dear.

(*CLIFFORD goes into the hall.*)

LIZ: Oh you clumsy, clumsy man.

FRANK: I couldn't help it.

LIZ: Let me see.

(*MAURICE flattens the nail in the tea-chest. LIZ puts her hat with her coat.*)

FRANK: It's alright, will be when I've sucked it.

ANNA: Thank you, Maurice.

CISSY: (*Going up.*) Come along, Frank, we'll go and bathe it and you can have a plaster on.

(*LIZ goes into the living-room. MAURICE follows.*)

FRANK: This'll ruin my putts.

CISSY: I think there are some in the bathroom, aren't there, Anna?

ANNA: On the top shelf.

CISSY: And I can tell you what has to stay and which things are ours.

(*CISSY and FRANK go into the bathroom.*)

MAURICE: Afternoon, aunty.

LIZ: Ha-aha.

(*CLIFFORD comes back. ANNA drags the tea-chest.*)

MAURICE: How about a selection, Clifford, a musical interlude to celebrate Aunt Elizabeth's engagement.

LIZ: That depends on Clifford.

MAURICE: He's been practising.

ANNA: (*Trying to get the tea-chest into the room.*) Help me with this, Maurice.

MAURICE: (*Lying down on the sofa.*) Clifford's available.

(*CLIFFORD takes over from ANNA.*)

LIZ: You're a lazy boy.

CLIFFORD: Hold the door...

(*CLIFFORD sets the tea-chest down. ANNA closes the door.*)

LIZ: Dear children – I shall miss you terribly.

MAURICE: They'll be along to see you whenever they can.

ANNA: (*Packing the china into the tea-chest.*) You'll be a real member of the family at last. I've always thought of you in that way.

LIZ: Well, yes, I can remember when you were born, Anna, and your mother was so ill, I practically lived here for a time.

CLIFFORD: You were like a second mother to us.

(*ANNA goes to the piano and picks up the wrapped dog.*)

LIZ: Your father certainly couldn't have coped with the three of you and poor Cissy as well. She seems to have got stronger as the years have gone by – thanks to all your care, Anna.

ANNA: That's reward enough.

MAURICE: Father will miss you more than any of us.

ANNA: (*Packing the dog.*) You've been a great help to him over the years, in so many ways.

LIZ: It's sweet of you to say so.

(*LIZ attempts to pick up the cardboard box.*)

ANNA: No, please, I can do this.

LIZ: You do so much, Anna.

ANNA: I'm glad to be able to. (*She packs the box.*)

LIZ: And she's always so cheerful.

CLIFFORD: I'm sure.

LIZ: I've never heard you once complain.

ANNA: Complain – ha – goodness no, I have an easy life when you think of it. I'm always busy shopping, cooking and the housework.

LIZ: And gardening when you can.

ANNA: (*Picking up the newspapers.*) Yes, and the Endeavour classes and Sunday School. Like Cinderella without Buttons. I have nothing to worry about, not like Cliff, for instance. I often think how worrying his work must be. Don't you find yourself wishing you hadn't any responsibilities sometimes, Cliff? Don't you wish sometimes that you could go off, leaving all your experiments to explode behind you? (*She dumps the papers into the tea-chest.*)

LIZ: As a matter of fact he has.

CLIFFORD: I lied to you all yesterday.

MAURICE: Shame.

CLIFFORD: I said I'd resigned.

MAURICE: And you were pulling our legs.

CLIFFORD: No, I have resigned. I even have a job to go to now... I couldn't explain over the tea table, your reactions took me by surprise.

ANNA: You mean you've left everything?

CLIFFORD: It wasn't difficult. There's no joy in the laboratory. Only molecules, formulae and apparatus.

LIZ: I still can't get over it. Your father's always told me such a lot about your work, he made it sound fascinating, absolutely fascinating.

ANNA: Father's a fascinating man. You know that.

MAURICE: And we all take after him.

CLIFFORD: In one way or another.

JACOB: (*In the hall.*) Hello – (*He hangs his umbrella on the banister rail.*)

LIZ: Ah!

CISSY: (*From the bathroom.*) Sounds like Jacob.

FRANK: (*From the bathroom.*) It will be.

MAURICE: If you're going to play, leave the door open, Cliff. (*He goes quickly up the stairs, before JACOB turns round to hang his coat up.*)

ANNA: I'll make tea.

CISSY: (*Calling, off.*) Is that you, Jacob?
(*ANNA goes into the hall. LIZ takes a sheet of music from her case and shows it to CLIFFORD.*)

JACOB: Yes yes, Cissy. Miss Mathews with you?

ANNA: In the room.

CISSY: (*Opening the bathroom door.*) We're upstairs. (*Appearing.*) Frank gave himself a nasty cut on his finger with a nail in a tea-chest.

JACOB: I'm sorry to hear that, Frank.
(*FRANK appears.*)
Have you received medical attention?

FRANK: I'm just getting it now from matron.

JACOB: Well done.
(*MAURICE is hammering tacks into the floorboards above. JACOB scowls.*)

ANNA: Clifford.

CLIFFORD: Yes?

ANNA: Bring the chest into the hall for me please.

CLIFFORD: Of course.

CISSY: (*For JACOB.*) It's Maurice.

FRANK: Carpet tacks.

JACOB: Everybody seems very industrious.

ANNA: There's such a lot to do.

CISSY: Oh Anna, love – I just remembered I knocked the little vase of French marigolds off the window-sill when I opened the cabinet door and it hit the sink and broke.

FRANK: My fault really.

CISSY: Bring a brush and the dustpan up –

ANNA: Alright.

CISSY: Oh and the floor cloth.

ANNA: (*Going into the kitchen.*) Yes.

CISSY: (*Calling.*) Have we another little vase we could put them in?

ANNA: (*Off.*) I'll see.

CISSY: (*Calling.*) A jam jar would do.

CLIFFORD: Hold the door for me, Elizabeth, would you please?

LIZ: One moment.

JACOB: Ask Maurice to hammer quietly.

FRANK: Maurice –

(He exits along the landing. The hammering stops. CLIFFORD comes down the hall with the tea-chest. JACOB moves out of the way ahead of him to the newel post.)

CISSY: Liz was saying you had a lovely book presented, dear.

JACOB: Gardening – Clifford – has Elizabeth given you a lesson? *(He takes his umbrella from the banister.)*

CISSY: He played to us earlier before Liz arrived.

JACOB: You must play again before she leaves.

(He goes into the room. ANNA comes from the kitchen with a dustpan and brush and a jam jar. She passes JACOB and goes to the foot of the stairs. LIZ is by the piano adjusting Bach's 'Sleepers Awake' on the music rest. CLIFFORD puts the tea-chest at the foot of the stairs.)

CISSY: *(As ANNA appears.)* Ooh, Anna, would you make the tea now father's home?

(JACOB goes to the vestibule and shakes the rain off his umbrella. LIZ closes the living-room door.)

ANNA: Before I clean the bathroom?

CISSY: How many are we? Liz – Clifford – Frank –

CLIFFORD: *(To ANNA.)* Will it be in the way here?

CISSY: Maurice – Jacob –

ANNA: *(Going up the stairs.)* That's fine. Cliff, put the kettle on, sorry.

CLIFFORD: Of course. How many?

ANNA: Seven. Thanks.

(CLIFFORD goes to the kitchen. FRANK reappears.)

CISSY: That's right, seven.

(MAURICE behind FRANK carrying a roll of carpet.)

MAURICE: All good children go to heaven.

CISSY: Where's my patient?

FRANK: Bleeding to death.

CISSY: Oh, you do exaggerate. It is a nasty cut.

(CISSY and FRANK return to the bathroom. JACOB leaves the open umbrella on the tiled floor of the vestibule.)

ANNA: *(On the small landing, blocking MAURICE's way.)* You can hammer now.

MAURICE: I've finished.

ANNA: You won't take me with you?

MAURICE: No. But take this. My return ticket to London. It's valid for three months. Use it.

ANNA: (*Taking the ticket.*) I want to go with you.

MAURICE: (*Trying to pass.*) You're on your own.

ANNA: (*Preventing him.*) Why else would I ask you?

MAURICE: (*Leaving the carpet on the top section of the stairs in exasperation.*) I must go and pack if I'm to catch the six o'clock.

> (*He goes back up. ANNA watches him go, then looks at the train ticket.*)

LIZ: It's unlucky, an open umbrella.

JACOB: Yes.

CISSY: (*From the bathroom.*) Anna, love –

> (*ANNA goes into the bathroom.*)

LIZ: This is probably the last time we shall be alone together.

JACOB: I shall miss you.

LIZ: Will you…

JACOB: I hope you'll be very happy with Frank.

LIZ: Frank's a happy man. I wish I'd married him years ago instead of waiting – hoping – even praying for Cissy to die.

JACOB: Eliza –

LIZ: Well, didn't we? I admit I did. I loved you enough in the past to wish it could be so. Now I feel ashamed somehow, as though I were in disgrace – especially in this house.

JACOB: Nonsense.

LIZ: Yesterday the children – hah the children – they made me feel so old. I *am* quite old now, I know. I hadn't felt it before. But yesterday, at tea, as I was sitting there with my life behind me, it seemed rather silly that I should still want to be your wife. I've got nothing much to show for my love towards you over the last twenty-five years, have I? We haven't got much, have we? Just the little shame of the wasted years we've spent; me preserving my honour and you your reputation as a Christian man.

JACOB: (*Touching LIZ's hand.*) Your loving friendship has meant a very great deal to *me*.

LIZ: (*Recoiling.*) Oh, I think you'd have managed alright without it. You will. You'll see. You'll have to. So will I.

JACOB: You'll have Frank to care for.

LIZ: Yes, I'll have Frank to care about instead, and you'll have Cissy and the children.

JACOB: Children! Clifford came home drunk last night.

LIZ: Oh.

JACOB: Under Maurice's contaminating influence.

LIZ: No I don't think so.

JACOB: He's immoral.

LIZ: He's your son.

JACOB: Any ordinary father would have disowned him years ago.

LIZ: Would he care if you had?

JACOB: Why didn't you wait while we'd gone?

LIZ: You won't have to preside at the ceremony.
    (*CLIFFORD comes from the kitchen carrying a tea tray with seven cups and saucers on it. He enters the living-room.*)

LIZ: I was just telling your father the truth – about your decision –

JACOB: What decision?

LIZ: His decision to leave his medicine – for good.

JACOB: And what does he intend to do instead?

CLIFFORD: Give piano lessons. (*He sets the tray down.*) I put the kettle on.

LIZ: He's taking over my pupils and my house, when I move to Frank's.

JACOB: What are you going to play for us?

LIZ: What would you like me to?

JACOB: I think Clifford should say.

CLIFFORD: The introit you played this morning.

LIZ: Did you like it?

CLIFFORD: You played it very well.

LIZ: I shan't play as well for the new minister. We made a good team, your father and I. I always came in on my cue. I have a little mirror above me that reflects the back of his head. Did you like the anthem as well?

CLIFFORD: Very much. Bach wasn't it?

LIZ: Yes. The introit is too. (*Indicating the music rest.*) See, it's waiting for you to play.

(*CLIFFORD sits at the piano.*)

(*Sad and vindictive.*) I only ever play it on special occasions.

(*CLIFFORD plays. MAURICE comes down the stairs carrying a large grip and his coat.*)

MAURICE: (*Calling as he passes the bathroom.*) Concert's started, Frank.

FRANK: (*Off.*) I'm coming. Thanks Cis. Hurry up.

(*He comes from the bathroom. MAURICE puts his things in the vestibule, then lies down on the sofa. FRANK comes downstairs into the hall. He puts his jacket on, goes into the living-room and sits on the fender box.*)

CISSY: (*Calling back, off.*) Yes. Bring the marigolds Anna.

(*She comes from the bathroom, followed by ANNA carrying the jar of marigolds.*)

Put them on the landing table in case they get knocked down again.

ANNA: Yes, we've had enough accidents. (*She goes up to the top landing.*)

CISSY: Ooh, look where they've left the carpet.

ANNA: (*Taking hold of the carpet as she comes down the stairs.*) That was Maurice. I'll take it down. (*She starts to drag the rolled carpet.*)

CISSY: Can you manage? (*She takes hold of the other end.*)

ANNA: It's not very heavy.

CISSY: (*Going backwards down the stairs.*) That's Liz playing, not Clifford, you can tell the difference. Just a minute –

ANNA: Leave it.

(*She jerks the carpet from CISSY's grasp. CISSY tries to hold on but has a heart attack and falls on to the small landing, her head coming to rest on the upper section. ANNA, still holding the carpet, steps over, bends down and shakes her, trying to bring her round. The carpet unrolls down the lower part of the stairs, dividing her attention. When CISSY doesn't respond ANNA goes down, trying to roll the carpet up again, fails and throws one end over the banister rail. She*)

*goes into the living-room. She goes up to CLIFFORD and
tugs his arm. He stops playing. She indicates the hall.)*
On the stairs...
*(CLIFFORD goes into the hall. He sees CISSY on the small
landing and hurries to her.)*
CLIFFORD: Mother. *(Calling.)* Frank –
(FRANK goes into the hall.)
Get Doctor Selby. *(He kneels.)*
FRANK: *(Going to CLIFFORD's side.)* What's happened?
CLIFFORD: Mum...
LIZ: *(To ANNA.)* What is it? *(She goes into the hall.)*
JACOB: Anna...?
ANNA: She fell –
(MAURICE gets up, bewildered.)
FRANK: *(To LIZ.)* She's fallen down and fainted on the stairs.
LIZ: I'll fetch a cushion. *(She goes back into the living-room.)*
FRANK: Yes, bring a few.
(MAURICE gets to the foot of the stairs.)
LIZ: Cissy.
JACOB: Is she alright?
FRANK: What can I do?
CLIFFORD: Fetch the doctor.
FRANK: Yes, right. Maurice...
(JACOB pushes LIZ out of the way.)
LIZ: Jacob –
*(She looks guiltily at ANNA, takes two cushions from the sofa
and follows JACOB. ANNA stands still.)*
JACOB: Oh God. *(He stands still by the stair cupboard.)*
FRANK: Come on – *(He takes a cushion.)* Here, can we
move her?
(CLIFFORD raises CISSY a little.)
CISSY: *(Opening her eyes like a mechanical doll.)* Ooh, Jacob
darling.
FRANK: She's alright, she's speaking. *(He pauses.)* What did
she say?
(CLIFFORD feels her pulse. All still and silent.)
CLIFFORD: She's dead.
(There is a pause.)

FRANK: Eh?

(*ANNA moves from the living-room into the hall.*)

JACOB: Dead?

(*ANNA moves slowly down the hall, passing LIZ and JACOB, to MAURICE.*)

FRANK: She can't be.

MAURICE: (*Two steps up.*) Mum.

(*There is a pause.*)

LIZ: Oh no.

MAURICE: Mum.

LIZ: I don't believe it.

MAURICE: Oh, Mum.

FRANK: Is she?

(*MAURICE sobs.*)

FRANK: Is it true?

CLIFFORD: True enough…

FRANK: What about the kiss of life?

CLIFFORD: She's gone.

JACOB: Cicely.

CLIFFORD: Maurice. Anna. Are you alright?

(*ANNA nods.*)

MAURICE: Dad. Can't you say a prayer, pray or something?

JACOB: I did. He heard. He must have – He's put an end to her suffering at last.

MAURICE: With a vengeance – with a vengeance. Oh, Anna. (*He turns away to ANNA and holds her to him as though she were CISSY.*)

ANNA: (*Embracing him desperately.*) Maurice.

(*The kettle starts to whistle, faintly at first but gradually getting shriller.*)

CLIFFORD: We'd better take her upstairs.

(*He lifts CISSY into his arms and starts upstairs. MAURICE realises ANNA's embrace is sexual and pulls away.*)

ANNA: (*Holding on.*) Stay with me, Maurice.

FRANK: Yes.

ANNA: I can't look.

LIZ: What a terrible thing to happen.

CLIFFORD: No, Frank, I can manage. Clear the carpet.

FRANK: Yes. We should've left them down.

(*CLIFFORD goes, carrying CISSY.*)

ANNA: It's my fault – oh…

(*MAURICE breaks free and moves away.*)

JACOB: Anna, come, Anna – have courage, we all must. Stay with her, Maurice.

FRANK: Bear up, love, she had to go sooner or later.

LIZ: My dear.

JACOB: The kettle – Anna… Make some tea, make tea for us, Anna. (*He passes her on to MAURICE.*)

ANNA: (*Joining MAURICE.*) I will, yes – yes.

JACOB: Take her, Maurice.

(*ANNA and MAURICE go into the kitchen. FRANK goes upstairs with the carpet.*)

FRANK: Are you alright, Cliff?

CLIFFORD: (*Off.*) Will you fetch the doctor then, please, Frank.

FRANK: (*Off.*) Yes of course right away.

(*The kettle whistle dies away. JACOB starts to climb the stairs. LIZ moves towards him. He picks up the cushion on the stairs and hands it to her.*)

LIZ: I'll go with Frank.

JACOB: Yes.

LIZ: You'll want to be alone.

JACOB: I suppose so. Yes. I suppose I will. (*He continues.*)

LIZ: When my father died, my mother told me to think that he'd gone on a very long holiday and that he wasn't coming back. I've never forgotten.

(*When JACOB has gone LIZ drops the cushions into the tea-chest at the foot of the stairs. The clock chimes five thirty as she goes upstairs to join the others. MAURICE comes from the kitchen into the living-room, still crying. He touches the back of the chair his mother had been sitting in. ANNA brings a full tea tray into the room. She moves close to MAURICE, then suddenly moves away from him to the sideboard. She crashes the tray down.*)

ANNA: I must go – I can't stay here any longer – I must be free, must leave the old woman upstairs, I'm afraid to be where she is – with him – afraid I'll grow like her – kind without reason – obedient because it's written – tolerant of indifference – (*She faces MAURICE.*)

MAURICE: And dead.

ANNA: Yes, dead –

(*She goes to MAURICE. He moves away from her trying not to cry. She follows him.*)

Don't shut me out any more Maurice – you're all I have – (*She touches him. He shrugs her off.*)

MAURICE: You don't have to stay now. You can catch the six o'clock.

ANNA: You mean I can go with you...you'll take me?

MAURICE: I'm not going.

ANNA: You must.

MAURICE: I want to see her buried.

ANNA: You sail tomorrow.

MAURICE: The ship does.

ANNA: The funeral won't be for days.

MAURICE: I'll wait. I'll go on the next.

ANNA: When?

MAURICE: Three weeks. A month – two.

ANNA: What will you do?

MAURICE: Hang around.

ANNA: Where?

MAURICE: With our father in Hockton, I suppose.

ANNA: (*Backing away.*) I see.

MAURICE: You can write to me. Tell me all your adventures.

ANNA: Yes.

MAURICE: You'll go?

ANNA: Yes.

MAURICE: Promise?

ANNA: Yes.

MAURICE: Swear it.

ANNA: (*Opening the garden door and standing up on the step of the vestibule.*) God's honour.

MAURICE: Cross your heart –

ANNA: (*Doing it.*) And wonder why.

MAURICE: Cross your fingers –

ANNA: (*Making the sign of a cross with her index fingers.*) And hope to lie.

MAURICE: Close your eyes –

ANNA: (*Doing so.*) And try to cry.

> (*FRANK and LIZ come down the stairs followed slowly after by CLIFFORD. He stands in the hall.*)

MAURICE: Matthew, Mark, Luke and John –

ANNA: Acts and Romans follow on.

ANNA/MAURICE: Gospel.

> (*ANNA folds JACOB's umbrella. FRANK takes his and LIZ's coats from the hooks in the hall. LIZ goes into the living-room.*)

LIZ: Children, I'm going for the doctor with Frank.

FRANK: We'll tell him to be as quick as he can.

> (*ANNA nods. MAURICE turns away.*)

LIZ: Your father's very upset, look after him – such a shock to –

FRANK: He's not going to evening service.

LIZ: (*Putting her coat on.*) It's too much to ask. Oh, what a dreadful thing to have happened just at this time…when they could have had a little comfort and leisure for once in their lives. Talk to him when he comes down, children. Talk to him. He needs you all, more than ever now. I'm not much use to him like this… (*She is crying.*) Shall I call round after the service?

ANNA: Perhaps it might be better if you didn't.

LIZ: Perhaps you're right.

FRANK: Yes. We'll call round in the morning.

LIZ: I'll get the doctor to bring some sleeping pills with him. (*She collects her handbag, gloves and hat.*)

ANNA: See you tomorrow.

LIZ: Goodbye.

FRANK: So long.

LIZ: Goodbye.

ANNA: Cheerio, Frank.

FRANK: Look after them.

LIZ: God be with you.

ANNA: Elizabeth. You'd better take this. Keep it as a souvenir. (*She gives LIZ the umbrella.*)

LIZ: Thank you.

> (*She passes the umbrella on to FRANK. They leave through the front door. JACOB comes down the stairs. MAURICE*)

picks up a wedding photograph of JACOB and CISSY from the top of the piano. ANNA goes to the tray and organises cups and saucers noisily.)

ANNA: We won't need all these cups.

JACOB: (*Outside the living-room.*) How's Anna?

CLIFFORD: (*Outside the living-room.*) She's in the room.
(JACOB comes into the room. CLIFFORD follows, closing the door behind him.)

ANNA: We made the tea.

JACOB: Ah yes.
(ANNA pours four cups of tea. When JACOB sits, CLIFFORD does.)

ANNA: Father…

JACOB: Mmm? Yes, Anna?

ANNA: (*Giving JACOB tea.*) Would you be alright if I went to Liversedge and stayed with Aunt Milly just for tonight?

JACOB: Yes – oh yes – I know, Anna, yes, go and tell her and we'll see you tomorrow.

CLIFFORD: I'll come with you.

ANNA: No – please, Cliff. No – I'll go alone. I'd rather.
(She gives CLIFFORD tea.)

MAURICE: Catch the six o'clock. You have time.

ANNA: Which train are you going on, Maurice?

JACOB: He won't want to leave tonight. He can't go now.

ANNA: (*Taking two cups and giving one to MAURICE.*) Yes, he can. Life must go on as usual, as though nothing had happened, as it always has in this house. We mustn't break the pattern for the last few days we're here. Mother would have wished things to go on as they were, wouldn't she, Father?

JACOB: Yes, yes she would.

ANNA: That's why you must go to evening service. We all have our duties to perform.
(MAURICE puts more sugar in his tea.)

JACOB: Yes, Anna is right. You, Maurice, must return to sea, Clifford to his – and I to my pulpit for the last time to lead the congregation in prayer for her and all of us, taking comfort in the knowledge that she's been taken

166

from us to travel to a more blissful retirement with our Father in heaven. I'm sure he'll say as he receives her spirit, 'Well done, good and faithful servant, enter into the joy of the Lord.'

MAURICE: She's just died, Dad.

JACOB: The Lord gave and now the Lord hath taken away.

MAURICE: The Lord hath taken away nothing. She's dead. There's nothing divine or preordained about it. It's happened and it's enough that it has without convincing yourself that death is heaven sent, hers or anyone else's.

JACOB: To those who have faith –

MAURICE: All the faith that ever was or is or ever will be world without end all put together can't weigh as heavy as she does here and now.

JACOB: Isn't it sacrilege enough that you must blaspheme against your mother?

MAURICE: My clichés are as good as yours. At least they don't insult her dead body prettying it up with gold wings and a halo of celestial light. You don't need to go through the ritual for our benefit. Have a little dignity and honesty for once in your two-faced ecclesiastical life, why don't you? You've wanted her in the churchyard ever since we came here.

JACOB: Clifford.

MAURICE: For twenty-five years you've made her your excuse for hibernating in this parish to collect the easy respect from the sheep that flocked into your sermons.

JACOB: Cissy's health –

MAURICE: For twenty-five years you've tantalised Liz Mathews with high hopes of marriage.

JACOB: She looked after you and cared for –

MAURICE: For a quarter of a century you've screwed down your natural instinct to flatter every woman in the neighbourhood into the awe-inspiring dark of the vestry to show them your tattoo.

JACOB: Frank –

MAURICE: I've got some, too –

JACOB: Frank told you –

MAURICE: I've got four of the damned things, it's better that we know.

JACOB: Your mother's death has affected us all, Maurice, you more than any of us no doubt, but I suggest you let Clifford take you upstairs and save us and yourself any further distress at this time.

MAURICE: This house is no more distressed than the Queen Mary in dry dock. Anna's right, we'll go on as though nothing had happened, as though we didn't know what a bloody hypocrite you are.

JACOB: Leave me alone. Clifford –

(*CLIFFORD goes to the piano.*)

You can't agree with him?

CLIFFORD: I have no feelings either way.

JACOB: No feelings…?

(*CLIFFORD sits on the piano stool facing into the room.*)

MAURICE: Clifford's too much of a gentleman, too educated, too full of wisdom and understanding to have feelings – Top-of-the-class Cliff, everything his father wanted him to be – sterile as the test tubes in his laboratory.

JACOB: I sacrificed my life for you all –

MAURICE: You sacrificed other people's for your own. You led mother up the garden path without love, then down the aisle to the altar in a fit of guilt, you stifled Clifford with the honour of learning and Anna with the virtue of servility – Liz – Frank – you know as well as any of us – and them.

JACOB: What you say sounds like the truth, it might be, it may be so – but don't let it be said, not now, eh?

MAURICE: When then, eh?

JACOB: Just let it be known between us in silence. Where there is silence we – I can imagine there's love.

MAURICE: What use is it to imagine love? God is love – imagine that. God to you's a magic word, a universal conscience, the reason for all things and the explanation of none. At best God's us, our equal, our reflection or more like he's nothing nowhere, and eternity, your everlasting eternity for ever and ever amen, is here and now or it never was nor ever will be world without end etcetera ad infinitum. (*The clock chimes five forty-five.*) There's no life after death, the best is here, not yet to come. Beats me why you haven't choked to death on platitudes.

(*JACOB slowly takes hold of his collar and pulls it off.*)

Get your coat, Anna, we'll catch the train together.

CLIFFORD: To Liversedge?

ANNA: To London. (*She goes to the hall and gets her coat and a headscarf.*)

JACOB: London – no. She's going to Liversedge. Aunt Milly's...

MAURICE: She lied. She never was, she never will again. She's served her sentence, twenty years of it, she's earned her release from this prison.

(*JACOB moves to the door of the living-room as ANNA returns carrying her coat. He stands in her way.*)

JACOB: You're not leaving me now? You wouldn't have gone?

ANNA: Yes. (*She collects her bag.*)

JACOB: What about your things – belongings – clothes and –

MAURICE: You'll have to send them on.

JACOB: Where to?

MAURICE: She'll let you know.

(*ANNA puts her coat on. JACOB helps her into it. Something to hold on to. An attempt to detain which speeds her departure.*)

JACOB: Write to me. Seldom if you like, but sometimes.

ANNA: Yes.

MAURICE: (*Moving to the vestibule and picking up his coat.*) Good-bye Father.

JACOB: God be with you.

MAURICE: You too. (*Picking up his grip.*) See you, Cliff.

CLIFFORD: Very likely.

(*ANNA joins MAURICE in the vestibule.*)

MAURICE: Dark outside.

ANNA: It's darker in here.

CLIFFORD: I'll put the light on. (*He switches a lamp on and joins them.*)

MAURICE: Genesis.

ANNA: Exodus –

(*MAURICE and ANNA go into the garden. CLIFFORD watches them.*)

CLIFFORD: Lamentations.

JACOB: Close the door. Fair wind blowing through.

CLIFFORD: The North.

(*He closes the garden door. The church bell tolls to rally a congregation for evening service.*)

You'll have to hurry if you're going to evening service, Father. You have ten minutes.

JACOB: Come with me. To chapel…

CLIFFORD: I must wait for Doctor Selby.

JACOB: Yes. Play something, Clifford. Practise.

CLIFFORD: Alright.

JACOB: I'll get my coat.

CLIFFORD: It's not raining.

JACOB: I'll take my umbrella in case.

CLIFFORD: (*Looking through the music in the piano stool.*) Elizabeth took it, Father.

JACOB: Oh – oh yes. Something to remember me by.

(*He hesitates to go into the hall. CLIFFORD finds a suitable sheet of music, puts it on the music rest and sits.*)

I hope the rain keeps off for the funeral. Makes it harder for the bearers when it's wet.

CLIFFORD: Father.

JACOB: Mmm?

CLIFFORD: What's tattooed on your thigh?

JACOB: A sword – and a serpent. 'For every man hath his sword upon his thigh, because of fear in the night.'

CLIFFORD: Solomon –

JACOB: Chapter three verse eight.

(*CLIFFORD starts to play the piano in slow tempo. Bach's Church Cantata 147 number 10, 'Jesu, joy of man's desiring'.*)

CLIFFORD: You mustn't worry about Maurice and the things he said, Father…he's not stable. Impetuous and a bit of a fanatic. Up to no good. You're right, you always were.

JACOB: You play very well, Clifford. See you soon.

CLIFFORD: Yes.

(*JACOB goes into the hall. He sits on the bottom stairs with his head in his hands. ANNA comes in from the garden. She moves to the piano and puts her bag on it.*)

ANNA: Where is he?

(*CLIFFORD nods towards the hall. ANNA crosses to the mantelpiece, takes CISSY's gloves and puts them on the fire to burn.*)

What are you playing that for?

CLIFFORD: It seemed appropriate.

JACOB: Anna.

(*ANNA goes out into the hall, takes JACOB's coat from the hooks and puts it over the banister. She takes JACOB's collar and silk from his hand. The church bell stops.*)

ANNA: We'll have to hurry. It's six o'clock. Turn round.

(*She clamps the collar in position round JACOB's neck as if to choke him.*)

JACOB: I don't want –

ANNA: Nobody wants, but they must.

(*CLIFFORD stops playing.*)

JACOB: Has Maurice come back?

ANNA: No. Just me.

JACOB: Why?

ANNA: Like you said. I've only one talent – looking after invalids.

JACOB: I'm not an invalid.

ANNA: You will be.

JACOB: You won't mind sleeping here tonight with your mother...

ANNA: I won't mind.

JACOB: You never liked her much, did you?

ANNA: All good children love their parents. It's only natural.

JACOB: You won't write to Maurice again, Anna...?

ANNA: (*Helping him into his coat.*) Not if you don't want me to.

JACOB: We'll go over to Aunt Milly's together in the morning, shall we?

ANNA: Yes. Alright.

JACOB: You're a great comfort to me Anna.

ANNA: I shall be – as long as you live.

(A train can be heard, leaving the station. JACOB and ANNA go up the hall and out through the front door. CLIFFORD hears the train and crosses to the garden door. He bolts it and closes the curtain. He goes back to the piano, sits and plays the concluding section of 'Jesu, joy of man's desiring' in its regular tempo. The end of the play coincides with the end of the music he is playing.)

The End.

A LILY IN LITTLE INDIA

Characters

GEORGE BLAND
a postman in his 30s

ANNA BOWERS
in her late 30s

JACOB BOWERS
aged over 70, her father

MRS HANKER
aged 40 plus

ALVIN HANKER
in his 20s, her son

AMBULANCE MAN

DOCTOR FRANKLYN

AUTHOR'S VOICE

A Lily in Little India was first staged at the Hampstead Theatre Club under James Roose-Evans and Richard Cottrell, 22 November 1965, and subsequently produced by Michael Codron, by arrangement with Peter Bridge, at the St Martin's Theatre, London, 20 January 1966, with the following cast:

GEORGE BLAND, Ken Jones

ANNA BOWERS, Jill Bennett

JACOB BOWERS, Leslie Handford

MRS HANKER, Jessie Evans

ALVIN HANKER, Ian McKellen

AMBULANCE MAN, David Cook

DOCTOR FRANKLYN, Raymond Mason

AUTHOR'S VOICE, Vernon Dobtcheff

Director, Donald Howarth

Designer, Kenneth Mellor

A note about the staging. The two houses are as separate islands, the Hanker's on three levels, the Bowers' on two; the stage between the unequal islands being the outside world. The rooms are tiered, Alvin's room with its window, door and wardrobe being the highest point from which the rest cascade. At front centre there is a low, three-sided box or step, for coal, soil, gravel and so on. An overall subdued light, reflecting the time of day or night, is heightened to anticipate and flow with the action wherever a scene is played.

ACT ONE

The darkness before daylight shrouds the winter frost over a small country town. Two homes: the BOWERS' and the HANKER's.

GEORGE BLAND, a lodger in MRS HANKER's house, sleeps, breathing noisily through his throat. A ticking clock gets louder until it rings. He wakes with a start, finds it and has to hit it twice before the alarm stops. The tick resumes.

GEORGE: Five o'clock already? Some clocks have nothing better to do but tick all day. I'm glad I'm not a clock, though. At least that's something to be glad of. I'm not a clock. (*He gets out of bed mechanically, puts his feet in his slippers, takes his clothes from the chair, yawns, stretches and bends his knees.*) I'm not wound or set the night before. I can get up in the morning when the alarm goes off. Nobody winds me. I'm not wound. Nobody has to wind me up to get me up. (*He goes to the bathroom.*)

(*The ticking stops. As the daylight grows ANNA BOWERS in a bungalow on the outskirts of town carries a breakfast tray into her father's bedroom. She puts it down and opens the curtains. She spoons Andrews Salts into a glass, adds water and stirs it.*)

ANNA: Father.

JACOB: Wednesday?

ANNA: Yes, Wednesday.

(*A clock chimes the half-hour.*)

Half past seven. Sit up.

(*JACOB struggles out from under the snowdrift sheets, a frost-bitten explorer imagining rescue. ANNA holds out the glass.*)

Don't spill it.

(*She unfolds a napkin as JACOB drinks the salts, takes the empty glass from him and spreads the napkin like a tablecloth on his chest. She picks up the tray. He throws the napkin to the floor. She repeats the ritual, gets the tray, places it in front of him, and slices the top off his egg.*)

It's likely to rain later today. Will you be getting up?

JACOB: Yes, I'll get up.

(*ANNA hands JACOB a spoonful of egg. He dribbles it. She pours his tea, then sits on the chair beside the window looking out as he eats his breakfast.*)

(*Music is heard from the radio in the HANKER's kitchen. ALVIN HANKER appears in his bedroom getting dressed. MRS HANKER comes into the kitchen from the back yard, picks up the garbage and goes into the hall.*)

MRS HANKER: (*Calling.*) Alvin. (*She goes out to the dustbin, collects the bottle of milk from the step on the way back and calls.*) Alvin.

(*A listless ALVIN comes down into the kitchen, sits and eats his cereal.*)

About time. (*She washes up.*)

ALVIN: What is?

MRS HANKER: You are.

ALVIN: I always am.

MRS HANKER: George never is.

ALVIN: What?

MRS HANKER: Late.

ALVIN: I'm not.

MRS HANKER: You can tell the time by George Bland.

ALVIN: Who wants to at five o'clock in the morning?

MRS HANKER: Those who have a mind to. He's always on time is George Bland. He's never late. He's the first to leave this house regular as a clockwork at half past five every morning on the dot.

ALVIN: On his bicycle.

MRS HANKER: On the dot, five thirty every morning.

ALVIN: Except Sunday.

MRS HANKER: Of course except Sunday. Nobody works on a Sunday.

ALVIN: A lot works on a Sunday.

MRS HANKER: Yes, but the majority don't. You know very well what I mean, very well you know it. As a postman Mister Bland's in the majority. Awkward.

ALVIN: I'm not being awkward.

MRS HANKER: Yes, y'are.

ALVIN: No, I'm not awkward.

MRS HANKER: You sound awkward.

ALVIN: I'm not, though.

MRS HANKER: I believe you. (*To herself.*) Every morning except Sunday he leaves this house on his cycle regular as clockwork.

ALVIN: What time is it?

MRS HANKER: You're late.

ALVIN: I didn't ask if I was late.

MRS HANKER: You're always late.

ALVIN: I said what time is it?

MRS HANKER: I heard you.

ALVIN: Is it eight o'clock yet?

MRS HANKER: George Bland's never late.

ALVIN: Is it eight?

MRS HANKER: You've got eyes, use 'em.

ALVIN: (*Going up to the clock and staring at it.*) I'm late.

MRS HANKER: I told you.

ALVIN: I'm off. (*He gets into his shoes, balaclava and donkey jacket.*)

MRS HANKER: You've missed this bus and you won't catch the next.

ALVIN: I'll get the one after.

MRS HANKER: It'll be full.

ALVIN: I'll get it.

MRS HANKER: The one after's always full. You have to be at the head of the queue for the one after. You know as well as I or anybody. You have to get there first.

ALVIN: I can stand.

MRS HANKER: George Bland's never late.

ALVIN: He has a bicycle.

MRS HANKER: I bet he's never stood on the one after.

ALVIN: He has a bike…

MRS HANKER: You'd still be last at the last push if you had a bike.

(*ALVIN dashes into the kitchen, snatches a thermos and sandwich box from the table.*)

What about your bread and jam?

(*ALVIN grabs it on the run.*)

ANNOUNCER: (*Through the radio.*) The time is eight-fifteen.

MRS HANKER: The time is eight-fifteen.

ALVIN: Ta-ra. (*He leaves through the back yard.*)

MRS HANKER: (*Clearing away his breakfast things.*) Always at the last push up. He'd never stand, wouldn't George. If George Bland went to work by bus instead of bike he'd get a seat. He'd be there first. He'd see to that. He wouldn't be at last push up.

(*ANNA takes a half-eaten slice of toast from JACOB, drops it on the tray with his napkin and takes it away.*)

JACOB: I haven't finished.

ANNA: Yes you have. You're getting fat.

JACOB: I'm not on a diet.

ANNA: You will be unless you cut down. Too many carbohydrates.

JACOB: You're too thin.

ANNA: I don't lie in bed.

JACOB: What time is it now?

ANNA: Winter.

JACOB: Er – no – er…

ANNA: Winter time. October, November, December.

JACOB: On the clock, the time.

ANNA: (*Leaving with the tray.*) Not breakfast time.

(*GEORGE rides in on his bike ringing his bell.*)

MRS HANKER: Oh – ha – hergh – ha – he he is silly.
(*She comes into the hall, takes a curler from her fringe and preens at her reflection before opening the front door. GEORGE parks, then tucks his hat under his arm and combs his hair.*)
Now, Mister Bland, what's all this? Why didn't you use your key?

GEORGE: (*Officially.*) Does Alvin Hanker live here?

MRS HANKER: Who wants to know?

GEORGE: Police.

MRS HANKER: Not the vice-squad are you?

GEORGE: Special branch.

MRS HANKER: Are you… Special. What do you specialise in?

GEORGE: My speciality?

MRS HANKER: Have you got one?

GEORGE: Private investigation.

MRS HANKER: You poke and probe, do you?

GEORGE: That's part of it.

MRS HANKER: A big part, I bet.

GEORGE: I quite, er, quite like taking suspects into my custody and giving them the once over.

MRS HANKER: Don't you need a warrant for that?

GEORGE: Not if they come quietly.

MRS HANKER: You'd have to handcuff me.

GEORGE: You better see to this first.

MRS HANKER: Not on the doorstep for all and sundry.

GEORGE: There's a registered for him.

MRS HANKER: Come in, daft.

GEORGE: Would you sign it, please?

MRS HANKER: I haven't got a pencil.

GEORGE: I have.

MRS HANKER: Sign it, then.

GEORGE: It wouldn't look right. Go on.

MRS HANKER: This the best you can do?

GEORGE: It does the job.

MRS HANKER: It's nearly a stub.

GEORGE: So long as it makes an impression.

MRS HANKER: Christian names?

GEORGE: No need.

MRS HANKER: Ivy Harriet Hanker. (*She exchanges receipt for letter.*) Nothing for me?

GEORGE: No.

MRS HANKER: Anything for you?

GEORGE: No.

MRS HANKER: What's this for Alvin?

GEORGE: Can't I come in?

MRS HANKER: What is it, do you think?

GEORGE: It says on.

MRS HANKER: *Hockton Weekly News.* He couldn't have won the criss-crossword puzzle without telling me.

GEORGE: No.

MRS HANKER: If you'd been a minute sooner he was here. I could have asked him and found out. Aren't you coming in this morning? There's tea already made – he's only just this minute gone.

GEORGE: Open it. (*He goes into the kitchen.*)

MRS HANKER: I would, but it's registered. I've signed for it. I can't open it as well. Takes all the pleasure out of getting it if it's opened *and* signed for. He'll get it tonight. (*She puts it on the hall-stand.*)

ANNOUNCER: The time is eight-twenty. Twenty min… (*MRS HANKER switches off the radio and pours tea.*)

GEORGE: (*Sorting letters on the table.*) I don't have so very many this morning.

MRS HANKER: I see. That's a lovely stamp.

(*ANNA comes back.*)

GEORGE: By air for Miss Bowers on Stroggen Hill Road.

MRS HANKER: What country is it? Your tea.

GEORGE: Ceylon.

MRS HANKER: Oh, lovely. Slice of bread?

GEORGE: No.

MRS HANKER: 'Anna Bowers, "Byeways", Stroggen Hill Road, Hockton, England.' Lovely.

(*ANNA takes a measuring stick, kneels beside the dressmaker's dummy and pins up the hem of the dress on it.*)

Any postcards today?

GEORGE: There's one with a joke.

MRS HANKER: Have you read it?

GEORGE: I saw the picture.

MRS HANKER: What does it say?

GEORGE: Read it.

MRS HANKER: Ohohi-haa-ha-he-ah. 'Mister, can I borrow your rubber mattress? That's not a rubber mattress, that's my wife in a bathing suit.' Ooerhha. You have to look at it to get the funny side. Here. I don't know how they dare print them.

GEORGE: I've seen worse.

MRS HANKER: I hope I never get as fat as that.

GEORGE: No, you're not that kind.

MRS HANKER: How do you know?

GEORGE: I'm a fairly good judge.

MRS HANKER: Are you?

GEORGE: I can tell if a woman's going to run to fat or not. You'll stay as you are for a long time yet.

MRS HANKER: You think so.

GEORGE: There's plenty of wear left in you for that. A good ten years, I'd say.

MRS HANKER: You make me sound like a second-hand carpet.

GEORGE: I didn't mean to.

MRS HANKER: I should hope not. I don't let anybody walk over me.

GEORGE: I know that.

MRS HANKER: Nobody wipes their feet on Ivy Hanker.

GEORGE: Unless they take their shoes off first.

(*As he drinks his mug of tea in one slow draught, they hold a look between them. MRS HANKER takes the mug from him like a bad Carmen, swirls the leaves round and looks into it.*)

MRS HANKER: I'll tell your fortune for you one of these days.

GEORGE: I can guess what it'll be.

MRS HANKER: I bet you don't.

GEORGE: I've a good idea.

MRS HANKER: (*Reading the leaves.*) Oh! I say!

GEORGE: What?

MRS HANKER: My goodness me!

GEORGE: What is it?

MRS HANKER: Well, I never!

GEORGE: Eh?

MRS HANKER: Fancy that now.

GEORGE: Is it bad?

MRS HANKER: That is interesting.

GEORGE: Is it good?

MRS HANKER: My word, it is unusual.

GEORGE: What?

MRS HANKER: It's all there, alright, crystal clear, cut and dried. Expanding, very bright and rosy pink.

GEORGE: What is?

MRS HANKER: Everybody's jealous.

GEORGE: Let me see.

MRS HANKER: I wouldn't dream.

GEORGE: Why not?

MRS HANKER: I wouldn't know where to look. (*She swills the mug out.*)

GEORGE: They were my tea leaves.

MRS HANKER: It's bad luck to see your own future.

GEORGE: If that's all you saw I don't mind. (*He collects his letters, post bag and hat from the hall.*)

MRS HANKER: Got your letters?

GEORGE: Yes. (*He steps outside.*)

MRS HANKER: Watch yourself.

GEORGE: You watch yourself.

MRS HANKER: I'm watching you.

GEORGE: Keep your eyes skinned, then.

MRS HANKER: Let me know if I miss anything.

GEORGE: I'll make sure you don't.

MRS HANKER: Cheeky devil.

GEORGE: Weather doesn't look very promising. I bet I get my feet wet.

MRS HANKER: Looks like we're in for a spot of rain.

GEORGE: I'll get my feet wet, I bet.

MRS HANKER: Then you'll have to take your shoes off when you come home.

(*GEORGE goes to his bicycle and 'freezes' in position, as does ANNA at her dummy. MRS HANKER goes upstairs to make GEORGE's bed up. She folds his pyjamas.*)

A walking man like George, never-late George, a man who rides a bike when he doesn't walk, he must have legs as heavy as pistons, calves as thick as thighs and lungs to breathe with. A pair of lungs locked away in a ribcage wider than Uncle Jack's. He carries a bag on a shoulder, too, and that's not empty. He's a forward man. Too much of it. Have a joke and he walks a mile. I'll take his shoes off and tickle his toes. He needs a peg or two taking out; too big for his boots by half a size. I'll have to be careful before I like him any more. If I've got to like him I'd better not show it.

(*GEORGE 'unfreezes'. He mounts his bike.*)

He should wear rubbers when it rains, I've told him before. (*She 'freezes'.*)

GEORGE: She's definitely pushing. She's certainly leading me on. She's almost too willing. Too eager, too. Too soon in some ways, if you like. Women are alright, but she has no manners with her; no proportion of when to stop going too far. I like to coax a woman. Fondle her fancy with a joke or a smile then try a bit more till, some months later, I know that I'm liked. When liking's achieved a man's confidence grows and who knows where that might lead to from there? A confident man who's liked – he's a valuable thing not easy to come by nor to meet with. Confidence can't be got quickly. A man needs time. She's too willing too soon, I think. Too eager. Putting me off, pushing me, leading me on. (*He looks at the sky.*) If it rains I should wear galoshes.

(*He cycles off on his rounds. MRS HANKER 'unfreezes'. She finishes GEORGE's bed.*)

(*ANNA 'unfreezes'. She rises, replacing the pins and measuring stick in the sewing-table. JACOB gets out of bed, puts slippers on and a dressing-gown. ANNA sees the postman coming, goes to the front door and opens it.*)

GEORGE: Airmail.

ANNA: Thank you.

GEORGE: Ceylon.

ANNA: (*Frostily.*) Do you collect stamps?

(*GEORGE rides off. ANNA closes the door.*)

Ceylon. (*She opens her letter and reads.*) 'Today's lesson is taken from Brother Maurice's epistle to St Anna of the Michaelmas Daisies, the only surviving Methodist nun west of Brighouse. Chapter six, verses one to eighteen – and after the monsoons came water in the swamps...'

(*She looks out of the imagined window by the sewing-table.*)

It can't rain in Ceylon. Not like it does here. Ceylon rain comes teeming, monsoonfuls at a time, tippling down on the jungle all at once, helter skelter, splashing in torrents, flooding the swamps. Rain like that's as good as thunder. Nothing so good in Hockton. Nothing so much as a flash in the sky. Just grey drizzle every fortnight for a week. (*She sits at the sewing-table, takes writing materials from the drawer, moving a vase of dead Michaelmas daisies to one side to make room.*)

(*MRS HANKER comes downstairs, puts her coat on at the hall-stand, picks up a shopping basket and leaves.*)

(*JACOB reaches for his walking-stick and comes into the room.*)

JACOB: Anna. Anna.

ANNA: What do you want?

JACOB: Nothing.

ANNA: Why call me then?

JACOB: I was on my own.

ANNA: You still are.

(*JACOB gets into his wheelchair and wheels to the magazine rack.*)

JACOB: Writing a letter?

ANNA: Yes.

JACOB: To Aunt Milly?

ANNA: Yes, Aunt Milly.

JACOB: Send her my love.

ANNA: I will.

JACOB: I never get any replies to my letters.

ANNA: You never write any.

JACOB: I do.

ANNA: Postcards aren't letters. Nobody answers postcards.

JACOB: Your brother, he never writes.

ANNA: Clifford does.

JACOB: Maurice doesn't.

ANNA: Why should he. You never got on.

JACOB: I wonder where he is.

ANNA: We'll never know – he won't write here.

JACOB: Couldn't you write to his old address – to that shipping line he used to work for?

ANNA: You told me not to.

JACOB: Yes, but I'm older now. Seven years.

ANNA: You're over seventy.

(*She fixes JACOB with a stare. He 'freezes'. She writes.*)
'My dear Maurice. Thank you for your letter which
I received this morning. Ceylon sounds nice. I went for
a walk last Sunday. The fish pond is frozen over. I still
get plenty of sewing to do. I'm altering an afternoon
frock at the moment for a fat customer. She could be
pregnant. Fat clients sweat more when they come for
fittings and use a lot of talcum. I do hate alterations.
There's no satisfaction in alterations. Especially letting
out and inserting. All seams and darts. Gussets and
pleats. I never have to take things in for people losing
weight, unless they're old children's frocks being handed
down to younger sisters or wedding gowns cut up for
make-do bridesmaids' stuff. People think they're doing
you a favour, too. Finding you a little job to do. Nobody
wants to pay for having alterations done. They expect
you to do them for nothing or next to nothing. Nothing
exciting has happened.'

(*A clock chimes five, breaking ANNA's reverie.*)

JACOB: Still raining?

ANNA: You woke up, then?

JACOB: Yes, I dozed off.

ANNA: These are dead, anyway, these daisies.

JACOB: What's the time?

ANNA: Five o'clock. Why don't you listen?

JACOB: I didn't count.

ANNA: You counted on me, you mean.

JACOB: Did the postman come this morning?

ANNA: No.

JACOB: I thought I heard him.

ANNA: Pamphlets, that's all.

JACOB: I wish Maurice would write.

ANNA: So do I, then maybe you'd shut up.

JACOB: I'd like to know where he is – what he's doing.

ANNA: You must expect to be ignored.

JACOB: How he feels. How he's getting on in the world. It's natural.

ANNA: Selfish.

JACOB: Old people are selfish.

ANNA: They shouldn't be. You talk as though old age were a licence for feeble behaviour. It isn't.

JACOB: I'm his father.

ANNA: Don't talk any more.

JACOB: I'm getting old.

ANNA: Read tonight's paper. It's there.

JACOB: I couldn't find last week's.

ANNA: I threw it away. (*She polishes a magnifying glass with the edge of her cardigan.*)

JACOB: But I hadn't finished the crossword.

ANNA: There'll be a new one tomorrow.

JACOB: I like to check it over with the clues. It's natural.

ANNA: (*Holding out the glass.*) Selfish.

JACOB: (*Snatching it.*) It's natural when a puzzle's part complete to check it over.

(*ANNA sits with her letter. JACOB reads the crossword with the magnifier.*)

Well over seventy. Over seventy clues. I did some across and I did some down. The easy years were filled in and there were others I couldn't attempt.

ANNA: (*Reading her letter.*) 'Our father, which art in Hockton, is sleeping.'

JACOB: I'm feeble at all hours of the day.

ANNA: 'He does all the time.'

JACOB: I want to be ignored.

ANNA: 'I'm sending you some cuttings from a local paper.'

JACOB: She knew and threw it away or lit a fire with it on purpose.

ANNA: 'The town is getting ready for the Flower Show although it's six months away. They've asked me to make baby clothes again for the White Elephant stall.'

JACOB: I don't like her.

ANNA: 'Any white elephants in Ceylon?'

JACOB: Spinster.

ANNA: Baby clothes.

JACOB: I never wanted a daughter.

ANNA: 'I suppose I shall have to.'

JACOB: She's an ugly woman with a dead mother. *De Mortuis nil nisi bonum.*

ANNA: 'Take care.'

JACOB: She's a daughter.

ANNA: 'Look after yourself.'

JACOB: I didn't want.

ANNA: 'Your ever-loving sister of the Michaelmas Daisies.'
(*She takes the dead flowers from the vase.*)

JACOB: I never liked.

ANNA: 'Anna.'

JACOB: I'm reading the paper if she looks.
(*ANNA takes her writing things into JACOB's room, sits by the window to write the envelope.*)
They're writing about the Flower Show already, Anna.

(*Rain. ALVIN runs in from the back yard through to the hall and wipes his feet on the door mat. He sees the letter and sits on the bottom stair to read it. MRS HANKER comes in to the hall with her shopping.*)

MRS HANKER: Well?

ALVIN: Well, what?

MRS HANKER: Tell us what?

ALVIN: Crossword prize, that's all.

MRS HANKER: What, first? (*Snatching the letter.*) First prize?
(*ALVIN snatches it back.*)
Tell us.

ALVIN: No.

MRS HANKER: Ah, come on.

ALVIN: No.

MRS HANKER: Have you won?

ALVIN: No.

MRS HANKER: I could see you hadn't. (*She hangs her coat up.*)

ALVIN: Third prize.

MRS HANKER: I might have known. I might have known you'd be a runner-up. Trust you.

ALVIN: (*Following MRS HANKER into the kitchen.*) It's not my fault.

MRS HANKER: It never is.

ALVIN: I got it right.

MRS HANKER: Why didn't you win, then?

ALVIN: That one wins who gets his envelope opened first.

MRS HANKER: And that one wins who gets his envelope
first into the post. First arrived is first opened. You were
allus a runner-up, allus were, allus will be. You're like
your dad in that respect. You take after him. Late for his
own funeral – died six weeks after they said he would.
I knew he would. 'You'll never make it,' I said. 'You won't
see death this side of ten weeks never mind four,'
I told him and I was right. (*Tearful.*) Late for his own
deadline in spite of my warnings; all I tried to do.
You get it from your dad.

ALVIN: Why drag him into it?

MRS HANKER: I don't want you to think you get it from
your mother, that's all.

ALVIN: Get what from you?

MRS HANKER: Don't pretend you don't know.

ALVIN: I don't.

MRS HANKER: Yes you do.

ALVIN: No.

MRS HANKER: And I say yes.

ALVIN: What for?

MRS HANKER: I'll give you what for.

ALVIN: Why?

MRS HANKER: You could have won if you'd put your
heart into it. If once you'd knuckle under and get down
to it I know you'd come out on top. But you won't. At
school you were bottom. Allus bottom. Best dunce they
ever had at Woodroyd Elementary. When you *did* move
up it was because of your age and even then you weren't
ashamed for a boy of your years. You never scored goals
in winter nor batted in June, you were a wash-out on
Whit Monday's sports.

ALVIN: I broke my ankle.

MRS HANKER: Running in a sack. You can neither swim
nor ride a bike, you couldn't yo-yo or spin a top, or even

chuck a frisbee, the army didn't want you, no girl'll have you, you lost all your marbles, you broke the string on your kite – you're a failure.

ALVIN: I wish I hadn't sent it.

MRS HANKER: Then you'd be nowhere, that's where you like. A nobody nowhere's where you'll end up.

ALVIN: When did you ever win anything?

MRS HANKER: I won you.

ALVIN: I wish you'd never.

MRS HANKER: May be.

ALVIN: Perhaps.

MRS HANKER: What do they give you for being third, anyway, is it owt worth having?

(*ALVIN bangs his sandwich tin down and goes upstairs.*)

Alvin – you can come back here and bang that door properly. Do you hear me?

(*She follows ALVIN up to his room. GEORGE arrives on bycycle and parks.*)

I asked you what you get for being third prize?

(*ALVIN locks his door. GEORGE lets himself in.*)

Mr Bland. You're home, are you?

GEORGE: Hello. (*He hangs his coat up.*)

MRS HANKER Did you get wet?

GEORGE: Yes.

MRS HANKER: Take your shoes off, then, before you tramp in there.

GEORGE: (*Removing his shoes.*) What's wrong with Alvin?

MRS HANKER: Came third in last week's crossword and sulks about it. He's a bad loser, that's all, like his dad. A bad loser. God, your feet smell. (*She goes into the kitchen.*)

GEORGE: What's for tea?

MRS HANKER: Wait and see.

GEORGE: (*Looking in the hall-stand mirror.*) I'm beginning to look old, ugly at the edges; if you look round the corners, into the crevices, you can see it isn't youth like it used to be. Close looks reveal age and a little bit of ugliness. I hope nobody notices.

MRS HANKER: (*Throwing his slippers at GEORGE in the hall.*) Wash your hands and feet before you eat.

GEORGE: (*Putting them on.*) She's very disapproving for teatime. I can't smell my feet, and if I could I wouldn't bring them up in conversation. Most days I wash between the toes and nobody tells me to. Nobody tells me what to do.

(*He goes to his room, then to the bathroom. ALVIN puts on a record and changes his clothes. MRS HANKER lays the table for high tea. GEORGE, topless, has come from the bathroom into his bedroom. He towels himself dry, jigging to the music. ALVIN also tries to dance with his hands in his pockets.*)

RECORD PLAYER: Number one, having fun
Number two, loving you
Number three, let me
Get more of your
Four and your five.
Six, had my fix
Seven's in heaven
Eight, can't wait for
Nine when you're mine,
One more time and then
We'll count to ten
All over again.

MRS HANKER: Alvin. Alvin, switch it off. Stop it. We don't want any more, understand? I'll break it over his empty head if he doesn't put its jacket on straight away. It's indecent at teatime with the neighbours listening. Please, Alvin. You know I hate the hooligan jives and you jerking on the ceiling. Stop it or I'll bounce you one. (*She goes upstairs.*) Are you hearing me? Do you listen? Mrs Raistrick'll be coming round again and not without reason, so stop it. I can't be bothered with her. George Bland doesn't like it, either – do you, Mr Bland?

GEORGE: (*Coming out.*) Hello?

MRS HANKER: (*Suddenly frail.*) Mister Bland…

GEORGE: I'm listening.

(*ALVIN turns down the volume, stands on a stool and looks through the glass fanlight to see what's going on.*)

MRS HANKER: Then I wish you'd tell our Alvin what you think of him before you come down. He needs a

man behind him to talk to him, to show him what's
what and what it's for. And that's where you come in,
Mister Bland, I can see that. Show him what you're
made of – you can show me an' all while you're at it
and ask him what does he think I feel. A woman can't
be doing it all the time alone.
(*GEORGE catches sight of ALVIN watching them.*)
It needs a man, it needs you to tell him, George.
(*She follows GEORGE's stare. ALVIN gets down and cowers
in the chair. GEORGE goes back to the bathroom.*)
(*Rattling the locked door.*) If only you'd read a book all
through for once or play cards – find yourself a hobby
like other people have to or go out to the pictures –
night school or Bert Shutt's dancing. Anything to get a
move on out of my sight.
(*ALVIN lifts the pick-up off the record.*)

ALVIN: Shut up!

MRS HANKER: You shouldn't have spoken like that,
Alvin, not to your mother.

ALVIN: Go away.

MRS HANKER: Mister Bland's here. Open this door. (*She
thumps on the door.*)

ALVIN: Stop it.

MRS HANKER: (*Having an imaginary conversation.*) Mister
Bland – belt him. Take your belt off and whack him. His
father never would. (*To ALVIN.*) Open the door. He never
had it. He never had a belting, that's why he needs it.
You have my permission.

ALVIN: (*Kneeling.*) You can't.

MRS HANKER: As you won't do what I say, Mister
Bland's coming to show you how about it. He's going to
belt you with his strap.

ALVIN: No.

MRS HANKER: It's 'no', is it?

ALVIN: I'm sorry.

MRS HANKER: Too late for sorry now.

ALVIN: I won't play it any more.

MRS HANKER: You've said that before.

ALVIN: I won't say it again.

MRS HANKER: Mister Bland's going to make sure this time. He'll knock some sense through you with the buckle end. You'll knuckle under for him. He'll make you get down to it.

ALVIN: I'm sorry I was third. I won't be if you go away. I'll win if you leave me alone.

MRS HANKER: Blackmail and threats won't make you top. Open up for Mister Bland.

ALVIN: I promise I'll make you glad I'm Alvin. I will. In the name of our dad I'll be first prize-winner, the best there is for ever and ever after.

MRS HANKER: We believe that.

ALVIN: I promise you – I swear it.

MRS HANKER: What on?

ALVIN: My record. (*He breaks it.*) My disc, on my pop that you don't like – (*He pushes the pieces under the door.*) Here – here, you see.

MRS HANKER: You're a lunatic.

ALVIN: I'm Alvin Hanker.

MRS HANKER: I shan't sweep it up.

ALVIN: I'll beat the world. I'll find something. If you can wait I'll be at the front. You'll look up – if you don't hit me – if you never use the buckle end.

GEORGE: (*Coming from the bathroom, belt in hand, putting his shirt on.*) I'm here. I'm ready.

MRS HANKER: Come along then, George, and have your tea. Put your belt on.

(*GEORGE and MRS HANKER go down into the kitchen.*)

GEORGE: What about Alvin?

MRS HANKER: Alvin's not worth bothering about. Fasten up and let's see what's on the table. I bet you're famished.

GEORGE: I could do with a bite.

MRS HANKER: What of?

GEORGE: What I fancy.

MRS HANKER: What's that?

GEORGE: What have you got?

MRS HANKER: What you fancy.

GEORGE: What's that?

MRS HANKER: It's all laid out on the table. You can pick
and choose where you like. Bread and butter plus a bit of
tongue. Half a plate of pie and tomatoes with it if you
want them, pineapple preserved while the custard's still
warm and lemon curd with the pastry. You can wash it all
down with a second cup of best Ceylon tea, fresh today.
I bought it for you to like. Two and fourpence.
(*ALVIN, still on his knees, opens his door to get the pieces of
record. The lights dim on MRS HANKER, GEORGE, ANNA
and JACOB. They 'freeze'.*)

ALVIN: You're silenced for ever if your groove's not joined.
I'm sorry I broke you in sacrifice. (*He puts the pieces back
in the sleeve.*) Never mind. I'll get you another one again.
'If only you'd read for once or play cards. Find yourself
a hobby like other people, go to the pictures, the night
school, the dancing, the football, the...' Night school.
If I went to night school I'd be a student. Alvin student.
There are too many. Students all trying. Besides, there's
only one for the top of the class. I might look well with a
hobby. If you have a private sideline, that's it. No one
expects you to present the result. You can do it when you
come home from work and you're alright at weekends.
I could dance. I could be taught. (*He mimics a young
woman's voice.*) 'Bert Shutt's Palais's no good for dancing
in with Alvin Hanker.' (*He takes an imaginary partner.*)
A dance floor's for partners. (*He dances.*) Four legs behave
as two on the ballroom boards. (*He trips on his partner's
toes.*) Never mind dancing. (*He sits.*) Too many dance. Too
many legs on ballroom floors, crowding each other out
on to the pavements. Dancing's overcrowded like the
pavements. All going to the pictures. I like the pictures.
Sitting in the pictures – getting dark and warm and
watching with the music all the time playing from
nowhere. Film stars are real and all first class with big
faces – and they're good at it. I get on well at the films.
It would be sitting at the pictures if I could have the
money to do it full time. I could borrow. But there's the
travelling to get to the one the night after and seeing a

different one every middle of the week. I couldn't afford the fares into town as well as a reasonable seat for sitting in. Playing at cards isn't for one, except patience. But I cheat so that's out. I could read. It's quiet. I could read a lot. Seven books a week. Library books. Long books – full of quiet reading far from Mrs Raistrick's ears. Books with photographs beside the print, beautiful, like film stars, but quiet. Slender, little thin-backed books with titles, books on buildings, books on ships, on bridges, books on end, books on wardrobes never dusted, books on gardening books. Flower books on flowers. (*He slides up on the chair until he is standing on it, turns to the wardrobe and pushes off the old books, comics, etc., before picking up the gardening book.*)

'What's that, Alvin?'

A secret.

'A secret what?'

Hobby.

'Hobby what?'

(*He sits on the back of the chair with his feet on the seat.*)

Just hobby.

'Come here.'

No.

'Where're you going?'

To hobby.

(*Calling.*) 'Alvin'

(*He slips on to the seat of the chair, curled up in it as the light dims in his room.*)

I can't miss it.

'Hurry up, then.'

I can't be late. I must get up. Mustn't forget.

'You won't.'

I can't.

'You shan't.'

I haven't.

(*GEORGE finishes drinking his tea as full light returns to the kitchen.*)

MRS HANKER: You aren't going to tell me you didn't enjoy that, 'cause I know you did.

GEORGE: A good tea.

MRS HANKER: Have some more tongue.

GEORGE: No more.

MRS HANKER: I'm putting it away.

GEORGE: I'm full.

MRS HANKER: You're sure?

GEORGE: I am.

MRS HANKER: Lemon curd?

GEORGE: No.

MRS HANKER: Or a third cup of tea?

GEORGE: Half a cup.

MRS HANKER: Hold it out under the spout.

GEORGE: Don't fill it up.

MRS HANKER: What are you doing tonight?

GEORGE: I'll have a drink.

MRS HANKER: At the pub?

GEORGE: Or the club.

MRS HANKER: I see. Sugar yourself. I'll clear these and
then I'll wash up.

GEORGE: I'll dry.

MRS HANKER: No, you won't.

GEORGE: Yes, I will.

MRS HANKER: You stay there.

GEORGE: I can help.

MRS HANKER: Drink your tea.

GEORGE: Where's the cloth?

MRS HANKER: Take your hook.

GEORGE: (*Picking up the teacloth.*) Might as well – now I'm up.

MRS HANKER: (*Snatching it from GEORGE.*) Sit you down.

GEORGE: (*Snatching it back.*) Give it me.

MRS HANKER: Do you hear what I say? (*She puts it on the
draining-board, challenging GEORGE to touch it.*)

GEORGE: What is it?

MRS HANKER: What?

GEORGE: Wrong?

MRS HANKER: Nowt.

GEORGE: Liar.

MRS HANKER: It's my house.

GEORGE: So?

MRS HANKER: I can lie if I want.

GEORGE: Why?

MRS HANKER: Don't ask.

GEORGE: I've a right.

MRS HANKER: Why?

GEORGE: I live here.

MRS HANKER: When do you leave?

GEORGE: (*Alarmed.*) Leave?

MRS HANKER: Go, then.

GEORGE: Where?

MRS HANKER: Off out drinking?

GEORGE: It's that, is it?

MRS HANKER: Three cups of tea and you're thirsty.

GEORGE: No.

MRS HANKER: Boozing.

GEORGE: No.

MRS HANKER: In the saloon.

GEORGE: No.

MRS HANKER: Tippling.

GEORGE: No.

MRS HANKER: Guzzling.

GEORGE: No. It's not the beer I go for.

MRS HANKER: What, then?

GEORGE: I go for the noise.

MRS HANKER: Too quiet for you here?

GEORGE: Not a bit.

MRS HANKER: It's Alvin puts you off.

GEORGE: Not a bit.

MRS HANKER: Doesn't he?

GEORGE: No.

MRS HANKER: Who, then?

GEORGE: That's right, he does.

MRS HANKER: I thought so. He's in your way.

GEORGE: He is a bit.

MRS HANKER: You feel awkward with him in the house.
I've noticed. You feel hemmed in, cooped up, tied hand
and foot, he drives you out all the time, he puts you off

what you're thinking. You should have complained, own
it, come on, own up.

GEORGE: Well, yes, I do feel a bit awkward with him in
the house.

MRS HANKER: You can never be sure when he won't
come in.

GEORGE: No.

MRS HANKER: If he's listening somewhere or watching to
catch you unawares.

GEORGE: You can't be sure.

MRS HANKER: The walls are thin in these houses.

GEORGE: Pre-war.

MRS HANKER: Mrs Raistrick listens, as well. No wonder
you feel you have to go out every night. You can't keep
your thoughts to yourself with Alvin behind the walls
everywhere you look. How can you relax?

GEORGE: I don't feel comfortable when he's in.

MRS HANKER: You'd stay if he weren't. You wouldn't go
out if he were.

GEORGE: I like the noise at the club, though, darts
dropped on the board, piano tunes off and on and the till
bell and the bitter glasses chinking as you count your
change.

MRS HANKER: But it's Alvin drives you to the bar –
you're not to tell me it's noise.

(*ALVIN slams his book shut, goes to the hall-stand for coat,
scarf and balaclava.*)

(*Simultaneously, ANNA is lit as she returns to the sewing-
table, puts the writing things back in the drawer, takes a torch,
gets her coat, scarf and gloves and puts them on.*)

JACOB: Where are you going?

ANNA: Not far.

JACOB: Walking?

ANNA: Post a letter.

JACOB: To Aunt Milly?

ANNA: Aunt Milly.

MRS HANKER: Alvin – where're you going?

ALVIN: To hobby.

MRS HANKER: You what?

ALVIN: Hobby.

MRS HANKER: Hobby what?

ALVIN: Just hobby.

MRS HANKER: I said where're you going?

ALVIN: (*Picking up his wellingtons.*) Walking.

MRS HANKER: And your tea? What about your tea?

ALVIN: I'll have it for supper.

MRS HANKER: You'll get it for breakfast if you don't.

ALVIN: Alright.

MRS HANKER: Come back late.

ALVIN: Alright.

MRS HANKER: You've got your keys?

ALVIN: Yeah.

(*MRS HANKER closes the front door behind him.*)

MRS HANKER: There – he's gone out.

GEORGE: Aye.

MRS HANKER: You can relax now.

GEORGE: I can. I will…

MRS HANKER: You don't need to feel you have to go to the club, and you can dry for me. Here's the cloth. (*She hangs it on him.*) We'll clear these away, bank the fire up, sit down, switch the wireless, read the paper, hark at the wind and be glad we're warm inside with – nothing but the hearth rug between us.

GEORGE: Nothing between us.

MRS HANKER: Snug, relaxed and comfortable.

GEORGE: Aye.

MRS HANKER: Lovely.

(*GEORGE tips the dregs of his tea into the sink, a hostage to his cowardice as light fades from the interior.*)

(*ANNA puts her beret on.*)

JACOB: Come back soon.

ANNA: I will.

JACOB: I worry.

ANNA: You needn't.

JACOB: I do.

ANNA: You shouldn't. (*She picks up her letter and the torch and leaves the house as light fades from the interior.*)

(ALVIN wheels GEORGE's bike to the front and removes the lamp, as ANNA appears and shines the torch beam on her letter. ALVIN checks the lamp by looking into its beam, and goes. ANNA looks up at the sky before setting off. Moonlight silhouettes the houses casting all in a dark shadow.)

(Sledgewick field. ALVIN is on his hands and knees putting earth into his wellington boots. The lamp lights the area in front of him. ANNA comes silently towards him and shines her torch into his face.)

ANNA: What are you doing?

ALVIN: Digging.

ANNA: At night?

ALVIN: Yes.

ANNA: Without a spade?

ALVIN: Yes. I haven't got one.

ANNA: Aren't you trespassing?

ALVIN: I don't think so.

ANNA: You are. This is farmland. This field belongs to Mister Sledgewick.

ALVIN: I didn't know.

ANNA: Where do you live?

ALVIN: Calcutta Street.

ANNA: Where's that?

ALVIN: Off Bombay Road.

ANNA: Oh – Little India.

ALVIN: Yes.

ANNA: How long for?

ALVIN: Always.

ANNA: Then you must have known you were in Sledgewick field.

ALVIN: Yes.

ANNA: So you're lying as well.

ALVIN: No, not really.

ANNA: Avoiding the truth is lying. You were avoiding answering me truthfully.

ALVIN: No. I wasn't.

ANNA: You're lying again.

ALVIN: Well I'm not, then.

ANNA: You said you didn't know you were –

ALVIN: I only know it's Sledgewick Lane along here, I meant. I never knew there was a field called Sledgewick as well.

ANNA: There is.

ALVIN: What are you doing here then, anyway.

ANNA: I was just passing.

ALVIN: Aye, well perhaps you were just tres-passing as well, like you say I am. You've got a torch like me as well.

ANNA: Don't be silly.

ALVIN: Where do you live any road? (*He shines his torch on ANNA's face.*)

ANNA: I live in Stroggen Hill Road.

ALVIN: That's the other one, isn't it?

ANNA: Along there, yes. At the junction.

ALVIN: I didn't know there was a man called Sledgewick.

ANNA: There is. He owns this land. He knows me.

ALVIN: I see.

ANNA: He's a farmer. This soil is his. You're stealing it, aren't you? Policemen come along here on their bicycles looking for couples. They shine their torches on the verge. Mister Sledgewick won't have his private property used as a meeting place for young people to – to see each other in the dark. The police come. (*She points with her torch.*) That's why it's deserted along here. There's 'Do Not Trespass' signs farther down with fines written on them.

ALVIN: Oh.

ANNA: You can be prosecuted and fined for trespassing.

ALVIN: I see.

ANNA: And you *were* stealing, weren't you?

ALVIN: He won't miss a little bit of dirt.

ANNA: If everybody took a little bit of Mister Sledgewick's field there'd soon be a hole.

ALVIN: If everybody took a bit, I wouldn't. I'd go somewhere else. Better. I'd go in the public woods higher up and get some there.

ANNA: What do you want it for?

ALVIN: It's my hobby.

ANNA: Collecting earth?

ALVIN: No. I grow plants in it.

ANNA: Oh. What kind?

ALVIN: Oh – flowers and things, you know, plants. Bulbs and flowering plants.

ANNA: I see. Your battery will run down. Hadn't you better turn it off?

ALVIN: 'S alright. (*He turns to go.*)

ANNA: If you're going into the wood to dig you'll need a strong light.

ALVIN: I'll manage.

ANNA: Why don't you have a trowel to dig with? It's so much easier.

ALVIN: I haven't got all the equipment I need – as yet. I will get one, though.

ANNA: Whose are those boots?

ALVIN: Mine.

ANNA: You'd better put them on if you're going into the woods.

ALVIN: I can't. I need them to put the dirt in.

ANNA: You should have a sack or a bag.

ALVIN: 'S alright.

ANNA: Why don't you buy soil from the shop?

ALVIN: It's not the same. It must be natural. A plant knows it's from the shop. It should be freshly dug up.

ANNA: I see.

ALVIN: Natural soil's best.

ANNA: Oh, I see. I grow daisies. Michaelmas daisies.

ALVIN: Ah, yes.

ANNA: What kind of plants are yours?

ALVIN: I don't remember their names. They're in Latin.
(*A torch flashes and wanders, searching.*)

ANNA: Ssshsh! (*She switches off and pushes ALVIN forward.*) Down! (*She checks before tapping ALVIN on the back with her torch to give him the all clear.*)

ALVIN: I'd better go to the woods and fill my boots.

ANNA: Yes.

ALVIN: I thought you were going to tell him.

ANNA: You go up Stroggen Hill Road. I'll walk you part way.

ALVIN: Switch yours off, we'll use mine.

(*He stamps the earth he has put back to make it level. ANNA waits. They leave together. Darkness. They reappear outside 'Byeways'.*)

ANNA: This is where I live.

ALVIN: You've got a gate.

ANNA: 'Byeways'. No number. What did you say your name was?

ALVIN: Alvin Hanker.

ANNA: Anchor?

ALVIN: Hanker – Haitch ay enn kay ee ar.

ANNA: Alvin.

ALVIN: Hanker, yes.

ANNA: I'm Miss Bowers.

ALVIN: I had thought at first it might be Sledgewick.

ANNA: You can take soil from my garden if you like.

ALVIN: I'd rather have it from the wood, thank you.

ANNA: I can lend you a shovel if you wait a minute.

ALVIN: I'll manage.

ANNA: Then take my torch. At least you'll be able to see what you're doing. (*She holds it out.*) You can bring it back tomorrow. Or the next day. When you like.

ALVIN: Well, alright. I don't want to finish this battery. It's borrowed from a bicycle.

ANNA: It doesn't matter if the battery runs out in this. I keep a spare indoors.

ALVIN: Well – thank you. Good night.

ANNA: (*Calling after ALVIN.*) There's plenty of leaf mould in the woods now. Better than Sledgewick's field. All clay there. And you won't need to hide from the policemen.

ALVIN: Good night.

ANNA: Good night.

(*ALVIN runs off. ANNA watches him before going in.*)

(*GEORGE is in the armchair. MRS HANKER, in her dressing-gown, stands in front of him with two mugs of bedtime drink.*)

MRS HANKER: This'll send you into sleep like the adverts.

GEORGE: Thank you.

MRS HANKER: We'll drop off smiling and wake up gladly the day after.

GEORGE: You can't improve on a good night's rest. I like a good night.

MRS HANKER: (*Reading the label on the tin.*) 'Induces sleep, deep and abiding.' (*She perches on the arm of the chair.*) There's other things do that besides hot milk.

GEORGE: Such as…?

MRS HANKER: Other things.

GEORGE: Like what?

MRS HANKER: More than hot milk.

GEORGE: For instance?

MRS HANKER: A day's work.

GEORGE: That makes you tired.

MRS HANKER: And makes you sleep.

GEORGE: And what else 'other things' besides?

MRS HANKER: Comforts. Warm comfort promotes rest in the dark.

GEORGE: That's two other things.

MRS HANKER: That's work, hot milk and comfort.

GEORGE: You know what I'm thinking.

MRS HANKER: Don't ask me.

GEORGE: I'm telling you.

MRS HANKER: I know.

GEORGE: So…

MRS HANKER: I hear you.

GEORGE: So you know I've told you and I'm saying now we'll get there in time, we'll come to that soon enough. There's plenty of nights left for snoring in together. (*He goes to the hall with his drink.*)

MRS HANKER: Where are you going?

GEORGE: I'm off up.

MRS HANKER: Why?

GEORGE: To get ready for the alarm. (*He goes to his room and winds the alarm clock and undresses. He gets into his pyjama bottoms. The ticking clock is heard in the background.*)

MRS HANKER: It's coming on. I can feel it – it's nearer than that. The taste's approaching like blood in the mouth from a bit lip. There's time soon enough, he says. I'll show him how to wait. I'll go after him. Out with the lights and follow him. Hot milk, work and comfort, there's three things to bring on the deep sleep and the law-abiding peace of a night-time. I'm getting to feel the pain of being on a different floor. I can't bear the ceiling between us. Don't let him leave you down here. Go on, up, go to bed, drink your milk, sleep if you can, rest in the dark. (*On the landing outside GEORGE's door.*) I'll have to put up with the walls for a time – so long as we're on the same floor. I must be on his level.

(*She listens outside GEORGE's imagined bedroom door. GEORGE also listens on the other side. Their ears are almost touching.*)

You know what he's thinking.

(*She goes to her room, puts her mug on her bedside table, switches on the lamp, turns back the bedcover, takes off her dressing gown and then gets into bed. GEORGE puts his pyjama jacket on and gets into bed.*)

The nights are drawing in and so's George. Things are nearly closer. In a short while he'll put the light out for me.

(*She switches the light off. GEORGE does likewise.*)

Beside. Next to. Don't palpitate. Good night, Ivy. Don't sleep, George. Don't leave me here – awake.

(*The clock still ticks. ALVIN appears and replaces the lamp on GEORGE's bicycle. He lets himself in, wipes his feet and drops a wellington. The noise alerts GEORGE and MRS HANKER. They sit up in bed anticipating each other.*)

He's coming now.

GEORGE: I didn't lock the door.

MRS HANKER: He's creeping for me in the dark.

GEORGE: If she's coming to crawl between the bedclothes without the light on, I can't prevent her.

MRS HANKER: I'll pretend to sleep.

GEORGE: She's in for a big surprise when she gets here. Bigger than she expects. I can't prevent it.

(*ALVIN picks up his wellingtons and goes upstairs, lighting his way with ANNA's torch.*)

MRS HANKER: Come on, George.

GEORGE: Here you are, Ivy.

(*ALVIN goes into his room. MRS HANKER and GEORGE hear the door close behind him and get the wrong idea.*)

MRS HANKER: If he thinks I'm going to lie here while he decides to go back to his bed, he's mistaken. (*She switches on her lamp and gets out of bed.*)

GEORGE: I don't think I locked the door. I'd better check. (*He puts his light on and gets out of bed. They go to their doors, pause to listen, then step out on to the landing at the same moment.*)

MRS HANKER: I thought you'd be over there.

GEORGE: I thought I'd locked the door.

MRS HANKER: I thought I heard you moving.

GEORGE: I thought you were.

MRS HANKER: Happen it was Alvin coming in. (*She calls.*) Alvin.

(*She moves to ALVIN's door, opens it and puts her head inside. ALVIN hides behind the door.*)

Alvin, did you come in?

(*Silence.*)

No, he's not back. (*She closes the door.*)

GEORGE: It must have been you I heard.

MRS HANKER: Or else I heard you, more like.

(*They look at each other. Stalemate.*)

It's cold out here.

(*GEORGE takes off his pyjama jacket and puts it round her shoulders.*)

There's not much warmth in a 'jama jacket.

GEORGE: Well, you're not getting the trousers.

MRS HANKER: I never asked for the jacket.

GEORGE: Good night, then.

MRS HANKER: My husband had a dressing-gown made of white towels that our Alvin gave him as a present. Lovely white towels that would have wrapped you up warm. You could have put it on if Alvin hadn't taken it as his own. (*Mesmerised by his chest.*) In fact, if you'll stay there shivering I'll get it and you shall have it to wear for the future.

(*She opens ALVIN's door and goes in. GEORGE stands by the door. MRS HANKER trips over one of ALVIN's boots, reaches behind the door for a white dressing-gown which is hanging there and falls over ALVIN. ALVIN shines the torch in her face. She staggers against the chest of drawers, screaming.*)

Aaaaaaarrhkk! Alvin! What are you doing crouched up in the dark for?

ALVIN: Get out.

MRS HANKER: What's all this –

ALVIN: Leave it.

MRS HANKER: – this dirt in your boots?

ALVIN: Take what you've come for and get back where you came from.

MRS HANKER: Where did you get that torch?

ALVIN: Stay out of me. Get away.

MRS HANKER: Why didn't you answer when I called?

ALVIN: Never say a word to me unless you're asked. It's my turn for that.

MRS HANKER: (*Concerned.*) Alvin…

ALVIN: Don't call me that.

MRS HANKER: What's the matter, love?

ALVIN: Nor that. (*He throws the dressing-gown at MRS HANKER.*) Here – take the dead man's towelling and get out.

MRS HANKER: Hoh!

ALVIN: (*Pushing MRS HANKER out.*) Drape it on Mister Bland and don't come back.

MRS HANKER: Alvin… (*She falls against GEORGE's chest.*)

ALVIN: If you touch this door knob again I'll unhinge it and bash your head in.

MRS HANKER: (*Whispering.*) George… (*She hides behind him.*)

ALVIN: You're wanted, Mister Bland. A wanted man, wanted without a reward.

MRS HANKER: George, don't let him.

(*GEORGE moves towards ALVIN.*)

ALVIN: (*Shining the torch in GEORGE's face.*) Never talk to me.

MRS HANKER: There's something wrong with him.

ALVIN: Never breathe in my room.

MRS HANKER: He's breaking down in pieces in front of us.

ALVIN: It's my room.

MRS HANKER: He needs to see the proper people to tell him what to do.

ALVIN: I live in my room. I'm entitled. I have permission...

MRS HANKER: He can't go on like this. Mrs Raistrick'll hear him and be able to tell what he's saying.

ALVIN: I put the paper to the walls, I laid the linoleum, I nailed the linoleum, the rugs are where I left them and I played the gramophone – I deserve these things.

MRS HANKER: You need a change.

ALVIN: I belong to my room.

MRS HANKER: Why don't you go abroad?

ALVIN: I'm the one for my room, you're for yours and don't you forget it.

MRS HANKER: Why don't you go mad and have done?

ALVIN: I'll do nothing for your peace of mind. Turn away. Please. Please turn the other way so I can close the door. (*MRS HANKER turns away, crying, her face in the dressing-gown. GEORGE rests a comforting hand on her pyjama-jacketed shoulder. ALVIN closes the door.*)

MRS HANKER: A chestful of skin like semolina pudding with a ripe raisin either side for stimulation. (*She puts the dressing-gown over GEORGE's shoulders.*) This is the one. Lovely white towels to wrap you up warm.

GEORGE: Close your door, then.

(*MRS HANKER switches off the light in her room and joins GEORGE in his. They undress each other in the dark. ALVIN reads the gardening book.*)

ALVIN: The dog-tail *Borealis – Obscurus – Floribisca – Ad Lybia Prim-ul-aris – Uvula-Laryh-gina – Somnambular-Omni-bus-cum – Orchis-Pa-eonie-Glutunus-Max-omus – Daf-odil...'* Daffodil. '*Ovular-ovum-Flori-bis-cus – Nomine-Sanc-tum-sarcofungus – Lili-orum Volvus – Liliorum Volvus –'* (*The slow scholarly voice of the AUTHOR of the book is heard.*)

AUTHOR: 'Dragon's Fang.'

ALVIN: Dragon's fang.

AUTHOR. 'This lily is a prime favourite with all true British flower lovers. It is thought to have been introduced to these shores by Alvin Alleynburgh, a minstrel and a player of the flute who served King Richard the Lionheart during that gallant monarch's crusades to the Holy Land.'

ALVIN: Alvin Alleynburgh.

AUTHOR: '*Liliorum Volvus* Culture. The Volvus Lily is best suited to a fibrous loamy soil. Textbooks tell us that Dragon's Fang likes leaf-mould and a little bit of decayed compost, and while I have no wish to dispute the verity of their recommendation nor argue with their authority I must record my experience that half a bushel of road scrapings, well watered, does this lily a power of good. Take any box...'

ALVIN: Take any box. (*Puts the open book on the stool in front of him and reads.*) 'Take any box.'

AUTHOR: 'Take any box and fill with the mixture.'
(*He tips the earth from the wellingtons into the empty box, pats it level then reads again.*)
'Make an oval in the centre, six inches deep – and twice the width of your bulb. Sprinkle the bottom with fine silver sand.'
(*He does so then reads.*)
'Add water till moist.'
(*He pours water from a milk bottle then consults the book.*)
' – and stir.'
(*He stirs with his finger.*)
'Place the bulb in the centre –'
(*He hurriedly scrapes the wet earth from his stirring finger on to the sides of the box, then picks up the bulb. He holds it delicately between finger and thumb and rotates his wrist, admiring the bulb.*)
(*Slightly irritated.*) 'Place the bulb in the centre –'
(*He kisses the bulb, places it in the box and tips the rest of the soil from the wellingtons on to it. The inner sole from the boot falls out and he throws it away.*)
' – and lightly pack with dry, turfy loam.'

(*He covers the box with the lid.*)

'*Liliorum Volvus* will not endure draughts in the early stages of its growth, so cover it in a warm and sheltered spot, out of harm's way.'

ALVIN: Out of harm's way... (*He puts it inside the wardrobe, gets the book and curls up in the armchair. The light fades from him as he reads.*)

AUTHOR: 'Water every seven days –'

ALVIN: Every seven days.

AUTHOR: '– for several weeks.'

ALVIN: For several weeks.

AUTHOR: 'At the end of two months, remove and repot.'

ALVIN: Remove and repot.

End of Act One.

ACT TWO

ALVIN takes a pot with a strong shoot growing from it and puts it lovingly on the stool. 'La Mer' plays on the kitchen radio. MRS HANKER comes from the yard into the kitchen, picks up the garbage and goes into the hall.

MRS HANKER: (*Calling.*) Alvin! (*She goes out and empties the garbage into the dustbin.*)
ALVIN: (*To the plant.*) See you tonight.
    (*He goes downstairs, puts his folded overall on the stand and sits at the kitchen table. MRS HANKER picks up a pint of milk from the step, re-enters and calls up the stairs.*)
MRS HANKER: Alvin! (*She goes into the kitchen and is annoyed to see ALVIN in situ. She pours milk on to his cereal.*) Well. How long is this going on?
    (*ALVIN ignores her.*)
When do you intend to stop it? Hoity toity. I'm addressing you, in case you hadn't noticed. Who bought your tie? You needn't think you worry us, not talking day in and out. We've got other things to do than get concerned about whether or not we should listen to your silence and not-speaking-to-us attitude. How do you get on at work? I expect you've plenty to say for yourself there, unless you've gone to Coventry.
    (*ALVIN holds out his empty bowl. MRS HANKER snatches it and washes up with her back to him.*)
When you think you'd like to use your tongue again and say a few words I hope you don't expect we'll listen to you. You'll fall on deaf ears. You'll wish you'd had your say before then, not before time or a day too soon either or words to that effect.
    (*ALVIN goes into the hall and looks into the hall mirror.*)
You'll talk to yourself. Anyone who's not bothered to talk to his mother or the postman for as many weeks as you have can't presume there'll be ears ready to listen to owt he has to say if and when he should want to some

time in the future. So don't presume it in this house. (*She finds out he's not there and goes to the hall.*) It's been a blessing to have you shut up. You can't think how glad we are that you've gone into yourself and left me alone, peaceful.

(*ALVIN sits on the stairs and puts on his shoes.*)

Mrs Raistrick's not had anything to knock on the door or bang the back gate, for four weeks or more. She's the only one who's missed your noises that you used to make. You should exercise your right to reply. When I pay attention you should reciprocate.

(*ALVIN walks around her to get his jacket.*)

You must think we don't like it to hear you not saying anything.

(*ALVIN puts his jacket on.*)

Well, you're wrong. It matters nothing to us. We have our own lives to live without unspoken interferences from you so you needn't think it.

ANNOUNCER: The time is five minutes to eight.

MRS HANKER: The time is five minutes to eight.

ANNOUNCER: Here is the weather forecast...

MRS HANKER: Here is the weather forecast... (*She switches the radio off, then picks up ALVIN's thermos and tucks it under her arm.*) If you go now you won't miss the bus nor not be able to catch the one after.

(*ALVIN picks up his sandwich tin, locates the thermos and takes it from MRS HANKER. He tries to leave by the back door. MRS HANKER bars his way. He goes into the hall.*)

(*Going after ALVIN.*) I suppose you know what you're doing, putting your coat on and leaving in good time so's you're not late, because *I* don't. Get inside. Come back here when I'm talking. Disobedient.

(*ALVIN goes in front of the house round to the back yard and away. MRS HANKER pursues him, leaving the door open.*)

At your age you're too old to be told in public you should be seen and not heard, that's for little boys only, not boycotters. Well, you'll not boycott Calcutta Street and Bombay Road with passive resistance. You're not

Ghandi. I don't care if you're on time to work or too
early for the one after or even if you get a seat. You don't
vex me with your silent punctuality, so you can grow out
of it as soon as you like. Insolence. What have you got
upstairs? What are you doing? (*She comes into the kitchen
from the back yard and through the house to shut the front
door.*) Scarcely three minutes before eight and he's left me
with the washing-up. He needn't think I'm won by not
opening his mouth in front of me. I'm his mother.
'Mummy' was the first perfectly formed figure of speech
he came out with. I always told him to speak when
you're spoken to, not before, and never with your mouth
full and always to voice an opinion based on reliable
sources and accepted principles. You'd think he'd thank
me for keeping a civil tongue in his head. Instead of
which he shuts up on me. Who does he think he is? The
pigging bleeder. I'll ruddy well find out what he's up to
upstairs. I'll find out and stop it. Put a good stop to it.
That'll make him talk. The donkey-nosed, stuck-up
muling fat ass. Nobody doesn't talk to me without saying
a word. He's not defective. He's not got mumps, nor
tonsilitis or or a stutter. He wasn't born dumb either,
thank God, like some poor kids. God let him have a
tongue and I'll have it out – as his mother I'll see he uses
it. (*She picks up a plate and crashes it down.*)
Hhoooohuohhoo! That's right, break my dinner plates.
You see what you've done? Smithereens. I'll tell George.
(*On her knees picking up the pieces.*) He's broken it, he'll
pay for it, I shan't. He'll have to pay for it. (*She goes out
and casts it in the dustbin.*) I'll cry till George brings the
post. I'll have to get rid of it somehow – or nobody'll
care a damn. (*Sobs.*)

(*The AUTHOR is heard in the darkness, coming from ALVIN's
room.*)
AUTHOR: 'At this stage in the growth of the *Liliorum
Volvus* the leaves should be uniformly elongated in
outline and pale green in colour.'

(*Daylight first hits the blue stool in ALVIN's room. The lily is no longer on it. ALVIN appears holding the pot. The lily is now in leaf as described. ALVIN puts it on the stool and positions it so the sunlight falls on to the plant.*)

ALVIN: Uniformly elongated. I wonder how pale pale green's supposed to be?

(*GEORGE reads a newspaper in the kitchen. ALVIN reads the gardening book. MRS HANKER listens to him on the stairs.*)

(*Reading.*) 'If any irregularities occur prior to bud growth, snip or twitch off every alternate leaf starting at the base of the stem.' You grow alright as you are without a book of rules. (*He slams the book shut.*) It's an old-fashioned book of rules, anyway. I'll get a new one. (*He strokes the leaves.*) You'll be the best ever grown when you've finished. Biggest – sharpest – widest – tallest – bestest.

MRS HANKER: (*Going to GEORGE.*) He talks to himself alright, all day.

GEORGE: He *never* spoke to me, so I don't miss it.

MRS HANKER: Won't you, can't you ask him, darling? Find out what it is he's got and let's get to the bottom of it.

(*ALVIN puts on his jacket and leaves his room. He locks the door.*)

GEORGE: We never had two words to rub together, Alvin and me. I doubt if anything I might say to him on your behalf would bring us into conversational terms now. It's something we went without. However…

MRS HANKER: I knew you would.

(*ALVIN leaves by the front door.*)

GEORGE: Too late. He's gone out.

MRS HANKER: You're always in time for getting out of things these days. It spells unwillingness to me.

GEORGE: Come here.

MRS HANKER: I have done. What now?

GEORGE: You see this thigh?

MRS HANKER: I do.

GEORGE: Well, sit on it.

(*MRS HANKER sits.*)

215

You'll find out soon enough when I'm unwilling. I'm the one to register any lack of readiness, not you. So sit quiet.

MRS HANKER: If and as how you're ready and willing still, why don't you do me a favour?

GEORGE: Like…?

MRS HANKER: Borrowing Raistrick's ladder next door and having a go at some upstair-window cleaning. With a leather and a ladling can, you could do them in ten minutes' time and they'd sparkle for the weekend. Don't forget, when this afternoon's over it'll be Saturday night.

GEORGE: You mean you'd withhold inclination?

MRS HANKER: I mean one good turn deserves the other.

GEORGE: You'll get your good turn whether or not I rub down the windows, I'll see to that. You think the day matters?

MRS HANKER: I do, it does and it will. Friday's bath night.

GEORGE: Well?

MRS HANKER: Saturday's psychological.

(*GEORGE gives in and goes to the back door.*)

GEORGE: Fill the ladling can and get the leather out till I get the ladder.

(*He goes for the ladder. MRS HANKER fills the ladling can and follows GEORGE.*)

(*An imagined bookshelf in the public library runs from left to right across the front. ANNA appears at one end, moving along as she surveys the titles on the shelves. She carries a book, a handbag and library tickets. She stands on the boxed step halfway along. ALVIN appears simultaneously at the other end, also looking as he moves along. He notices ANNA.*)

ALVIN: Hello.

ANNA: Hello.

ALVIN: I've still got your torch.

ANNA: Shshshsh! You're not supposed to talk in libraries.

ALVIN: You can whisper.

ANNA: (*After a pause.*) I don't need it.

ALVIN: What?

ANNA: My torch.

ALVIN: You said you had another one.

ANNA: You got the earth you wanted?

ALVIN: Leaf mould, yes.

ANNA: Good.

ALVIN: And I planted a bulb.

ANNA: Did it grow?

ALVIN: Yes, very much, thank you. It's called *Liliorum Volvus*.

ANNA: Dragon's Fang.

ALVIN: How did you know?

ANNA: My father has a book. An encyclopaedia. I read it once.

ALVIN: I've seen you in here before.

ANNA: I wondered where we had.

ALVIN: Met before?

ANNA: Where we'd met before, yes.

ALVIN: Before we met in the field?

ANNA: Yes, before last time. When we met last time I thought I'd seen you before somewhere else.

ALVIN: It was in here. Lending books.

ANNA: Borrowing.

ALVIN: So was I. What are you taking out?

ANNA: I haven't decided.

ALVIN: Those are Geographical.

ANNA: My brother's a seaman. I chart his voyages on maps.

ALVIN: I want Botonikel.

ANNA: Botanical. Over there.

(*ALVIN goes, then comes back.*)

ALVIN: If you come with me to my house you can have your torch back. If you want it now. Or later. I could fetch it if you like. Even though you don't need it. You might. It's not far.

ANNA: Alright. (*He steps off the box.*)

ALVIN: I'll wait for you at the 'Way Out'.

ANNA: I'm going now.

ALVIN: Oh.

ANNA: Shall I wait there for you?

ALVIN: Alright. (*He goes to Botanical.*)

217

ANNA: (*Approaching ALVIN, hesitant.*) If you come with me
   to Byeways you could borrow my father's gardening
   encyclopaedia. It's all in one. Volume. One volume. You
   could get something else then instead. As well. And you
   won't need to renew it. No fines.

ALVIN: Alright.

ANNA: Do you want to?

ALVIN: Yes. I said. Alright, then, I will if that's alright.

ANNA: As long as you're not too long.

ALVIN: You can keep them for two weeks from here before
   you have to renew. Is that too long to keep yours?

ANNA: Of course not. You can have it as long as you need.

ALVIN: I thought you said you didn't want me just now to
   have it too long.

ANNA: No, I meant don't be long. Choosing something else.

ALVIN: I don't want anything else.

ANNA: That's alright then. We can go now.

ALVIN: You've got yours?

ANNA: I'm renewing.

ALVIN: You were looking when I saw you.

ANNA: Browsing.

ALVIN: Shall we go to where I live first?

ANNA: Lead the way.

   (*They go.*)

   (*GEORGE appears, balancing a heavy extending ladder and
   smoking a cigarette. MRS HANKER is in attendance with
   the can and a wash leather.*)

MRS HANKER: That's right. Careful. Hold it up. There
   you go. My word. Here's your can.

   (*GEORGE and MRS HANKER disappear behind the house,
   making a confusion of bangs, clatters, warnings and instructions.
   GEORGE rests the ladder against ALVIN's window-sill,
   climbs it and peers in.*)

   Well, what do you see?

GEORGE: Nothing to mention.

MRS HANKER: Open up and climb in. Exploring's the
   only way to discovery.

(*GEORGE opens the sash, puts a leg over the sill and sits astride it. MRS HANKER appears from behind his thigh, clinging on. GEORGE reaches in and puts the can and leather on the chest of drawers.*)

You ought to have been a window-cleaner, it suits you from below.

GEORGE: What does?

MRS HANKER: Sitting astride it like that, one in, one out.

GEORGE: One what?

MRS HANKER: You know what.

GEORGE: Say it, then.

MRS HANKER: You always pester me to mouth it.

GEORGE: Because you hold back.

MRS HANKER: Because I'm not forward.

GEORGE: You've reformed, then.

MRS HANKER: Who said it was a drawback being forward? Holding back's nothing to reform to nor be proud of.

GEORGE: Say it, then.

MRS HANKER: What?

GEORGE: Sitting astride, you said.

MRS HANKER: Window-sill, I meant.

GEORGE: One in, one out, you said.

MRS HANKER: You like to hear the sound of your own body, that's your trouble.

GEORGE: One what?

MRS HANKER: Thigh.

GEORGE: Where?

MRS HANKER: In. One thigh in.

GEORGE: And out?

MRS HANKER: The other. One thigh in the other out. Are you satisfied? I always have to clarify. You'd kill anyone's spontaneity you would. You strangle me dry. I have enough of your thighs at night without having them forced down my throat in broad daylight.

GEORGE: You brought them up.

MRS HANKER: I never mentioned them.

GEORGE: You hinted.

MRS HANKER: Not by name, though.

GEORGE: A hint's as good as done.

MRS HANKER: No. Spontaneous hinting's allowed. It's different to naming. (*She runs her palm along GEORGE's thigh.*) I said sitting astride suits you. It does. Just look at that. Did you ever see such a thigh on a window-sill? Curving up to the knee before dangling over the edge. It's worth climbing anybody's ladder to look at. (*She peers into the room and notices the plant.*) What's that?

GEORGE: What?

MRS HANKER: That. That's it. That's what he's got that he won't let me discover. That's what he won't tell me. Get in. (*ALVIN and ANNA appear. ALVIN points out the lamp on GEORGE's bike. They enter the hall. GEORGE has trouble swinging his leg into the room and sprawls, knocking the plant off the stool. ALVIN rushes upstairs and unlocks the door. ANNA stays in the hall.*)

You're not clumsy, are you? Blind hunchbacks aren't a patch on you.

(*Still on his knees, GEORGE picks up the plant and is about to put it back on the stool when the door opens.*

GEORGE: I was cleaning your windows. It got knocked by accident. I am sorry. It's alright. No damage. No damage done. It's very nice. We were admiring it. Your mother and me. We were saying how tall it was for a plant that size. What sort is it? With soot off the windows you should get more sunlight through – do it good.

MRS HANKER: George.

GEORGE: Ivy?

MRS HANKER: Why do you let him listen to you without replying?

GEORGE: He makes me feel guilty.

MRS HANKER: He thinks he's getting at me through you. Pass me that plant. I'll make him talk with it. Go on – reach over and give it to me here. We'll see what it's like from the first floor. Dropped out from the ladder top. When it's down on the flags in the back he'll find his God-given tongue. He'll call out and use it like he used to then. If you want to hear his voice, pass it over,

George. We'll make him live with us. I'm waiting. If you
don't do it, George, if you don't do as I ask you're a
postman. Not worth a lick on a stamp.

(*GEORGE picks up the plant. MRS HANKER reaches out
to receive the plant. ALVIN picks up the can and throws the
water and leather into MRS HANKER's face. She clasps her
face, screams, falls backwards away from the ladder on to the
paving stones in the yard below. ALVIN throws the empty
ladling can out after her. It clatters as it lands in the yard.*)

GEORGE: Oh my God, what's happened?

(*ANNA goes halfway up the stairs. GEORGE thrusts the
plant into ALVIN's hands, climbs out and down the ladder.
ALVIN slams the window shut, picks up ANNA's torch and
goes downstairs still clutching the plant.*)

ALVIN: (*Handing over the torch.*) Here you are. (*He goes into
the hall.*)

ANNA: Thank you.

ALVIN: This is my plant.

ANNA: Looks very strong.

ALVIN: Yes, but it needs the sunlight.

ANNA: I thought I heard a scream.

ALVIN: My mother fell off a ladder round the back.

ANNA: Does she have a weak heart?

ALVIN: No.

ANNA: My mother fell down a flight of stairs and died at
the bottom, but she had a weak heart.

ALVIN: She was throwing it away. It's not safe to leave. It's
getting too big and needs the sunlight. I'll turn it loose.
I'll plant it in the woods.

ANNA: There's a greenhouse in our garden. You can use it
if you like.

ALVIN: To live in, you mean?

ANNA: No. For your plant.

ALVIN: It's not only that. I'm getting past living here as
well. It's not safe for either of us.

ANNA: (*Alarmed.*) Oh.

ALVIN: I'm sorry your mother had a weak heart when
she died.

221

ANNA: That's alright. She was old.

(*GEORGE rushes in through the kitchen into the hall.*)

GEORGE: Alvin… Oh – hello. It's Miss Bowers, isn't it?

ANNA: Yes.

GEORGE: I can always place the name when I see the face. 'Byeways'.

ANNA: And place the name of the place – as well as put one to the face.

GEORGE: Nearly.

ANNA: Postman's knack.

GEORGE: Goes with the territory.

ANNA: Part and parcel if you have to deliver.

GEORGE: (*Chuckling.*) Oh yes. Excuse me. Alvin, she's knocked out or something, concussed and bleeding, too, a bit. You'll have to fetch the doctor.

ALVIN: I haven't got a bicycle. You'd get there first on the bike.

GEORGE: Well, alright, but you get her inside.

ANNA: You shouldn't move her unless she's dead.

ALVIN: I can't stop now, anyway. I have to get an Encyclopaedia.

GEORGE: There's no time to read up about it. It's an emergency. We have to get her to the hospital.

ANNA: Call an ambulance.

GEORGE: She's not on the telephone.

ALVIN: You pass the kiosk.

ANNA: Someone should get her to the hospital.

GEORGE: Alvin –

ALVIN: I'm going to Stroggen Hill Road before it's too dark.

GEORGE: Not now –

ALVIN: Yes.

GEORGE: Too dark for what?

ALVIN: That's not my torch.

GEORGE: You can't leave.

ALVIN: I can.

GEORGE: We both can't go.

ALVIN: Miss Bowers –

ANNA: Yes, Mister Hanker?

ALVIN: – could I let a room in your house, do you think?

ANNA: Yes, I think I could arrange it.

ALVIN: Tonight?

ANNA: Yes.

ALVIN: Thank you. (*He goes outside.*)

GEORGE: You have to stay, Alvin. She's your mother.

ALVIN: Ask Mrs Raistrick. It's her ladder she climbed.

ANNA: Good afternoon.

(*ALVIN waits for ANNA as she seems to hesitate.*)

GEORGE: No. Alvin. Please.

ALVIN: Lead the way.

(*ANNA and ALVIN go. GEORGE gets on his bike and rides off.*)

(*ANNA and ALVIN come through the front door into Byeways. ANNA moves to the sewing-table, puts her torch in the drawer, positions a protective mat and indicates to ALVIN to put the plant on it. He does so.*)

ANNA: It'll be alright there tonight.

ALVIN: Where will I be?

ANNA: Not in the greenhouse.

ALVIN: In here?

ANNA: In the guest room.

ALVIN: We've always slept together.

ANNA: I'll show you. Not now. Tea?

ALVIN: Alright?

ANNA: Make yourself at home.

ALVIN: Will that be alright?

ANNA: What?

ALVIN: To have it in the guest room with me?

ANNA: I won't come between you.

ALVIN: Alright.

ANNA: Plants are free if accompanied. No pets.

ALVIN: I sell pet food.

ANNA: In a pet shop. You said.

ALVIN: You asked me.

ANNA: That's why I said.

ALVIN: What?

ANNA: No animals.

ALVIN: Alright.

ANNA: There's enough to do looking after birds.

ALVIN: We sell bird seed.

ANNA: There's a tom cat called Tim next door eats them. You have to be vigilant.

ALVIN: Alright.

ANNA: Shall I take your coat?

ALVIN: Thank you.

(*ANNA takes ALVIN's coat and then hangs up her own. ALVIN looks at the unclothed female figure of the tailor's dummy, then turns to communicate with his plant.*)

(*GEORGE appears, preparing the way for MRS HANKER to be wheeled in by an AMBULANCE MAN. Her right arm and her neck are encased in plaster of Paris so that her arm, supported by a brace and strut, is held out horizontally in front of her at right angles in a bent Hitler salute. This is covered for the moment by her dressing-gown and a blanket which cloak her. They help her out of the chair and park her by the newel post. GEORGE goes to her room and turns down the bedcovers. The AMBULANCE MAN helps her up the stairs to her bedside. They co-operate to lift off the blanket and dressing-gown, get her under the covers and prop her up with pillows so she can maintain a sitting position. GEORGE offers her a magazine. She eyes him. He places it beneath the salute, reaches over, takes hold of her good hand by the wrist and lays it on the cover page. She stares ahead. GEORGE goes down with the AMBULANCE MAN, gives him the blanket and helps him out with the chair.*)

(*Evening. JACOB and ALVIN are playing snakes and ladders. JACOB is seated in his wheelchair. ANNA is knitting baby clothes.*)

ALVIN: You to fifty-eight. I'm on forty-two.

JACOB: I haven't played snakes and ladders since I was a child.

ANNA: Yes, you have. He has. Many a time. With Maurice and Clifford when they were boys. You used to have contests. The three of you.

JACOB: (*Throwing.*) Six and two.

ALVIN: Eight. To sixty-six.

JACOB: (*Moving his counter.*) Missed it.

    (*ALVIN and JACOB 'freeze' as ANNA speaks.*)

ANNA: They used to have contests, between them, the three of them. I wasn't allowed as a girl because I was young, too young and a girl.

    (*ALVIN and JACOB resume. ALVIN shakes and throws.*)

ALVIN: Three one.

JACOB: Three and one.

ALVIN: Four – to forty-two, forty-six. Down.

JACOB: You've hit a snake. You're eaten, beaten. Down to fourteen. Bad luck. Never mind. My turn.

    (*ALVIN and JACOB 'freeze'.*)

ANNA: When I *was* old enough to join them they'd grown out of it, my brother and he, so I played by myself for two players. Alone but as two, with one red one green. For the red counter I shook them with my left hand and for the green I used the right. Red nearly always won, which was strange. I'm not left-handed.

    (*ALVIN and JACOB resume. JACOB throws.*)

JACOB: Three and three. Six. And a double shake for a pair. Six to sixty-six. (*He moves his counter.*)

ALVIN: Seventy-two.

ANNA: Sounds like father's ahead.

    (*JACOB shakes.*)

ALVIN: Yes. He is.

ANNA: Shake with the left hand, that's how to win.

JACOB: (*Throwing.*) And nine is eighty-one. (*He moves his counter.*) Two rungs up to ninety-four. Your turn.

ANNA: How did you play your games without any brothers and sisters?

ALVIN: My dad would play. He liked a game indoors. (*He throws.*) To twenty-five and up to fifty-seven. (*He moves his counter.*) Ludo, draughts, tiddly-winks and a Lexicon pack.

    (*JACOB collects and shakes frantically.*)

You need six to win, no more. He bought them for both of us. The bagatelle was my birthday surprise.

    (*ALVIN and JACOB 'freeze'.*)

ANNA: Father gets too excited. He forgets it's only a game. He forgets the time and what the doctor tells him. Come along. Put it away. (*She collects the counters, puts them in the shaker with the dice, folds the board and boxes it.*) It's only a game and father has won.

(*ALVIN and JACOB 'unfreeze'.*)

JACOB: I don't want to go.

ANNA: Come along. There's nothing more to bring from Calcutta Street?

ALVIN: I cleared everything out.

ANNA: I'll make a space in the stair cupboard. We'll keep them in there. Except the record-player, of course.

JACOB: How's your baby knitting for the Elephant stall?

ANNA: (*Wheeling the chair.*) I'll worry about that when you're tucked in bed. Say good night. (*She helps JACOB to his room.*)

JACOB: Good night.

ALVIN: Good night.

JACOB: Good night. I haven't played since I was a boy.

ANNA: You played with Maurice and Clifford many a time. You had contests.

(*JACOB gets out of his dressing-gown and into bed. ANNA closes the curtains, picks up the dressing-gown from the floor and kisses him on the forehead. ALVIN takes the torch from the sewing-table and goes out. ANNA comes back into the room, sees the drawer is open and the torch gone, then collects her cardigan and goes. ALVIN appears in the greenhouse. He is holding a small stepladder, with a thermometer attached to it. The lily, now big and strong, is on the top of the ladder. He brings it forward, placing it in the spill from an artificial light. He checks it over in the light from the torch.*)

ALVIN: You're the tallest that ever grew.

(*He fondles the leaves up to the bud, caressing it then brushing his lips against it. He cups his palms round it and inhales as if to coax the bloom from the bud and syphon off its future fragrance from the stem. ANNA enters, and watches. She carries a small coal shovel and glove.*)

ANNA: I couldn't find the torch.

ALVIN: I borrowed it.

ANNA: I see. I came for a few pieces of coal.

ALVIN: I'll bring some.

ANNA: Thank you.

ALVIN: Close the door. The heat escapes.

(*ANNA moves into the shadow then comes back.*)

ANNA: It doesn't stick any more.

ALVIN: Winter made the wood swell. It was damp.

ANNA: The heat's dried it.

ALVIN: That's right.

ANNA: What's the temperature?

ALVIN: Sixty-eight.

ANNA: It's very strong.

ALVIN: Yes.

ANNA: So tall.

ALVIN: It's going to flower soon. You can see the petals.

ANNA: If it weren't going to flower before July you could have put it in the Show.

ALVIN: I thought about it.

ANNA: It will flower, though.

ALVIN: I know, and die before then.

ANNA: You encouraged it too much too soon for July.

ALVIN: If it hadn't been going to flower then and if I'd put it in, would it have won first place, do you think?

ANNA: I don't suppose so. But it would have been nice for it to be there with the others. (*She touches it.*)

ALVIN: I wouldn't have liked it to be second best or third or without a place altogether.

ANNA: Nothing is.

ALVIN: After the way it's grown it deserves to be more.

ANNA: Nothing can. If it's grown it has and that's it.
You don't compete, you can't. You grow and put in for the display.

ALVIN: Plenty go in for the prize.

ANNA: Never too many enter.

ALVIN: Only one is first.

ANNA: The one that wins is all the others. They call it first but it's never there on its own. If it's by itself it's without a place altogether. It can only be first with the others.

ALVIN: But there has to be one best.

ANNA: The display is best. The green smell rising. Moving through the tents, pale and cool under the canvas wide above. Sunlight filters through. There's a shadow of haze and the plants almost suffocate with sweetness. Too much colour for one day. Too much for once. Like being abroad. I see the petals. It should be out soon. You must have encouraged the sun when you washed the soot and moss from the windows. We've had good weather for a month.

ALVIN: (*Picking up the shovel.*) It's not just the weather that's brought it on. The old man's book has everything in it to do with it.

ANNA: I'm glad it's been helpful. (*She hands ALVIN the glove.*)

ALVIN: It says in the front that he was a vicar. (*He kneels by the box.*)

ANNA: A Reverend, father, yes. The book was a present from one of his parishioners where we lived before we came here. She gave it to him on his retirement.

ALVIN: (*Taking coal from the box.*) He doesn't talk like a churchman.

ANNA: What did you think he was?

ALVIN: Well, I thought he'd been a representative or salesman like an insurance man. I mean, he doesn't seem like a vicar to me.

ANNA: If you'd known him long enough you'd think so.

ALVIN: It's the last thing I'd have suspected him of. He never speaks of it. He doesn't look like one, either.

ANNA: He tried to.

ALVIN: He's like my dad and he hated churches. He said they weren't Christian. He looks like him a bit except my dad was younger and a lorry driver for a building firm.

ANNA: You don't look like a lorry driver's son.

ALVIN: You look like a… You look all right.

ANNA: I'll take the coal.

(*ALVIN gives ANNA the glove, shovel then the lit torch. She leaves. He picks up the ladder and goes into the shadows.*)

(*ANNA appears carrying her father's breakfast tray as before. She opens the curtains, spoons Andrews salts into a glass and stirs.*)

ANNA: Father. It's Tuesday. Father – Father…?

(*She stares at JACOB, backs away, puts the glass on the tray and takes it away. The clock chimes all quarters, then the hour, nine, as ANNA opens the door to DOCTOR FRANKLYN. They go to JACOB's corpse. The DOCTOR feels the pulse, then listens with his stethoscope. He turns to her and shakes his head.*)

ANNA: I knew he was.

(*She goes into the living-room, stops by the dummy and dresses it with her cardigan. The DOCTOR draws the sheet over JACOB's face and pulls a screen round the bed.*)

(*GEORGE cycles on and away across the front.*)

(*The clock chime ends. ANNA goes to answer the door to GEORGE.*)

GEORGE: I'm sorry to bring you to the door when there's no post but I wanted to ask you if Alvin's out, if you'd ask him to call in at Calcutta Street to see his mother.

ANNA: He's gone to work.

GEORGE: I didn't think he'd be in. She's been asking, his mother, where I think he is and why he doesn't bother to visit. She says she doesn't care and doesn't want to see him and wouldn't talk to him if he came in and tried to, but I know she would. So could you ask him to call round on his own and not to say I asked him to, but pretend he comes of his own accord to see how she was?

ANNA: How is she?

GEORGE: Very well. I've looked after her and the neighbours have, too.

ANNA: What happened?

GEORGE: She broke her arm and her shoulder blade, fractured her finger bone, was shocked with concussion and had injections. Then out she came in a bright red rash, her flesh blew up, all swollen with fluid – she put on weight and got fat. She lies in bed, propped up, waiting to be cared for. I do my best but she's not my responsibility.

(*The DOCTOR comes downstairs with his bag.*)

Good morning, doctor.

DOCTOR: Mister Bland – good morning. How's Mrs Hanker?

GEORGE: I was just saying – she's very well.

DOCTOR: I'll be in to see her on Thursday.

GEORGE: I'll tell her. Thank you. You will ask him to call for me?

ANNA: Yes.

GEORGE: Very much obliged. Thank you.

ANNA: Goodbye.

(*GEORGE cycles off.*)

What must I do?

DOCTOR: Make yourself some tea, take one of these tablets every three hours to help you relax, and I'll do the rest. The coroner will call and he'll arrange for the undertaker. Don't worry.

ANNA: Thank you.

DOCTOR: Would you like me to inform any relatives?

ANNA: No. There aren't many. I'll let them know after the funeral.

DOCTOR: Chin up.

ANNA: Of course.

(*The DOCTOR goes. ANNA picks up JACOB's magnifying glass, polishes it with the sleeve of the cardigan and puts it in the drawer. She goes into his room and closes the curtains against the day.*)

(*GEORGE takes a pot plant upstairs and puts it in ALVIN's room. He sprays the air with perfume from a vanity bottle with a tassled rubber bulb. MRS HANKER is turning the pages of the magazine singlehanded. ALVIN lets himself in. He wears a mackintosh. GEORGE hears and welcomes him.*)

GEORGE: Alvin! You have a visitor, Ivy. (*On the landing.*) Let me take your coat, Alvin.

(*He helps ALVIN out of the coat, takes it down and hangs it up, then goes to his room and smokes. ALVIN goes in to MRS*

HANKER's room. He stands beside the bed. He puts a bag of sweets on the magazine. MRS HANKER pushes it aside, and continues to turn the pages.)

ALVIN: Does it hurt? I'm living up Stroggen Hill Road, now. Old Mister Bowers' house. (*He waits.*) He died this morning. It looks as though it should be painful. My plant that you saw's got some buds on it. It's three feet tall, the stem. You're a lot fatter. Are you glad I came? Pleased to see me? I'm sorry I didn't come before. I'm sorry I threw water at you. I didn't mean you to get hurt. Don't you want to talk? I'll go, then.

(He pretends to leave. GEORGE comes on to the landing.)

(Returning.) Would you like me to call often?

(He leans over and finds a way of getting past the salute to kiss MRS HANKER on the cheek. She wipes it off. ALVIN goes on to the landing.)

GEORGE: Thank you for coming, Alvin.

ALVIN: 'S alright.

GEORGE: I hung your coat up.

(He beckons ALVIN into his room and offers him a cigarette. ALVIN shakes his head. GEORGE lights another for himself.)

You didn't tell her I asked you here, did you?

ALVIN: No.

GEORGE: She's looking a lot better than she did a month back. I've done my best looking after her but she's not my responsibility, really, you know. We're not married. I'm not her husband. There was no oath for in sickness, health, richer, poorer, better or worse taken between us. We just fell in together for a while, like. I never expected I'd have to look after her. I never wanted responsibility, just the good time of it was enough for me. Understand? Sit down, Alvin.

(They sit side by side on GEORGE's bed.)

I'm not the type for serious development or changes. I'm set in my ways. Always have been. I like things to stay as they are at the start. Besides, it was all her doing. I've been cheated if you look at it. You can see I've been cheated. I'm a victim. She made the running. I'm involved unwillingly through her. I'm the innocent party. She's the injured one but I'm not to blame. I have to get out. That's why I want you to have this because I'm leaving next week. (*He picks up the white dressing gown.*) I never asked her to give it to me. (*He points to the back of the chair.*) My coat. (*He gets up and puts on his coat.*) Next week the plaster comes off her arm and next week I go to Denbridge. I've got transferred to an indoor job. Registered parcels and express department.

ALVIN: I see.

GEORGE: I knew you'd understand, Alvin. You're a good lad. She'll soon be on her feet again. You can advertise for a lodger straight away. She'll perk up with you and a new lodger pottering about the house.

ALVIN: Yes.

GEORGE: Just one thing. I haven't told her yet. I didn't want to until I was sure you'd see things straight. So you'll let her know, then, would you? Explain the position to her. I have to go to the club now. Darts and that.

ALVIN: Yes, I'll tell her, Mister Bland.

GEORGE: Good lad. (*He shakes hands with ALVIN.*) Good night.

(*He goes down and out through the front door. ALVIN goes on to the landing holding the gown.*)

MRS HANKER: (*Calling.*) George. Are you there, George? Has he gone? Was that him banging the door, the dirty, snotty little runt. George.

(*ALVIN goes in.*)

Where's George?

ALVIN: Gone out.

MRS HANKER: What are you doing with that gown?

ALVIN: He gave it to me.

MRS HANKER: What for?

ALVIN: He's leaving next week. Got a job in Denbridge. He asked me to tell you.

MRS HANKER: He's not.

ALVIN: You have to advertise for a new lodger.

MRS HANKER: George wouldn't leave, he's not that sort.

ALVIN: He said your plaster comes off next week.

MRS HANKER: He can't leave. I need him. Anyhow, he's
no right to push off, we're supposed to be in love.

ALVIN: He's gone to the club.

MRS HANKER: Don't tell me I've been wasting my time
on him. Don't tell me *that* after all these months.
(*ALVIN goes on to the landing, and stands still.*)
(*Calling.*) Alvin. Get him back here. Alvin. Fetch him.
Alvin. Where are you? Go to the club, find him and
fetch him.
(*ALVIN goes down the stairs, takes his coat from the hall-stand,
and puts it on.*)
He can't leave. I love him too much for that. He has
to marry me. I won't be left. I can't be. He has to care.
If I do, he must. Somebody has to care as much as
I do. Somebody has to care more than I know how.
George. Alvin. Don't make me any more. I'm tired,
worn out and away. Mrs Raistrick'll start knocking.
(*ALVIN hangs the robe on the hall-stand and leaves, banging
the door.*)
Come back. They've gone. I know when I'm alone. I can
tell from past experience. I'll never get used to it, though.
I'm damned if I'll ruddy get used to it. I'll have to cry
like hell to remember how lonely I am. Nobody joins
in with me for long if they can help it. Nobody joins me for
long. (*She whimpers.*)

(*ANNA opens the curtains. The screen has been folded away.
The bedding is piled on the bed. She gathers it up and dumps
it outside the living-room. She goes back and bags JACOB's
clothing, including his clerical bib and collar, a hot-water
bottle, his teeth, etcetera. ALVIN is standing by the front
door with a suitcase when ANNA returns. She looks at the
suitcase, then dumps the rest of the things.*)

ALVIN: I *have* to go and look after her.

ANNA: (*Removing the pillowslip.*) You won't be coming back,
then?

ALVIN: She's hurt, very hurt. It's awful to see her.

ANNA: I shall miss your plant.

ALVIN: Can't I leave it in the greenhouse?

ANNA: (*Folding things.*) I don't want it. If you do, take it. I'd only throw it in the dustbin.

ALVIN: Why?

ANNA: To avoid remembering, I suppose.

ALVIN: I should take it then, if you'd throw it away.

ANNA: (*Tossing medicine bottles into a shoebox.*) Yes, take it.

(*ALVIN takes his donkey jacket from the hall-stand.*)

ALVIN: I'm sorry you won't remember.

ANNA: (*Throwing her own tablets into the shoebox.*) Aren't you going to take your games and things?

ALVIN: I thought they could go to the White Elephant Stall at the Flower Show.

ANNA: Alright. I'll see to it.

ALVIN: Thank you. Do you want me to come back and stay with you tonight?

ANNA: No.

ALVIN: You won't mind being in the house alone?

ANNA: It won't make any difference with him gone. He was old.

ALVIN: I see.

(*ANNA holds the hot-water bottle.*)

Shall I come with you to the funeral?

ANNA: No. I lived with him. I'll bury him.

ALVIN: Yes, alright, if you like. I'm sorry.

(*He leaves, re-appearing in the back yard, going through the kitchen and taking the robe from the hallstand. He goes to his room, dumps everything, comes downstairs and goes out.*
Distant nondescript organ music can be heard. ANNA puts on a black headscarf and her raincoat which has a mourning band on one arm. She pulls on her gloves, picks up a Bible and leaves the house.)

(*A churchyard. ALVIN appears walking backwards, reading gravestones. When he turns round moving forward, he reveals the lily in full flower. The stem is almost as long as his torso, making him carry the pot with his arms hanging at full stretch.*

ANNA comes from the opposite direction. They come together at either side of JACOB's grave.)

Aren't you going to get him a headstone?

ANNA: I've ordered one.

ALVIN: Oh yes.

ANNA: How's your mother?

ALVIN: Alright.

ANNA: I hear we're going to have a new postman next week.

ALVIN: Yes. Mister Bland's going to Denbridge to work.

ANNA: They called round this morning about those things of yours. The games and things.

ALVIN: They'll sell them easily, don't you think?

ANNA: Oh yes, I'm sure.

ALVIN: It's a nice day.

ANNA: Oh. Yes.

ALVIN: Shall we walk up Stroggen Hill?

ANNA: What for?

ALVIN: Why not?

ANNA: Stop off on the way back and I'll make tea.

ALVIN: Alright. *(He puts the plant on the grave and steps back.)*

ANNA: It's lovely now, isn't it?

ALVIN: Yes. It's alright.

(The organ music is now not so distant and helps to fill the silence as the light wanes, leaving all in silhouette, except for the lily on the grave. No more.)

The End.

THREE MONTHS GONE

For George W. Goetschius

Characters

ANNA BOWERS
in her late 30s

MAURICE BOWERS
in his 40s, her brother

MRS HANKER
aged 40 plus

ALVIN HANKER
in his 20s, her son

DOCTOR FRANKLYN

A MILKMAN

Three Months Gone was first presented by the English Stage Company at the Royal Court Theatre, London, on 28 January 1970, and subsequently at the Duchess Theatre, London, in association with Bob Swash and Leon Gluckman on 4 March 1970, with the following cast:

ANNA, Jill Bennett

MAURICE, Alan Lake

MRS HANKER, Diana Dors

ALVIN, Richard O'Callaghan

DOCTOR, Kevin Stoney

MILKMAN, Warren Clarke

Director, Ronald Eyre

Designer, Jocelyn Herbert

A note about the staging. The action of the play passes in a bungalow called Byeways, the home of Anna Bowers. The main room has a French window into a glass extension which leads to the garden, a hatch to the kitchen and a door into the hall, which is no more than a passage to other rooms and the front door.

ACT ONE

*The main room of a bungalow called Byeways, the home of ANNA
BOWERS. Although it is late summer the bungalow is being spring-
cleaned. Furniture is stacked and covered, the curtains are down,
rugs rolled up, boxes, books, china, old magazines and newspapers,
etcetera, are piled in the hall, cluttering the usual routes. Nothing is
where it should be. A clock chimes ten.*

*ANNA is on her knees polishing the lino. She backs into view, stops
work, sits back on her haunches listening to the chimes and sighs.*

ANNA: I'll never do it. He'll be here before I'm ready.
    (*A ship's hooter, seagulls and waves washing on a shore can
    be heard.*)
MAURICE: (*Off.*) Hello, anyone at home? Anna?
    (*MAURICE BOWERS appears outside the confines of the
    living-room, waiting in limbo. He carries a kitbag.*)
ANNA: Maurice.
MAURICE: What's going on here?
ANNA: I'm trying to clean up.
MAURICE: Before I get here tomorrow.
ANNA: Yes, you didn't give me much warning.
MAURICE: Couldn't.
ANNA: You said you'd be here late. If you are late like you
    said, everything will be done.
MAURICE: I'll arrive late tomorrow, then.
ANNA: Yes. Go away and come back. I can't wait for you to
    get here. I suppose you'll be docking just about now.
MAURICE: Probably.
ANNA: What have you brought me?
MAURICE: Just say.
ANNA: Silk.
    (*MAURICE pulls several yards of diaphanous silk from his
    kitbag. ANNA smiles as it swirls in the air above.*)
    Who do I look like?
MAURICE: Samson Bowers's infamous sister.
ANNA: Delilah Bowers.

MAURICE: Spinster.

ANNA: Notorious spinster.

MAURICE: Of Byeways, Stroggen Hill Road, Hockton.

ANNA: Hockton.

MAURICE: It's bigger than Donisthorpe.

ANNA: Spinster.

MAURICE: Why don't you get married?

ANNA: There's no one suitable. (*She polishes the floor.*)

MAURICE: Out of all Hockton and Donisthorpe?

ANNA: Out of all Donisthorpe and Hockton and
   Donisthorpe and Donisthorpe and Hockton and Hockton
   – or Hockton either.

MAURICE: How about Donisthorpe?

ANNA: There's no one I'd accept as your brother-in-law.

MAURICE: (*Putting the silk back.*) Has anyone offered?

ANNA: Yes.

MAURICE: In Hockton?

ANNA: Yes. In Hockton and Hockton.

MAURICE: I see.

ANNA: You won't bring me any silk. I know you. I'm too
   old. Too selective and old. I'm above the age of consent.
   I could be violated if I was below it, but I'm not. I'm
   over age these days, instead of under. I shan't marry him.
   (*There is a knock at the front door.*)

MAURICE: Why are you kneeling there? You've so much
   to do.
   (*The knock is repeated. MAURICE leaves. ANNA checks herself
   in the mirror then goes to the front door.*)

ANNA: Who is it?

ALVIN: (*Off.*) Me.

ANNA: Alvin?

ALVIN: Yes.
   (*ANNA opens the door. ALVIN HANKER stands on the
   doorstep. He doesn't say anything.*)

ANNA: Come in.

ALVIN: Thank you. (*He comes in with difficulty and finds
   somewhere to stand.*)

ANNA: (*Closing the door.*) I'm very busy.

ALVIN: I know it's late.

ANNA: I couldn't think who it was.

ALVIN: I won't stop.

ANNA: I'll make some cocoa.

ALVIN: Yes, please.

ANNA: I was going to. (*She goes into the kitchen.*)

ALVIN: I knew you were in.

ANNA: The light was on.

ALVIN: I knocked a few times.

ANNA: I didn't hear.

ALVIN: I *did*.

ANNA: If you say so. (*She returns to the living-room.*) What do you want?

ALVIN: Where were you?

ANNA: I must have dozed off.

ALVIN: All night?

ANNA: Just now.

ALVIN: Why didn't you come, then?

ANNA: I said. I didn't hear you knocking.

ALVIN: No, not the door. Why didn't you meet me at the Carlton?

ANNA: Oh yes. I'm terribly sorry.

ALVIN: You're not sick?

ANNA: No, I wasn't sick.

ALVIN: I waited.

ANNA: I'm terribly sorry. I would have let you know.

ALVIN: 'S alright.

ANNA: No, it's awful of me.

ALVIN: As long as you weren't sick.

ANNA: Did you wait long?

ALVIN: Over an hour.

ANNA: Oh dear.

ALVIN: As you said you would and as you said you'd read the book of it, I was sure you'd come eventually.

ANNA: I would have.

ALVIN: When I did go in eventually, I kept thinking you'd have come and be waiting for me. I went out once to look. I told the usherette I was going out to look so she'd let me in again. I missed the news and the trailers and all the short film and a quarter of an hour of the big picture and as I haven't read the book like you, I don't know what happened to start with.

ANNA: I'm terribly sorry.

ALVIN: 'S alright.

ANNA: Get the book from the library. I did.

ALVIN: Yes, I will. Thank you.

ANNA: It wasn't raining, anyway.

ALVIN: No.

ANNA: That's one good thing.

ALVIN: Yes. Although you can stand underneath in front of the Carlton unless the queue sticks out and you're late for it, but I was there early, so I got a good place well under.

ANNA: As it wasn't raining, it wouldn't have mattered anyway.

ALVIN: Why not?

ANNA: Well, you wouldn't have got wet even if there had been a pathetic queue sticking out.

ALVIN: There weren't many there.

ANNA: I should have let you know.

ALVIN: 'S alright.

ANNA: Don't look at me. I feel worse.

ALVIN: I thought you might not have been feeling very well, or something.

ANNA: You said.

ALVIN: I came to see.

ANNA: Thank you.

ALVIN: What time is it now?

ANNA: Nearly quarter past ten.

ALVIN: It was ten minutes past seven when I got there and started to wait.

ANNA: So you went in at eight o'clock? (*She takes the blanket from the sofa and gets a chair.*)

ALVIN: A quarter past.

ANNA: Sit down somewhere.

ALVIN: You're not moving? (*He sits in the chair where ANNA has left it.*)

244

ANNA: No. Tidying up. (*She folds the blanket.*) Was it a good film?

ALVIN: I missed the first part.

ANNA: It didn't spoil it too much for you, though, did it?

ALVIN: No.

ANNA: I can usually do without the first half-hour of most films. I like to guess what's gone before. Especially if it's a particularly bad film.

ALVIN: This was a good film, though.

ANNA: I'm glad you enjoyed it.

ALVIN: It was alright.

ANNA: (*Folding an eiderdown.*) Anyway, you liked what you saw of it.

ALVIN: Yes, and you'd have liked it, too, as you've read the book it was from.

ANNA: It couldn't be as good as the book.

ALVIN: You should see it.

ANNA: I'll go another night.

ALVIN: It's not on any more.

ANNA: I'm sorry I missed it.

ALVIN: It might come again.

ANNA: Yes, if it's that good.

ALVIN: It's a musical in colour tomorrow for six days. I didn't see the trailer, though.

(*ANNA doesn't respond.*)

If you weren't feeling sick, why didn't you come?

ANNA: I had a telegram late this afternoon. (*She takes it from her pocket.*)

ALVIN: Oh.

ANNA: From Maurice. He's coming home to see me. Here.

ALVIN: It's from overseas.

(*The kettle whistles.*)

ANNA: A cable, of course. No stamps for you this time.

ALVIN: 'Viggo'.

ANNA: Vigo (*She goes into the kitchen to make cocoa.*)

ALVIN: Vigo.

ANNA: A Spanish port.

ALVIN: Is it alright to read it?

245

ANNA: Yes, of course.

ALVIN: Funny, isn't it?

ANNA: Yes.

ALVIN: I mean it's like a code message from a secret agent.

ANNA: Not really. (*She switches off the kitchen light and comes back.*)

ALVIN: It is, though. 'Prodigal returns on the fourteenth Southampton stop prepare the fatted calf stop expect to eat it late on the fifteenth stop.'

ANNA: Tomorrow.

ALVIN: Fatted calf?

ANNA: It's a kind of joke we have.

ALVIN: A joke?

ANNA: Yes. (*She takes back the telegram and continues to tidy up and place the furniture.*) A joke. You said it was funny.

ALVIN: I didn't mean I thought it was a funny joke, though. I meant it's funny.

ANNA: It's biblical, that's why it's funny.

ALVIN: The Bible's not funny.

ANNA: You can't have read it.

ALVIN: I've heard it at school and on the wireless.

ANNA: You have to be religious to appreciate the jokes.

ALVIN: Is your Maurice religious?

ANNA: Oh yes, he's a fanatic.

ALVIN: Why, like? What does he do?

ANNA: Sings hymns and prays.

ALVIN: I didn't think he was that sort at all from what you said before.

ANNA: What sort did you think he was, then?

ALVIN: Well – I thought he was alright.

ANNA: He is.

ALVIN: I mean not religious.

ANNA: He's devout. He goes into brothels all over the world. That's his religion.

ALVIN: Brothels is?

ANNA: Temples of delight. He's a non-conformist body worshipper.

ALVIN: He sounds alright. I wish I could be religious like that.

ANNA: You have to be dedicated. It's a vocation. Talk to
    him nicely and he might convert you.

ALVIN: I'd be no use. You have to be good-looking.

ANNA: You're not bad-looking.

ALVIN: Is he very?

ANNA: Yes, very. And sunburnt. All over. A terracotta
    colour.

ALVIN: That's because he's outdoors so much at sea in
    hot climates.

ANNA: His hair's thick and black. He's strong. He's
    tattooed. He's nice. You'll like him.

ALVIN: He won't like me, though.

ANNA: Of course he will. He takes a lot of trouble putting
    different stamps on his envelopes just to please you.

ALVIN: Because you asked him to.

ANNA: He'll like you.

ALVIN: How long will he stay for?

ANNA: The weekend, I expect.

ALVIN: Perhaps he'd like to see the musical on Saturday
    night.

ANNA: He won't want to go to the pictures. I haven't seen
    him for seven years.

ALVIN: No.

ANNA: Will you be going?

ALVIN: I like to see the trailer before I decide.

ANNA: As you missed it, you'll never be able to make up
    your mind.

ALVIN: Yes, I will. I've read about it.

ANNA: Musicals are all the same.

ALVIN: I'd like to see it, but I don't like to see them on my
    own – musicals.

ANNA: Take your mother.

ALVIN: I could do, yes. We could all go with your brother.
    Take him, like, as it's Saturday. I could pay for all of us.

ANNA: No, Alvin. You couldn't pay for us. We can't go.

ALVIN: I don't expect I shall see him, then, if he's only
    here for the weekend.

ANNA: Why not? You can call. Come on Sunday for lunch.

ALVIN: Thank you.

ANNA: I must buy some beer. He likes a drink.

ALVIN: What did you say about me in your letters?

ANNA: Just that we were friends.

ALVIN: Did you tell him we'd slept together?

ANNA: No.

ALVIN: Why not?

ANNA: It wouldn't mean anything to him.

ALVIN: Will you tell him?

ANNA: Why should I?

ALVIN: I thought you'd be glad to tell him, as he goes in
for body worship and that.

ANNA: You're not suggesting you're in the same category?

ALVIN: No.

ANNA: Our little night together was just embarrassing.

ALVIN: I'd never done it before.

ANNA: I'm surprised you want me to tell anyone about it.
Especially Maurice. I'd have thought you'd be rather
ashamed to have him know.

ALVIN: I liked it.

ANNA: That's alright then.

ALVIN: I could get better at it if you'd let me try more
often.

ANNA: I can't. I can't. I really can't.

ALVIN: Why?

ANNA: You're not mature.

ALVIN: I know I'm not very big physically. I'm not strong
like Maurice is, but maybe I could grow bigger perhaps.

ANNA: You'd still be Alvin.

ALVIN: Don't you like me at all?

ANNA: I don't want to talk about it. If you do, drink your
cocoa and go home.
(*She takes the blankets and eiderdown to MAURICE's room.
ALVIN puts the cocoa down.*)
(*Returning to the living-room.*) What's the matter with it?

ALVIN: Nothing. But it's just that if I drink you'll think I
want to go home as well as that I want to go on talking
about it – you, you I mean, and I don't want to go home,

yet if I don't drink it, my cocoa, then you could think I
don't want to talk about you, although I do.

ANNA: You're full of problems, aren't you?

ALVIN: I don't want you to think the wrong thing.

ANNA: Thank you. That's very considerate.

ALVIN: It's not. You don't have to tell him.

ANNA: Alvin, I'm very touched. (*She hands ALVIN his cocoa.*)
Don't be miserable.

ALVIN: Have you got a photo of him?

ANNA: Somewhere.

ALVIN: Show us.

ANNA: There in an album some place.

ALVIN: Where?

ANNA: In that sideboard.

ALVIN: I like snap albums.

ANNA: Get it, then. (*She takes the pillows to MAURICE's room.*)

ALVIN: (*Finding the album.*) I'd have thought you'd have
kept lots of pictures of him all over the house in each
room and on the walls, too.

ANNA: (*Returning and arranging things.*) Father didn't get on
with him. Having his pictures on show would have
aggravated him. He threatened to burn them once.

ALVIN: I wish I were him.

ANNA: Whatever for?

ALVIN: You never stop talking about him.

ANNA: Neither do you. (*She indicates MAURICE's photo.*)
There.

ALVIN: That's you with him, too, in shorts.

ANNA: Playing tennis in Low Moor Park.

ALVIN: Your hair's changed.

ANNA: You're supposed to be looking at Maurice.

ALVIN: I wish I'd known you then.

ANNA: You were a child.

ALVIN: I can't play tennis.

ANNA: He always won.

ALVIN: I've played table tennis.

ANNA: He made me run all over the court.

ALVIN: He looks a good player. Bridlington.

ANNA: We ran on the beach at Scarborough.

ALVIN: 'Flamborough Head swimming.'

ANNA: Splashing all the way and cold but laughing.
Pebbles and the hurry of the ocean making me sick.
Pools, crabs, warm seaweed and shells. Never again.
(*MAURICE appears in the kitchen and comes into the living-room, fresh from the sea in his swimming trunks.*)

ALVIN: He looks a good swimmer.

ANNA: Yes.
(*MAURICE moves between them.*)
That's Alvin.

MAURICE: Hello.

ALVIN: Hello.

ANNA: He's looking forward to meeting you.

ALVIN: It's hard to tell what he's like from these snaps.

ANNA: He won't have changed.

ALVIN: He's a bit like I thought he'd be from what you
said.

ANNA: I'm sorry your first meeting has to be so informal.
I'd rather have introduced you fully clothed. I don't like
other people poking their eyes into your flesh.

ALVIN: Liar.

ANNA: Alvin!

ALVIN: There's nothing you like better than showing him
off. You swank with him to make me feel inferior.

ANNA: Don't stand up when you speak to me. Don't listen
to him, Maurice; he's the true liar, lying because he feels
inferior to me in your presence. Sit down. I can't stand
lies. I shouldn't have introduced you.

MAURICE: We ought to shake hands.

ALVIN: (*Shaking hands with MAURICE.*) How do you do.

ANNA: I should have kept him out of your letters.

ALVIN: I suppose you left your clothes on the beach.

MAURICE: My hand's bigger than yours.

ALVIN: Am I like you thought I'd be from what she said in
her letters?

ANNA: He's a stamp collector, standing over a hot kettle
steaming them off, scalding his fingers with care, licking
hinges, fixing them into a seven and sixpenny book. He's

humourless, too. He could do with a few years at sea, toughen him up. Strengthen his weakness. Make him like you. A man of the world.

ALVIN: I'll go if you like.

ANNA: I wish you would. Shove off while the tide's in, else you'll be here all night.

MAURICE: How do you get on with her?

ALVIN: Not bad. We slept in the same bed once.

ANNA: Don't tell him that.

ALVIN: She doesn't like me much.

MAURICE: Why don't you like him?

ANNA: I like him.

MAURICE: She says she likes you.

ALVIN: Not as much as I like her, though. I wish she liked me as much as she likes you.

MAURICE: You can't expect that. She's my sister.

ANNA: He's my brother.

MAURICE: We're brother and sister.

ALVIN: Would you show me how you kiss her, please, so I can watch and try and make her like me more.
   (*MAURICE and ANNA turn to each other, close their eyes and come together in a slow passionate embrace.*)
   People can see in.
   (*The kiss ends. MAURICE leaves.*)

ANNA: You'll have to go, Alvin. There's so much to do. I'll be up all night getting things ready. (*She puts the album back in the sideboard.*)

ALVIN: You've got all day tomorrow.

ANNA: I have to go shopping tomorrow.

ALVIN: I could help you.

ANNA: I have to shop alone.

ALVIN: I meant now I could help.

ANNA: Oh.

ALVIN: Let me. (*He removes his mackintosh and jacket.*)

ANNA: You could stack the things from the hall in the small room.

ALVIN: Yes, alright.

ANNA: The hall bulb's gone.

ALVIN: Yes.

ANNA: You'll need the ladder.

ALVIN: What shall I do first?

ANNA: Fix the curtains. People can see in. I'll give you a hand.

ALVIN: Thank you.

ANNA: The hooks are on. I'll hold the ladder steady.

ALVIN: No need. (*He sets up the ladder.*) If we finish before twelve o'clock, can I stay till one?

ANNA: Have you got permission to stay out late?

ALVIN: No.

ANNA: I had to at your age.

ALVIN: Can I put you to bed?

ANNA: I'm too old for that. (*She gets the curtains from the ironing-board.*)

ALVIN: I don't care. I like you.

ANNA: I can't.

ALVIN: Let me try again, please. (*He starts to hang the curtains above the French window.*)

ANNA: It's not your fault. I'm no good at it either. We just don't work together.

ALVIN: We're working together now.

ANNA: That's not what I meant.

ALVIN: I was joking.

ANNA: They're a lot brighter than the other curtains.

ALVIN: I'm sure we could work together if I tried harder.

ANNA: It isn't something that improves with effort.

ALVIN: If I practised on someone else for a bit, would you let me try again, then?

ANNA: Who else?

ALVIN: Well, there's a girl on the cash register in the supermarket who sometimes comes into the shop to buy goldfish food. I don't think she's got any goldfish, because her mother's got a cat. She just comes in to see *me*. She asks me about goldfish just to talk. Anyway, she wants me to go out with her. She's been to Calcutta Street once. My mother likes her.

ANNA: Good.

ALVIN: I don't, though.

ANNA: Why? What's wrong with her?

ALVIN: She's too young. She's not like you. But I could
try with her and get better. I'm sure she'd agree to.

ANNA: You mean you'd tell her you were practising?

ALVIN: I could, couldn't I?

ANNA: I suppose you could. She might like the idea.
It's not usual though, is it? Sounds a bit functional.
And she'd be bound to ask who you were in training for.

ALVIN: That's no good, then, is it?

ANNA: Look – why don't you go with her – what's her
name?

ALVIN: Maureen Wilcock.

ANNA: Why don't you go with Maureen for a bit, try to like
her, and don't think about me like that at all any more,
and I bet you in no time you'll be getting on like houses
on fire together. You'll stop wanting to keep seeing me and
feeling bad because I don't want to sleep with you.

ALVIN: You really don't want to?

ANNA: I really don't want to talk about it. The stuff to go
in the small room's in the hall.

ALVIN: I've nearly done.

ANNA: They do look better.

ALVIN: This window frame's dirty.

ANNA: Nobody sees.

ALVIN: I'll paint it for you if you like.

ANNA: Not now.

ALVIN: I meant in the near future some time.

ANNA: Yes. Alright. Some time in the future.

ALVIN: All the woodwork. A nice colour. Blue. Or a nice
green perhaps.

ANNA: I don't like gaudy colours.

ALVIN: A nice green's not gaudy.

ANNA: Suppose not.

ALVIN: Nor's a nice blue.

ANNA: Your ideas of nice aren't as nice as mine.

ALVIN: (*Collapsing the ladder.*) You'd choose the colour
anyway. I wouldn't want to. I just said I'd paint it. I don't
care what colour it is. It could be the same as it is now.

I was just suggesting. I painted a buffet blue in my room at home. I think it looks quite nice. I think you'd like it. I've got a small quantity of paint left in the tin still. I'll bring it up and show you. Coat Dazzer it's called. Coat Dazzer gloss. There won't be anything like enough to do in here though, of course. It's a small tin I got to start with, just for the buffet. Have you got any paint brushes?

ANNA: Somewhere.

ALVIN: I'll do the light bulb and move the stuff in the hall now. (*He takes the ladder into the hall.*)

ANNA: Why am I sitting here? There's so much to do. I wish he'd go home.

(*ALVIN starts moving things from the hall into a room off the passage. MRS HANKER enters from downstage, then moves into the living-room.*)

MRS HANKER: Is our Alvin here?

ANNA: Mrs Hanker!

MRS HANKER: Is he here – our Alvin?

ANNA: No.

MRS HANKER: You're not lying, are you?

ANNA: He's not here.

MRS HANKER: He went out with you tonight.

ANNA: I haven't seen him.

MRS HANKER: He went to the pictures.

ANNA: Not with me.

MRS HANKER: He said he was.

ANNA: I didn't go.

MRS HANKER: Well, he's not in our house.

ANNA: He might be when you get back.

MRS HANKER: If I go.

ANNA: You can't stay here.

MRS HANKER: Stalemate then, isn't it.

ANNA: I'm so sorry I can't help you.

MRS HANKER: Liar.

(*ALVIN takes the bulb from the hall light.*)

ANNA: Some lies are justified in the name of good manners and expediency.

MRS HANKER: Well, they don't cut any sugar icing with Ivy Hanker, sweetheart. You're neither sorry you can't help nor politely justified and don't imagine you're any better than you should be just because you won't co-operate. A lie's a lie and a liar a liar, expedient or otherwise.

ALVIN: It's sixty watt.

ANNA: Kitchen cupboard.

(*ALVIN goes into the kitchen.*)

MRS HANKER: There's some muck about here, by God. Hasn't been touched for a month of Sundays nor Mondays either, I bet.

ANNA: What does your son look like?

MRS HANKER: Guilty, if I've had 'owt to do with it.

ANNA: Very well. If I should see him about in the next hour or so.

MRS HANKER: Don't sleep with him.

ANNA: I'll do my best –

MRS HANKER: I'm sure you will.

ANNA: – to deter him.

MRS HANKER: Is your best good enough?

ANNA: Enough for Alvin.

MRS HANKER: One thing is all he's after.

ANNA: Thank you for your cautionary advice.

MRS HANKER: Think on what I've said.

ANNA: With all the power at my disposal.

MRS HANKER: With all the power at your elbow.

ANNA: I don't have unlimited powers. I can go so far and no further.

MRS HANKER: You can muster up enough to throw him out.

ANNA: I'll summon what I can.

(*ALVIN enters the hall with the bulb, then continues to tidy the hall.*)

ALVIN: I'll put it in.

ANNA: Thank you.

MRS HANKER: You don't know where he could have got to, do you?

ANNA: No.

MRS HANKER: I worry about him.

ANNA: You should go to the police station.

MRS HANKER: Why for?

ANNA: He might have been knocked down and taken to hospital.

MRS HANKER: Oh God! Don't say that.

ANNA: You'd better hurry.

MRS HANKER: Our Alvin involved in a fatal accident from which he has since died!

ANNA: Don't you mean recovered?

MRS HANKER: Not if they took him to hospital. They die in the ambulance so they're dead on arrival.

ANNA: Any witness who can give any information please contact the police.

MRS HANKER: No. I can't see him mixed up in anything like that. He hasn't got it in him.

ANNA: I'm so glad to see you worry about him.

MRS HANKER: You're always either glad or sorry about something, aren't you?

ANNA: I was brought up to concern myself with other people's emotional distress.

MRS HANKER: Well, concern yourself with this, then, before you go any further. I don't worry about our Alvin suffering injuries on the road. That's not what frets me, clever miss.

ANNA: Then I'm so sorry I was so glad to see you worry about him.

MRS HANKER: You needn't take it back. I can still do with your concern for my emotional distress, not so much for cars knocking him down as him knocking it off. Him coming up here and messing around with you, that's the seat of my distress.

ANNA: Anything I can do to alleviate –

MRS HANKER: You'll leave him alone. I won't have it. You're old enough to be his mother and that's my look-out not yours. Oh – and please don't think I'm a prohibitive parent. I don't clamp down on him.

ALVIN: She's always clamping me. (*He puts the bulb in the hall light and turns it on.*)

MRS HANKER: I don't care who he sleeps with or how often, so long as it's sensual and lecherous with a bit of love feeling on the side to make him think it and life has a meaning, but he's daft if he thinks he'll get any bliss down your way. Chicken bone and gristle stew'd make a better meal.

ALVIN: I've done the light.

ANNA: Mrs Hanker.

MRS HANKER: Yes, love?

ANNA: I've had enough of you *and* your son.

MRS HANKER: You *have* had him then...?

ANNA: Once.

MRS HANKER: You can own up to your achievements, I see. I see you are principled in that direction.

ANNA: I never balked at facts.

MRS HANKER: No, you don't look a balker. I'll give you that. And anyone who didn't balk at Alvin'd balk at nothing. Once, you say?

ANNA: That's correct.

MRS HANKER: And once was enough?

ANNA: No, quite inadequate.

MRS HANKER: About ten weeks ago, right?

ANNA: Twelve.

MRS HANKER: A mother's intuition. I didn't need *you* to let me in on it. My Alvin doesn't slip past his mother without her knowing he's had it and still goes on wanting it.

ANNA: I shall open the front door and close it in your face.

MRS HANKER: You might want to, but you won't. I'm waiting here till he comes.

ALVIN: I'm moving the stuff in the hall now.

MRS HANKER: I know he'll be here somewhere. He's on his way.

ANNA: Leave this house.

MRS HANKER: Not without our Alvin.

ANNA: You're trespassing.

MRS HANKER: You're poaching.

ANNA: You're common.

MRS HANKER: You're genteel.

ANNA: Coalman's wife.

MRS HANKER: Vicar's daughter.

ANNA: Piss off!

MRS HANKER: Right.

> (*ALVIN picks up an old radio and turns it on. MRS HANKER and ANNA do a competitive cha-cha, ending with MRS HANKER pushing ANNA victoriously on to the sofa.*)

ANNA: Help.

ALVIN: (*Going to his mother and grabbing her arm.*) Leave Miss Bowers alone.

MRS HANKER: You're the one who should do that.

ALVIN: Lay off her.

MRS HANKER: And that.

ALVIN: Let go.

MRS HANKER: Don't bruise your mother.

ALVIN: You stand over there. (*He moves MRS HANKER aside.*)

MRS HANKER: I'm on your side.

ALVIN: Anna, come here. (*He takes ANNA to him manfully.*)

ANNA: (*Sheltering in ALVIN's arms.*) Make her go, Alvin.

ALVIN: You calm down. I'll see to her.

MRS HANKER: You'll have a job on, turfing your mother out of a strange house into the small hours of the morning. It won't sound very much in your favour in front of the magistrate.

ALVIN: (*Pointing.*) Return to Calcutta Street.

MRS HANKER: It's rude to point. I never taught him that.

ALVIN: I'm making you go.

MRS HANKER: I see no signs of it.

ALVIN: Be off.

MRS HANKER: I'm staying here. (*She sits.*)

ALVIN: You're provoking me to use force.

MRS HANKER: It's *my* goat you're getting.

ANNA: Be careful, Alvin.

ALVIN: I'll be all right.

ANNA: Don't make too much noise.

ALVIN: I'll gag her first.

ANNA: (*Handing ALVIN a duster.*) Yes. Use this.

ALVIN: I'll put my hands round her throat.

MRS HANKER: Put your coat on and get yourself down Stroggen Hill Road, sharp.

ANNA: Get rid of her for me.

MRS HANKER: You're not staying here.

ALVIN: Mother.

MRS HANKER: What?

ALVIN: Will you go?

MRS HANKER: No.

ALVIN: (*Kneeling in front of MRS HANKER.*) Please.

MRS HANKER: I have a sacred duty as your mother to see you don't get into trouble without me and you know what I mean by trouble. You don't want to be cornered like I was for the rest of your life just because of a slip of the tongue one night, as you might say.

ALVIN: I'm old enough to make my own decisions.

MRS HANKER: A slip of the tongue's not a decision.

ALVIN: I'm old enough.

MRS HANKER: I know you're old enough, love, but she's old enough to be your mother and I don't want you to go with her. I wouldn't expect it of you myself and I'm not only old enough to *be*, I *am* your mother. As such I want a nice young girl for you like Maureen Wilcox at the supermarket – who could want fairer than that?

ALVIN: She's got brown hair. And she's cock not cox.

ANNA: Alvin.

ALVIN: Wilcock. (*He starts to remove his pullover.*)

MRS HANKER: Why are you taking your pullover off for?

ALVIN: I'm trying to go to bed with Miss Bowers.

MRS HANKER: In front of your mother?

ALVIN: Watch if you like.

(*MRS HANKER makes herself comfortable on the chair.*)
What you doing?

MRS HANKER: Sitting down.

ALVIN: What for?

MRS HANKER: We're never too old to learn. I'm not proud. Come on. Get on with it.

ALVIN: Don't sit there.

MRS HANKER: Where would you like me?

ALVIN: Aw, mother, go home, please.

MRS HANKER: I've got nothing more to say.

259

ALVIN: I'll put the ladder outside. (*He takes the ladder from the hall, through the living-room and out into the lean-to. As he does so he sneezes.*)

MRS HANKER: You've got a cold coming on.

(*ALVIN sneezes.*)

I see you've been doing a bit of spring-cleaning.

(*ALVIN sneezes.*)

That's more than I can get him to do at home.

(*ALVIN sneezes.*)

Not a bad little bungalow, is it?

(*ALVIN sneezes.*)

ANNA: Are you alright?

ALVIN: I got some dust in my – (*He sneezes.*)

MRS HANKER: Have a glass of water backwards.

ANNA: That's for hiccoughs.

MRS HANKER: I'm not sitting here in a draught. I'm off. I'll leave a cup of Bovril on the grate, tell him – and send him straight home.

(*MRS HANKER leaves. ALVIN comes in from the garden, closing the door behind him.*)

ALVIN: It's cold out (*He puts his pullover on.*)

ANNA: There's a frost coming down from the north.

ALVIN: It's early for frost.

ANNA: If you're cold, put this on. (*She hands him a reindeer sweater from the sofa.*)

ALVIN: Whose is it?

ANNA: Yours if you want it.

ALVIN: Really?

ANNA: It's had the moth in it.

ALVIN: It's like Eskimos have.

ANNA: You can darn it.

ALVIN: Reindeer.

ANNA: Stags.

ALVIN: It's a bit big for me.

ANNA: You don't have to have it.

ALVIN: (*Putting it on.*) I like it. Thank you very much.

ANNA: It looks good on you.

ALVIN: Makes me look wider.

ANNA: Yes, it does. You could be Maurice.

ALVIN: Yeah.

ANNA: From the back. Alvin, I've had enough for today.

ALVIN: Oh.

ANNA: It's late. I'm tired. I'm going to bed.

ALVIN: Yes. Well, if you want to go to bed I'd better go.

ANNA: Thank you for helping.

ALVIN: 'S alright.

ANNA: Your jacket.

ALVIN: If you'd let me stay over I'd be here first thing in
the morning. I could go to the shops with you and carry
your things.

ANNA: No, Alvin. (*She helps ALVIN on with his coat and
pushes him towards the door.*)

ALVIN: I could stay on in case he got here early.

ANNA: He won't be.

ALVIN: Are you going to meet the train?

ANNA: It's safer to wait here.

ALVIN: He'll never find it.

ANNA: He's not a child – he's been all over the world.

ALVIN: Yes.

ANNA: Your mother will be getting worried about you.

ALVIN: She won't.

ANNA: She might be looking for you.

ALVIN: She'll most likely be in bed with Mister Verity.

ANNA: I know she doesn't like me.

ALVIN: You've only met her once.

ANNA: She doesn't approve of me.

ALVIN: She doesn't know you like I do, that's why –
that's all.

ANNA: I knew she didn't like me.

ALVIN: She does like you.

ANNA: I don't like her.

ALVIN: If you'd come for tea or just call in sometimes,
she'd get to like you.

ANNA: I don't want her to. Can't you understand? I don't
want her to like me. Why should I? I don't want you to
like me either. I'm alright, thank you. Leave me alone.
Go home.

ALVIN: Ta-ra then.

ANNA: Good night.

ALVIN: I'll see you.

ANNA: Sunday lunchtime.

ALVIN: (*After a pause.*) Good night. (*He opens the front door and waits.*)

ANNA: Good night.

(*ALVIN closes the front door as though he has left, and slips into the room being prepared for MAURICE. ANNA puts ALVIN's cocoa mug through the kitchen hatch, picks up her dressing-gown and a magazine, turns out the living-room light, then the hall light, and goes into her bedroom. The light goes on. ALVIN comes into the living-room. ANNA comes from her bedroom, senses something in the darkness, and enters the living-room.*)

Maurice…? Maurice.

(*ALVIN darts forward and embraces ANNA frantically, desperately kissing her as she struggles to be free of him. She is not immediately aware of the situation, suspended for a moment between imagination and reality.*)

ALVIN: It's me. Alvin.

(*ANNA laughs.*)

It's only me. I didn't want to go. I didn't want to frighten you. Don't make a noise. I didn't hurt you, did I? I wouldn't ever hurt you. Did I hurt you? Are you alright? What's the matter?

(*ANNA drops on to a chair, laughing. She shakes her head.*)

You're alright. (*He kneels.*) I thought if I didn't say anything, if I didn't talk, if I only kissed, you might not send me away. I only kissed you. I only held you. I'm sorry. I know I don't say anything right, but I thought if I only kissed you wouldn't mind me so much; you might like it more if I held you. I want to all the time. Don't laugh at me. I'm glad you're laughing. I wish you wouldn't. (*He tries to laugh but ends up crying, takes his handkerchief out and rubs his eyes violently, angry with ANNA yet more angry with and sorrier for himself in his predicament. He finds it hard to stop crying, even with the help of the handkerchief.*) Can I stay, please?

ANNA: You don't have to cry.

ALVIN: I don't want to.

ANNA: Why are you?

ALVIN: I don't know.

ANNA: It's got nothing to do with me. It's all in you.

ALVIN: I know.

ANNA: You've made it all up.

ALVIN: Yes.

ANNA: You must want to carry on.

ALVIN: I don't.

ANNA: I can't help you.

ALVIN: You can.

ANNA: I can't, Alvin. Absolutely.

ALVIN: You could.

ANNA: I've just got nothing to do with it.

ALVIN: You have.

ANNA: You're imagining things.

ALVIN: I'm not.

ANNA: You're just fed up with your dreary little life and you've decided I'm the one who's going to make the stars twinkle in broad daylight.

ALVIN: Yes. You could. You do. You do that.

ANNA: I can work miracles.

ALVIN: Yes. You do. You can. For me.

ANNA: What's the use of miracles if you're the only one who benefits?

ALVIN: You know what I mean.

ANNA: I don't.

ALVIN: I mean – I mean I like you. Don't laugh.

ANNA: I'm not.

ALVIN: Can I stay now?

ANNA: If you stop crying, yes.

ALVIN: I have, yes.

ANNA: Well then.

ALVIN: I won't any more. (*He struggles with the challenge.*)

ANNA: Oh God.

ALVIN: What?

ANNA: Where am I going to put you? You can't sleep in Maurice's room and you can't have sheets.

ALVIN: Can't I stay in your room?

ANNA: No.

ALVIN: On top of the eiderdown.

ANNA: I'll get you some blankets and you can sleep where you used to.

ALVIN: I can't.

ANNA: Why 'can't'?

ALVIN: I've piled everything up on the bed. It was the only place.

ANNA: You'll have to unpile it again, won't you?

ALVIN: Let me sleep on the floor in your room.

ANNA: No.

ALVIN: I might as well sleep at home if I can't sleep with you – I mean where you are.

ANNA: Go, then.

ALVIN: I didn't mean it. I'd still rather be here.

ANNA: Stay, then.

ALVIN: Couldn't you let me rent my bedroom again when your brother's gone back?

ANNA: What about your mother?

ALVIN: She won't mind. She'd be glad, I expect. I expect she'd be able to have two fellers staying then. She likes renting out. Especially to contract workers.

ANNA: Mm?

ALVIN: Contract men only come for so long until their job's done, then they move on. She likes the demolition men best, then scaffold erectors, cement mixers and road wideners. She has this Mister Verity staying now who came a month back. He mends high-tension cables. He has to spend all day climbing up these telegraph poles in the country, climbing and hanging on by leaning backwards away from it at the top, with a wide strap and belt round him. He comes home with the back of his shoulder muscles aching where the strap's been pulling on him and at first Mam massaged where it hurt in front of the fire and then later on up in his room.

ANNA: How do you know all these details?

ALVIN: I'd listen at the bottom of the stairs. He'd groan when she rubbed and then he'd stop. Then she'd groan as though she was getting rubbed.

ANNA: Maybe her shoulder straps pulled too tight as well.

ALVIN: I tried to watch through the keyhole, but they drew the curtains and that was that. A few times they left the light on, but I could only ever see little bits of them.

ANNA: Which bits?

ALVIN: It was hard to tell.

ANNA: I'm sure.

ALVIN: I saw his bottom once. Very big with hollows in the side when he moved it. Like big dimples, and some of his legs I saw, but that's all. I never got the whole picture. I never saw much of her ever because Mister Verity or whoever it is covers most of her up.

ANNA: I see.

ALVIN: So she wouldn't mind if I came and lived here. She'd have more rent and be able to make them jealous of each other.

ANNA: (*Going to MAURICE's room for blankets and pyjamas.*) I can't have you staying here. I'm sorry. It would start people talking in the neighbourhood. It was different when father was alive.

ALVIN: It wouldn't matter what they said.

ANNA: It would to me.

ALVIN: They wouldn't know the truth.

ANNA: Exactly.

ALVIN: I wouldn't care. I'd like them to think things.

ANNA: Here. Blankets and pyjamas. You can sleep there.

ALVIN: Thank you.

ANNA: What time have you to be at work tomorrow?

ALVIN: It's my Saturday off. I thought I said.

ANNA: I'll bring you tea in the morning.

ALVIN: Thank you.

ANNA: Have a good night's sleep.

ALVIN: Yes, I will.

ANNA: You know where everything is.

ALVIN: Yes. (*He goes to the bathroom.*)

ANNA: Good night.

ALVIN: Good night.

(*ANNA starts to undress, taking off her smock, shoes and stockings during what follows.*)

MRS HANKER: (*Off.*) Ooh – hoo – hergh-hergh.

MAURICE: (*Off.*) Eh? Awhh – sofcha.

MRS HANKER: (*Off.*) Hoh – You're alright, aren't you.

MAURICE: (*Off.*) Hrmm.

MRS HANKER: (*Off.*) Mmmmmh.

MAURICE: (*Off.*) Take it off.

MRS HANKER: (*Off.*) Hoh no.

MAURICE: (*Off.*) Take it off.

MRS HANKER: (*Off.*) It's cold, love.

MAURICE: (*Off.*) Open it.

MRS HANKER: (*Off.*) There's frost on the ground.

MAURICE: (*Off.*) I like it bare.

MRS HANKER: (*Off.*) We all like it bare within reason.

MAURICE: (*Off.*) I'll keep you warm.

MRS HANKER: (*Off.*) I'm weak, but I won't lie down.

MAURICE: (*Off.*) You're standing.

MRS HANKER: (*Off.*) So are you.

MAURICE: (*Off.*) I'll stay standing till you lie down.

MRS HANKER: (*Off.*) I'd best stay on my feet, then.

MAURICE: (*Off.*) You're too covered up.

MRS HANKER: (*Off.*) I'm properly dressed.

MAURICE: (*Off.*) You're going to be exposed.

MRS HANKER: (*Off.*) No, not now, not here.

(*MAURICE and MRS HANKER appear from the shadows lit by a moonbeam shining into the living-room.*)

MAURICE: You're a tart in a field.

MRS HANKER: Don't say that.

MAURICE: Why?

MRS HANKER: We're not in a field.

MAURICE: You're a tart against a tree trunk.

MRS HANKER: I'm up against it alright.

MAURICE: It's coming off.

MRS HANKER: No.

MAURICE: I like it bare.

MRS HANKER: Not in a public place.

MAURICE: Bare.

MRS HANKER: Don't keep saying bare.

MAURICE: Without.

MRS HANKER: I've said no.

MAURICE: No clothes.

MRS HANKER: I know what you mean – barely no clothes
on – exposed without; you've made your point – I take it
– but not in a shop doorway, love. It's cold, a sheet of
plate glass on the arse – catch your death; you have to
think twice.

(*ANNA goes to her bedroom.*)

MAURICE: Let's find that tree trunk, then.

(*MRS HANKER and MAURICE take over the middle of
the room.*)

MRS HANKER: There's a park full of trees locked up for
the night.

MAURICE: Cut down some trees.

MRS HANKER: Shut.

MAURICE: Make a house with the logs.

MRS HANKER: Don't reach down there here, love.

MAURICE: Strip off the bark.

MRS HANKER: You're losing your hat.

MAURICE: Make a fire with the wood.

MRS HANKER: I have hold of your hat, but don't bend
your knees.

MAURICE: Burning.

MRS HANKER: You've torn open my blouse.

MAURICE: Saw down the trees.

(*They sit on the sofa.*)

MRS HANKER: They're locked up in the parks.

MAURICE: Chop down the parks.

MRS HANKER: You can't spoil the parks. Kiddies play
there, sit on the swings and slide. Mothers perambulate
in among the gardens where the flower beds grow bigger
and better all summer. Lately, with September out of the
way, the leaves drop off, but still the mothers keep
going, pushing their prams in spite of them blowing
about, and the pond gets full. A man with a broom keeps
the paths swept clear, but still the pond fills up with the
leaves, curled at the corners like potato crisps, drifting
on past the ducks. They soon go limp and sink to the

mud bed at the bottom, from four to five to six feet deep in the middle. And then, by the end of the year, there's only the twigs and branches still left on the trunks. Reflected at first in the top of the pond, and soon, not even that when the ice covers them all over.

MAURICE: What?

MRS HANKER: The reflections. You can't see 'owt in a pond full of ice.

MAURICE: Where are the ducks?

MRS HANKER: Hiding out of sight in among the laurels.

MAURICE: Where are we now?

MRS HANKER: In your sister's little house.

MAURICE: Already?

MRS HANKER: Doesn't take long once you set off.

MAURICE: We'll have to be quiet or we'll wake the old man.

MRS HANKER: Old Mister Bowers?

MAURICE: You know him?

MRS HANKER: Your father?

MAURICE: Yes.

MRS HANKER: He's dead, love.

MAURICE: Dead?

MRS HANKER: Yes, he's dead, love.

MAURICE: Oh. Did he die?

MRS HANKER: He did. He died, love.

MAURICE: He would.

MRS HANKER: I never saw him.

MAURICE: It's just like him, stubborn sod.

MRS HANKER: You don't need to keep quiet for fear of waking him now he's disposed of, unless you think he'll turn in his grave.

MAURICE: I don't believe in life after death.

MRS HANKER: I know what you mean.

MAURICE: He won't show up if he's dead.

MRS HANKER: He sank to the bottom of the pond.

MAURICE: Dad's dead.

MRS HANKER: Elegiac. I've still got your hat.

MAURICE: Some find consolation in the resurrection.

MRS HANKER: I know, love.

MAURICE: Others don't believe in life after death.

MRS HANKER: Some say the hereafter's heavenly
   beautiful, others wouldn't give you tuppence for it.

MAURICE: There's only beauty here.

MRS HANKER: Beauty's lovely.

MAURICE: Beauty lives, ugliness dies.

MRS HANKER: But the memory lingers on.

MAURICE: Dead memories are ugly.

MRS HANKER: If it's dead, forget it.

MAURICE: Living memories are beautiful if they're not
   nostalgic.

MRS HANKER: And romantic if they're faithful.

MAURICE: Thank you.

MRS HANKER: (*Taking her coat off.*) You get warmer inside.
   We can get fully unclothed together and be comfortable
   with each other on the sofa. We won't wake your dad and
   there's no frost or wind.
   (*They start to take each other's clothing off, sitting on the
   sofa. ANNA comes from her bedroom, wearing her dressing-
   gown, and switches on the light.*)

ANNA: So. This is it.

MRS HANKER: Oh. Hello, love.

ANNA: Mrs Hanker.

MRS HANKER: Yes, it's me again. I'm back.

ANNA: I won't have it.

MRS HANKER: It's not an offer.

ANNA: I'm disgusted with you, slobbering, both of you.
   Appalled.

MRS HANKER: Oh dear, I am sorry to hear that. That's
   not how we feel, is it, darling?

ANNA: Maurice!

MAURICE: Hello.

ANNA: You're drunk.

MAURICE: Blind drunk.

MRS HANKER: Don't exaggerate. He does exaggerate.
   You do exaggerate. Slight inebriation doesn't qualify for
   squiffy, never mind blind drunk or even plastered.

ANNA: I've been watching you.

MRS HANKER: Spying through the keyhole?

ANNA: I followed your besotted progress along the banks of the canal.

MRS HANKER: You must have heard us singing, then.

ANNA: Probably.

MRS HANKER: Lovely voice your brother has, haven't you?

(*MAURICE sings, and MRS HANKER joins him in a duet.*)

ANNA: No. Please. Alvin will hear.

(*ALVIN comes from the bathroom wearing the pyjamas and carrying the clothes he was wearing.*)

MRS HANKER: Magical.

MAURICE: Undying.

MRS HANKER: I've still got your hat.

ALVIN: So. This is it!

MRS HANKER: Alvin!

ALVIN: Get dressed.

MRS HANKER: I've only just this minute taken them off.

ALVIN: I've caught you this time. Red-handed.

MRS HANKER: How come you're here in your pyjamas?

ALVIN: How come you're here in your brassière?

MRS HANKER: We'll each mind our own business, shall we?

ALVIN: They're not my pyjamas, anyway.

ANNA: They're yours, Maurice.

MAURICE: How come you're here in my pyjamas?

ALVIN: How come you're here in my mother?

MAURICE: I borrowed her.

ALVIN: Aye, well – that's funny, 'cos I borrowed your pyjamas.

ANNA: Go back to bed, Alvin. (*She pushes ALVIN to the door.*) Leave this to me.

MRS HANKER: So. This is it! Back to bed, is it?

ANNA: I'll deal with them.

MRS HANKER: I've caught you both. One hotfoot, the other red-handed.

ANNA: You're the one who's been exposed.

MRS HANKER: I thought I asked you to send him straight home.

ANNA: (*To ALVIN.*) Go to my room and wait for me.

MRS HANKER: Stay where you are.

MAURICE: Who's the kid?

MRS HANKER: My only son, Alvin.

MAURICE: Do as your mother says, Alvin.

MRS HANKER: My one and only son flagranting himself in front of us, and not even in his own pyjamas. You're not *fit*. Come on, put your clothes on and let's have you out of here, down Stroggen Hill Road.

(*ALVIN takes his pyjamas off and starts to get dressed, helped by MRS HANKER.*)

ANNA: What have you to say for yourself this time?

MAURICE: I got the dates mixed up.

ANNA: I had a feeling you'd arrived tonight.

MRS HANKER: I had a feeling.

ALVIN: So did I.

MAURICE: I had a feeling I got in at ten o'clock.

ANNA: Why didn't you come straight here?

MAURICE: How was I to know where you were in the dark?

ANNA: Byeways.

MAURICE: But how to get there? Byeways aren't on the main road. They're off the beaten track.

ANNA: Byeways is on a road. Stroggen Hill Road. The drive is crazy paving and it leads to the road. The road is an ordinary public road. It ends at Byeways. It takes you there. All the way. You can't miss it.

MAURICE: If you've never been before, it's hard to find.

ANNA: It's not my fault you're not familiar with this area. You should have come before. Besides, as I was saying only this evening, you're not a child. You've travelled all over the world. I should have thought you'd have found your way here instinctively.

MAURICE: To tell the truth I was thirsty. I went for a drink.

MRS HANKER: He comes into the Junction, opposite Saxbys, you know.

ANNA: No.

MAURICE: The Junction.

MRS HANKER: In Jowett Street. You know, Alvin.

271

ALVIN: Yes. I know where you mean.

MRS HANKER: He knows where I mean.

MAURICE: I know where you mean.

MRS HANKER: We all know. Madam knows where I mean, but chooses to play dumb. She wants to be set apart from us.

ANNA: I know where you mean.

MRS HANKER: I knew you did.

MAURICE: I go into the Jowetts Arms.

MRS HANKER: The Junction Pub.

MAURICE: In Junkett Street.

MRS HANKER: Jowett Street. He has a drink and he asks his way to Stroggen Hill Road. Well, of course, up pricks my ears right away. There aren't many lives up this way and when he said Byeways I chips in, didn't I?

MAURICE: She chips in.

ALVIN: She's always chipping in.

MRS HANKER: I said, 'Excuse me, but did I hear you say Byeways?'

MAURICE: (*As in the pub.*) 'Yes.'

MRS HANKER: 'Off Stroggen Hill Road?'

MAURICE: 'Stroggen Hill, yes.'

MRS HANKER: 'I know precisely where that is.'

MAURICE: 'You'd better have a drink, then.'

MRS HANKER: 'Do you insist?'

MAURICE: 'Give her a drink.'

MRS HANKER: 'As I'm forced, I'll have a gin.'

MAURICE: 'One large gin.'

MRS HANKER: 'Who said large?'

MAURICE: 'I said large.'

MRS HANKER: 'Large it is.'

MAURICE: 'Anyone who knows where Stroggen Hill Road is must be worth a large one.'

MRS HANKER: 'Flatterer.' And I gave him his hat.

ANNA: You drank all night.

MRS HANKER: Till they closed, love.

MAURICE: From ten o'clock.

MRS HANKER: You should have come back with me to my house; then we'd have had none of this explaining to do.

MAURICE: Must see my little sister first.

MRS HANKER: Yes, well, now you've seen her, can't we go back to my place?

MAURICE: Let's ask.

MRS HANKER: (*To ANNA.*) Excuse me –

MAURICE: (*To ANNA.*) Excuse me –

MRS HANKER: Would you have any objection…
(*To MAURICE.*) Raise your hat.

MAURICE: Would you have any objection if I raised my hat?

MRS HANKER: If I went with this lady…

MAURICE: If this lady raised my hat.

MRS HANKER: This lady to her house.

MAURICE: Raised this lady to her hat.

MRS HANKER: House. Take this lady to her house.

MAURICE: Have this lady in her house.

ANNA: No objections.

MRS HANKER: Come on. Let's get moving. We could have gone there in the first place, avoided all this alibi-ing. Now we'll never hear the end of it. Tuck your shirt in and don't forget your hat.

MAURICE: I haven't got a hat.

MRS HANKER: Well, whose is it, then?

ANNA: He never wore a hat.

MRS HANKER: How was I to know? I never set eyes on him before.

ANNA: You'd better be quiet when you creep in together at Calcutta Street or you'll wake Mister Verity.

MRS HANKER: Oh, my God. You've hit it. Thanks for reminding me. The very reason I didn't want to take him back there in the first place. Two birds beating about the bush and I might end up with neither – one in the hand's well worth two you don't end up with.

MAURICE: Changed your mind?

MRS HANKER: My mind's like a bed. Once it's made up I get into it and stay there, tucked in at the edges and snug inside, quick as a flash.

MAURICE: Not too quick. I don't like to rush.

MRS HANKER: Whatever you say, we shall do.

ALVIN: I'm staying now, then?

MRS HANKER: Have you a spare bed for the night, dear? He's awfully tired, your brother.

ANNA: His room isn't ready yet.

MRS HANKER: We'll cope so long as there's a bed and blankets.

ANNA: If you'll kindly follow me. (*She goes to MAURICE's room.*)

ALVIN: You can't let them stay.

(*A red light comes on in MAURICE's room.*)

ANNA: If I send her away, she'll take you both with her. This way, please.

MRS HANKER: (*To MAURICE.*) Come on, kindly follow me. Steady. Mind, Alvin, we're coming through there.

ALVIN: No.

MRS HANKER: You wouldn't grudge your mother a bit of sex-making.

ALVIN: Not with Miss Bowers's brother.

MRS HANKER: Why not? You've had his sister.

ALVIN: Not tonight. She refused.

(*MRS HANKER and MAURICE go into the bedroom. ANNA returns.*)

ANNA: Here, blankets and pyjamas. You can sleep there.

ALVIN: Thank you.

ANNA: What time have you to be at work in the morning?

ALVIN: It's my Saturday off, I thought I said.

ANNA: I'll bring you some tea in the morning.

ALVIN: Thank you.

ANNA: Try and have a good night's sleep.

ALVIN: Yes, I will.

ANNA: You know where everything is?

ALVIN: Yes.

ANNA: Good night.

ALVIN: Good night.

(*He goes to the bathroom. ANNA peeps through the keyhole to MAURICE's room and gasps. The door opens. ANNA rushes to the living-room, followed by MRS HANKER in her slip.*)

MRS HANKER: What do you want?

ANNA: What will you do?

MRS HANKER: Comfort each other where we left off.

ANNA: Why do you do it?

MRS HANKER: The reality of sexual encounter gives my imagination a rest. I always say there's nothing so beautiful as feeling flooded right through by sexual experience with a man. And then, for a woman there's the added comfort of knowing you yourself are causing comfort – passing it on, like, in the process of receiving.

ANNA: You told him his father had died.

MRS HANKER: Yes, and he got a bit upset. The bereaved are always available for a bit of comfort. Stimulation's very good for it.

ANNA: Very well, I'll allow you to proceed on this occasion because I don't want to appear puritanical about the sexual impulse. I disapprove, but only of you doing it in my bungalow with my brother. I, too, need stimulation and comfort in these trying times and I'm just as capable of dispensing it as you are. In future I shall have priority.

MRS HANKER: I don't blame you. You've got a lovely brother. I'm very grateful, bless you, good night.

ANNA: Good night.

(*MRS HANKER goes back into the bedroom. ANNA feels sick and goes to the sideboard. DOCTOR FRANKLYN appears from ANNA's bedroom carrying his doctor's bag.*)

Thank you, Doctor Franklyn.

DOCTOR: Not at all.

ANNA: I'm sorry *you* had to come and see *me* but...

DOCTOR: Of course, I understand. Any time.

ANNA: I wasn't feeling too good, anyway.

DOCTOR: No. You might feel a bit off colour – dizzy from time to time, but don't worry. It passes. Just do what you did, in fact. Hop into bed with a warm drink and forget about the world.

ANNA: I didn't want to wait around in the surgery. People wonder what's wrong with you. You don't know who you might meet. If it's someone who knows you, they might ask what's the matter.

DOCTOR: Some patients ask whether they know you or not. They often ask me. I sometimes think that's all some of them come for, to find out who's got what. You might call it misplaced hypochondria on their part.

ANNA: Yes.

DOCTOR: Well. Is there anything you'd like me to do about it?

ANNA: Not for another six months.

DOCTOR: Oh yes. (*He sits.*) We shall call round before then, of course. I see. Well, have you any relations near at hand?

ANNA: Not in Hockton.

DOCTOR: Oh.

ANNA: They're in Donisthorpe.

DOCTOR: Will you be going to stay with them?

ANNA: I haven't decided yet.

DOCTOR: I ask because – and I don't want to alarm you – you're not a young woman; you could have a painful delivery.

ANNA: A bit of pain never hurt anyone.

DOCTOR: I thought it might be wise for you to have someone close to you when the time comes, for that extra bit of support and comfort.

ANNA: I'll manage.

DOCTOR: There's no chance of the father...

ANNA: No. No chance. I don't know who it was.

DOCTOR: Oh. Ah. I see. Well.

ANNA: I'll do all the things you said.

DOCTOR: One thing.

ANNA: What?

DOCTOR: Well – these days a woman in your position, I mean in your condition physically, of your age, from a health point of view alone – you understand – if I advised it.

ANNA: What?

DOCTOR: The hospital is allowed to perform the operation free – on the health scheme, that is.

ANNA: Oh, I know that.

DOCTOR: Quite a few of my unmarried patients have had it done.

ANNA: You mean abortion?

DOCTOR: Yes.

ANNA: Oh no. I wouldn't do that. I want to have it.

DOCTOR: Good. I'm glad.

ANNA: I want to know what it's like.

DOCTOR: I'm sure he or she will be a beautiful child.

ANNA: I meant I want to know what it's like to have it.

DOCTOR: Yes. It's quite an experience.

ANNA: You sound as though you've been through it yourself.

(*The DOCTOR chuckles.*)

I'm looking forward to it. It could be the making of me.

DOCTOR: Oh yes, indeed.

ANNA: Make or break.

DOCTOR: I'll call whenever you want me to. Just telephone.

ANNA: I'll send a message. I'm not on the phone.

DOCTOR: Of course. I forget.

ANNA: Good morning.

(*They shake hands.*)

DOCTOR: It's afternoon already.

ANNA: Is it. Good afternoon, then.

DOCTOR: Good afternoon, Miss…

ANNA: Goodbye.

DOCTOR: Goodbye, goodbye, goodbye, goodbye.

(*He leaves by the front door. ANNA locks it, moves the blankets and tidies the sofa. ALVIN comes from the bathroom, wearing pyjamas and carrying his clothes. He goes to ANNA's bedroom door, his back to the room. ANNA goes into the kitchen.*)

ALVIN: I've finished in the bathroom now. (*No reply.*) I had a bath as well. Was that alright? Hello? Good night.

(*He comes into the living-room, closes the door, turns out the light, puts his clothes on a chair, fixes his blankets on the sofa, takes off his socks and smells them, turns off the fire, opens the curtains, and settles down on the sofa. ANNA comes into the living-room.*)

ANNA: Good night.

ALVIN: Eh? Oh. I had a bath.

ANNA: I heard.

ALVIN: You don't mind?

ANNA: Course not.

ALVIN: Thank you.

   (*ANNA puts her hand out and lets it rest on ALVIN's shoulder.*)

   What's the matter?

ANNA: Nothing.

ALVIN: Are you feeling alright?

   (*ANNA kisses him on the forehead.*)

   Thank you.

ANNA: Good night.

ALVIN: Yes. Thank you. Good night.

ANNA: Good night.

   (*She goes to her room. ALVIN leans forward, listening, hears her door close, then sleeps.*)

   End of Act One.

ACT TWO

The same. The next morning.

ALVIN still on the sofa. ANNA is in the kitchen. Sparrows are heard, and a rook. A man whistles. Milk bottles rattle in a crate. ANNA comes into the living-room, picks up her purse, goes to the front door and opens it. The MILKMAN appears.

MILKMAN: Not a very nice day, is it? (*He steps inside.*)

ANNA: No.

MILKMAN: A trough of low pressure in the Midlands, the forecast said.

ANNA: Does that mean we're in for a deep depression?

MILKMAN: Something like that.

ANNA: I thought so.

MILKMAN: So long as the rain keeps off I'm happy.

ANNA: It won't get me down if it doesn't.

MILKMAN: That's right.

ANNA: Four and six?

MILKMAN: Please. (*He takes the money.*)

ANNA: And I'd like two pints until further notice.

MILKMAN: As and from today?

ANNA: Yes.

MILKMAN: Right.

ANNA: And a jar of cream now.

MILKMAN: Single?

ANNA: Double.

MILKMAN: Small?

ANNA: Large.

MILKMAN: Large. (*He takes cream from the crate and gives it to ANNA with the milk.*)

ANNA: I'll leave a note for eggs.

MILKMAN: Very good, thank you. Building yourself up for the winter?

ANNA: My brother's coming to stay for a while.

MILKMAN: Oh yes. Very nice. Two's company.

(*ALVIN comes from the living-room in his pyjamas. He yawns and goes into the bathroom.*)

(*To ALVIN.*) Morning!

ANNA: That's not him.

MILKMAN: Oh. Oh no.

ANNA: He's coming tonight.

MILKMAN: Ah, of course. I'll put these extras on next week's bill.

ANNA: Do.

MILKMAN: Right.

ANNA: Thank you.

MILKMAN: Good morning. (*He goes, whistling.*)

ANNA: Building myself up – damn cheek. (*Calling.*) The milkman saw you.

ALVIN: Eh? What did you say?

ANNA: Nothing. (*She puts the cream and one pint of milk on the hatch, her purse on the sideboard, then goes with the second pint to the garden door.*) Tim. Come on, Tim. Timmy-tim-tim. Meeow. Pussy pussy puss-puss. Come on, then. Dink o' milky. (*She bends down and pours milk into a saucer. She comes back into the room. She feels her breasts.*) I suppose I ought to build myself up. (*She sings the tune of 'Oh my baby' as she goes to the kitchen.*) 'Oh da-dee-dum, da-da-da-da-da-dee-dum. Da-dee-da-dee-da-dee-da-dee-da-dee-da-dee-da-de-oo-oo-oo, OO-OO-OO' –

(*MRS HANKER comes from MAURICE's room, feeding a baby from a bottle and picking up the song where ANNA left off – full-throated.*)

MRS HANKER: (*Entering the living-room.*)

'So loo-la-loo-la-loo-la-loo-la bye bye,

Do you want the moon to play with,

Or the stars to run away with?

They'll come if you don't cry.'

ANNA: (*Returning to the living-room.*) Where did you get that?

MRS HANKER: Oh, hello. You mean this demonstration model?

ANNA: Yes. Whose is it?

MRS HANKER: These things will happen.

ANNA: Not after one night.

MRS HANKER: After just one night.

ANNA: I don't believe you.

MRS HANKER: Please yourself. It's a fact. Here's the proof, sucking away. Come on, drink it all up – nearly gone. Sucky-sucky-sucky.

ANNA: Disgusting.

MRS HANKER: Lovely.

(*ALVIN comes from the bathroom still in pyjamas.*)

ANNA: Did you have a good sleep?

ALVIN: Yes, thank you.

ANNA: I'll get your breakfast. (*She lays a tablecloth.*)

ALVIN: I dreamt about you.

ANNA: Nightmares?

ALVIN: I dreamt I held on to you. I stepped off the pavement into the road, only it wasn't the kerb, it was a cliff, and to stop myself from falling I clung on to you.

ANNA: You do rather.

MRS HANKER: Must you talk to him like that?

ANNA: He's used to it.

MRS HANKER: It hurts his feelings.

ANNA: Pity. I dreamt I held on to Maurice.

MRS HANKER: I *did*. Whoops, slipped out, didn't you. Never mind, poppet. Here you are, pop it in again, in you go. It *is* a nice bit of rubber teat – isn't it lovely?

ANNA: Must you talk like that to him?

MRS HANKER: I'm used to it.

ALVIN: I'll say you are.

MRS HANKER: I can't help it if it's always slipping in and popping out, can I? No. They like it, don't they? Eh? Someone talking to them while they're eating.

ANNA: What would you like for breakfast?

ALVIN: Oh – anything.

MRS HANKER: Dynamic.

ANNA: Porridge?

ALVIN: Alright.

ANNA: Toast – bacon?

ALVIN: Thank you.

MRS HANKER: He usually has cornflakes and an egg.

ANNA: You could have an egg.

ALVIN: No, thank you.

ANNA: What do you usually have?

ALVIN: Bread and jam and shreddies.

    (*ANNA looks at MRS HANKER.*)

MRS HANKER: (*Putting the bottle on the table.*) Nobody's always right *all* the time. Shall we play patta-back now? Shall we? Yes. Come on then, ups and over.

ALVIN: What about you?

ANNA: I've had my breakfast.

MRS HANKER: There you are. (*She holds the baby over her shoulder.*) One two three pitta-patta-pitta-patta-pitta-patta –

ANNA: (*Taking the bottle to the kitchen.*) This house is too small for the three of us.

MRS HANKER: I'm in accordance with that.

ANNA: Why don't you join the navy and set sail?

ALVIN: My sense of duty keeps me here, tied hand and foot.

MRS HANKER: She doesn't want you staying here because you're supposed to as the other guilty half, you know. You must feel free to bugger off whenever you like – free as the driven wind as blows – whoops – there, he did one. She won't nail you down to obligations just for the one night. You're younger than her, you have a life of your own to live on the ocean wave exploring your fatal destiny. Go on, hop it. And why should you be forced to change your job to earn more money to buy a bigger house to live out the rest of your life in with a woman who's not fussy whether you do or not...?

    (*ANNA brings in his breakfast.*)

ALVIN: You talk as though I know about it.

MRS HANKER: What?

ALVIN: The baby.

MRS HANKER: You don't mean you haven't told him yet?

ANNA: If I tell him he'll practically force me into marriage.

    (*ALVIN eats.*)

MRS HANKER: Isn't that what you want, 'forcing'?

ANNA: Nobody's going to make me do anything against
  my will.

MRS HANKER: You've nothing to worry about then,
  have you?

ANNA: No. Unfortunately.

MRS HANKER: You're not likely to do any better, if you
  ask me.

ANNA: Oh shut up, nobody ever asks you if they can help it.

MRS HANKER: I'm not offended.

ANNA: I won't marry him.

ALVIN: I'd be uxorious.

ANNA: Not with me.

MRS HANKER: Oh, go on, dear, wed him for *me*. You'll
  get on. We all know the sexual aspect of nuptial
  arrangements is the least little part of it – with *some* men
  an infinitesimal portion, proportionately speaking, of
  that which is needed or sought after the first six weeks'
  hard bashing's over and done with. And I would just like
  to say this on behalf of all happy housewives listening in
  – namely we feel sure you both have all the excellent
  qualities needed to keep your ship of marriage away
  from the rocks of disillusion. And also, that even if you
  do get fed up in a few years' time you can always seek
  marriage guidance and advice from your fellow citizens.
  If that's no good you can indulge in mental cruelty for a
  bit to liven things up or have individual breakdowns or
  be unfaithful or reconciled or, in the last resort, divorced.
  There are various solutions before pension and death and
  despair set in for good. The main thing is so long as you
  enjoy these things together, as one flesh. And don't
  forget, I'm cradling your victim here. Offsprings are
  very good for interposing between parents in unhappy
  marriages and forcing them to stay together till they're
  all choked off. Asphyxiated with frustration.

ANNA: All this is premature. The baby isn't born yet.

MRS HANKER: That *is* a point.

ANNA: If I marry him before it is and something goes
  wrong before the delivery date, our marriage would be a

dead loss. I'd never be able to try again, being so old,
and Alvin would live on in wedlock, the last of his line.

MRS HANKER: That'd be no loss to evolution.

ANNA: He'd never know the joy of fatherhood.

MRS HANKER: You could adopt. There's plenty of
waiting lists.

ANNA: I wouldn't impose that as a condition. No. If the
baby's born alive and well, then I'll consider marrying
him, but if there's anything wrong with the child, if I
miscarry or have an abortion, then he has to promise to
leave me alone. I shall never want to see him again.
I never want to see him again.

MRS HANKER: It's a bargain. You can't ask fairer than
that, Alvin.

ALVIN: I could, but I wouldn't get anywhere.

MRS HANKER: Right. You're a red brick, Miss Bowers,
one of the old unglazed wire cuts. They don't make them
like that any more.

ALVIN: The porridge is nice.

ANNA: I put cream on it.

ALVIN: It's nice.

ANNA: There's more if you want it.

ALVIN: I'll see.

ANNA: I couldn't eat mine.

MRS HANKER: Now, Alvin, you must see she eats enough
for two.

ALVIN: You said you'd had breakfast.

ANNA: A biscuit – I felt a bit...

ALVIN: What?

MRS HANKER: Now's your chance. Tell him now.

ANNA: I didn't feel hungry.

MRS HANKER: You felt nauseous. Tell him nausea; you
felt nauseated because you're going to have his child.

ANNA: I felt – excited.

MRS HANKER: Nauseated.

ANNA: I was nearly sick this morning.

MRS HANKER: Morning sickness.

ALVIN: What for?

ANNA: Because Maurice is coming, I expect. I haven't seen him for seven years.

ALVIN: You look alright.

ANNA: I'm alright now.

MRS HANKER: How far gone are you?

ANNA: Three months.

MRS HANKER: Is that all!

ANNA: Seems like ten.

MRS HANKER: Of course, he'll never be right if he's bottle fed. Little boys prefer the breast.

ANNA: At that age?

ALVIN: I've had enough porridge, thank you.

ANNA: There's a bacon sandwich under the grill.

ALVIN: I'll get it, thank you. (*He picks up his plate and is about to go into the kitchen.*)

MRS HANKER: Here, grab hold and present him with it now as a matter of fact.

(*ANNA takes the baby and holds it out awkwardly to ALVIN.*)

ALVIN: What's that for?

ANNA: Us.

MRS HANKER: It's your mother's grandchild, dear. You're a proud father.

ALVIN: Does he look like me?

MRS HANKER: He's a bit like your dad about the mouth.

ANNA: He dribbled a lot, did he?

MRS HANKER: I'll say. All snot and dribble.

ALVIN: What's his name?

MRS HANKER: Harry.

ANNA: Harry's an ugly name.

MRS HANKER: He's an ugly baby.

(*ALVIN takes the bowl into the kitchen.*)

ANNA: He takes after you.

MRS HANKER: Your photo gives the lie to that.

ANNA: Beauty is skin deep.

MRS HANKER: And ugliness goes a lot deeper.

ANNA: You should know.

MRS HANKER: I'm not here to argue and abuse.

ANNA: (*Going to fetch her coat.*) I must think of a different name. It could be a girl. (*She puts on the coat.*)

MRS HANKER: Had I been born a little boy child I would have been a Harry. It's the only drawback I have. When I shall be asked at the last judgement to repent, to own up to the one bad thing in all my life and take it back, that one big regret would be that I had only been just a little girl from birth and not just a little boy as well. (*She goes into the hall.*)

ALVIN: (*Returning to the living-room.*) What have you got your coat on for?

ANNA: I'm going shopping. You stay here. I won't be long. If you go before I get back, just drop the latch on the door.

ALVIN: I expect I'll still be here, if that's alright with you. It's Saturday.

ANNA: (*Going to the kitchen for her shopping-bag.*) As you like. Alvin…

ALVIN: What?

ANNA: What's your favourite name?

ALVIN: I haven't got one.

ANNA: You must have.

ALVIN: No.

ANNA: Supposing you got married and your wife had children. You'd have to choose names for them.

ALVIN: I'd leave it to her.

ANNA: Supposing she didn't have any favourite names either?

ALVIN: Well – they call children after your relations, don't they?

ANNA: Why were you called Alvin?

ALVIN: My dad wanted me to be sensitive.

ANNA: He overdid it.

MRS HANKER: (*With her coat on in the hall.*) He's too sensitive to wipe his own arse.

ANNA: What was your father called?

ALVIN: Derek.

ANNA: Suppose you had a daughter?

ALVIN: I've got an Aunt Edna.

ANNA: I've got an Aunt Milly.

MRS HANKER: You'll not have a girl.

ANNA: I might have one of each.

MRS HANKER: If you're going off out shopping, come on.

ANNA: I shan't be long.

(*She goes into the hall. MRS HANKER opens the front door.*)

Mrs Hanker...

MRS HANKER: Yes, love?

ANNA: There are many great men whose names begin with H.

MRS HANKER: Such as Cuthbert.

ANNA: Hector.

MRS HANKER: Humphrey.

ANNA: Hadrian.

MRS HANKER: Horace.

ANNA: Horatio.

MRS HANKER: Herbert.

ANNA: Hypolitus.

MRS HANKER: Houdini.

ANNA: Homer.

MRS HANKER: Hamlet.

ANNA: Hieronymous Bosch.

MRS HANKER: Henry the eigth.

ANNA: And – Harry.

MRS HANKER: I thought you'd come round.

(*They link arms and leave by the front door.*)

ALVIN: (*Sitting on the sofa.*) How should I know what to call babies? I wonder why she asked for? Perhaps she's having one. Perhaps she's having mine, then. I did try, briefly.

(*MRS HANKER enters from the spare room, goes into the living-room, sits at the table, and pours herself a cup of tea.*)

MRS HANKER: What time do you call this?

ALVIN: Saturday morning.

MRS HANKER: Where've you been?

ALVIN: Stroggen Hill.

MRS HANKER: Miss Bowers.

ALVIN: Byeways, yes.

MRS HANKER: You slept there.

ALVIN: Yes.

MRS HANKER: Coming on, aren't you?

ALVIN: Not really.

MRS HANKER: It's about time, mind you.

ALVIN: She's going to have a baby.

MRS HANKER: Whose?

ALVIN: Mine.

MRS HANKER: Congratulations. When's the happy day?

ALVIN: A long time, I'd say. Six months about or else
when she starts to get big enough, you know, around the
proper time.

MRS HANKER: I didn't mean when is she having her
happy day delivering. If I had I'd have said when's the
happy event. What I meant was, when do you come out
of the cathedral as one flesh? I must know, I have to buy
the rice to pelt you with like confetti.

ALVIN: Why pelt me?

MRS HANKER: To express the vehemence of my joy at
getting shut of you out from under my feet.

ALVIN: Can't you buy those little bits of coloured paper
and just gently toss it at us?

MRS HANKER: Don't change the subject.

ALVIN: What was it?

MRS HANKER: I asked you to name the day.

ALVIN: Oh – well, that's the thing.

MRS HANKER: Crucial.

ALVIN: The important thing.

MRS HANKER: The most.

ALVIN: That's the thing you see, the one thing, just the
thing, the very thing, the main thing, the big thing,
the thing –

MRS HANKER: What is, what thing, who's thing, which
bloody thing are you talking about?

ALVIN: She doesn't want to marry me.

MRS HANKER: She what!

ALVIN: That's it. That's the thing.

MRS HANKER: She won't 'not marry' you. Over my dead
body she won't. She'll make a respectable married man
of you or I'll sue her on your behalf for breach of pre-

marital relations. She got herself into trouble, thanks to you; she must pay the consequences and make it legal. A wife only owns half in the eyes of the law, you know, and the husband gets the other half. Think of your good name.

ALVIN: Alvin's a bad name to start with.

MRS HANKER: It'll be worse if she doesn't marry you. Mine too. Your bad name'll drag mine down with it. Alvin dirt and Ivy mud it'll be. I'm not having a bastard for a grandchild. What would Mrs Raistrick be able to say? No fear. You kept your side of the bargain getting her in the family way; now it's up to her to do the right thing by you. Your chances are ruined if she doesn't. You'll be looked down on as second-hand goods, another woman's cast-off. No girl'll marry a chap who's been in trouble. You'll never hold your head up again.

ALVIN: You encouraged me. (*He starts to fold up the blanket.*)

MRS HANKER: I never said be careless.

ALVIN: I shan't do it with anyone else ever.

MRS HANKER: That's a good lad. Loyal and faithful to your heart's desire, like your mother would be, given half the chance.

ALVIN: You make sure you're not.

MRS HANKER: It's only 'cos the lodgers don't stay that I'm obliged to change horses in mid-stream.

ALVIN: You see they're not long between the shafts.

MRS HANKER: Don't. I'll not be criticised for avoiding monotony. A mother's always right.

ALVIN: Why don't you go up and see Miss Bowers for me? Tell her off, not me. Tell her she's got to marry me. Oh. But you can't tell her she's going to have a baby. She doesn't know yet. I made it up.

MRS HANKER: How can I blackmail her, then?

ALVIN: I've never known you stuck for an argument.

MRS HANKER: Flatterer. Why don't you tell her to marry you.

ALVIN: She'd laugh and say no straight away.

MRS HANKER: You mean to stand there in your pyjamas and tell me you haven't proposed yet?

ALVIN: I daren't.

MRS HANKER: What's to be afraid of?

ALVIN: She might say she would. (*He piles the dishes on the tray.*)

MRS HANKER: You'd be daft not to marry her. She's not without a bit in the bank, I dare say, and that bungalow must be worth a three thousand pound mortgage. You could sell off the garden as a couple of plots and make a fortune. Your mother knows what side to butter bread. Put your heart where the money is.

ALVIN: But she doesn't want it.

MRS HANKER: Every woman wants it. It's up to the man to make them want it. Put your foot down.

ALVIN: I have done.

MRS HANKER: And?

ALVIN: She tells me to go home. (*He takes the tray to the kitchen.*)

MRS HANKER: Well, if you will do it in your stocking feet, of course she'll refuse you. Buy a pair of clogs or a club boot. Make her jump when you bring it down. No woman ever resisted an insisting man eventually.

ALVIN: But mother – please – listen, please – try and help me… (*He puts on his socks and shoes.*)

MRS HANKER: Yes, love.

ALVIN: You see, if I'm like you say and bang my foot down and have my way, I'll have to ignore her feelings.

MRS HANKER: That's right.

ALVIN: I'll have to hurt her.

MRS HANKER: Yes.

ALVIN: She might cry.

MRS HANKER: Hit her.

ALVIN: She might laugh at me.

MRS HANKER: Hit her harder.

ALVIN: She might hit me back.

MRS HANKER: Hit her till she bleeds.

ALVIN: You mean hurt her?

MRS HANKER: Right.

ALVIN: It seems wrong.

MRS HANKER: If things weren't like that you'd never get anywhere. And you must. A man must get on in life. Evolution says so. He must rise up and overcome with deliberate malice. Stand astride on his mighty feet and bash his way into the gates of paradise, revenging himself for his predicament on all the obstacles that block his way.

ALVIN: Even if he's wounded and bleeding?

MRS HANKER: Even if he's crippled and dying.

ALVIN: Even if he cries?

MRS HANKER: Men's tears are salty.

ALVIN: What if he doesn't want to?

MRS HANKER: Any man worth his salt *can't* not want to.

ALVIN: I'd like to be salt worthy, but I don't want to cause pain.

MRS HANKER: You won't see or feel it if you bash on selfishly regardless.

ALVIN: I don't want to get hurt.

MRS HANKER: How can glory hurt you?

ALVIN: Well – you know I'm not circumcised.

MRS HANKER: So what?

ALVIN: It hurts me when the skin's pulled back.

MRS HANKER: You're supposed to enjoy that.

ALVIN: I don't, though.

MRS HANKER: That's the mystery of life rearing its ugly head, uniting all the universe in spectacular sensation.

ALVIN: I don't like pain.

MRS HANKER: You've got to get used to pain, love. You'll never be a man if you don't stop wincing. Grit your teeth and establish yourself.

ALVIN: But why must I have to be forced against myself?

MRS HANKER: Nature does it with all living things. Most people don't have this trouble you know. They just pretend they're in love and imagine they're using their instincts to achieve their own ends. They tell themselves it's just human nature and get round the inexplicable that way. Can't you pretend you're in love, love?

ALVIN: You mean hoodwink myself into taking being hurt for granted, as though pain was natural.

MRS HANKER: I don't know what you mean – pain.
Just enjoy it, relish it.

ALVIN: (*Folding the tablecloth and putting it in the sideboard.*)
It's not enough. I have to know what it's all for.

MRS HANKER: You're never satisfied.

ALVIN: No, I'm not, that's right enough.

MRS HANKER: You know I want your satisfaction as well
as anybody's.

ALVIN: They should give you lessons at school. What to
do and how to be. Boys and girls.

MRS HANKER: If they did I might get a job demonstrating
with the headmaster. I should qualify as headmistress.

ALVIN: You wouldn't like our headmaster.

MRS HANKER: So long as I got paid.

ALVIN: I tried to learn by watching you at it through the
keyhole. I never learnt a thing.

MRS HANKER: Are you insinuating I put up a bad show?

ALVIN: I never saw details, so I couldn't say.

MRS HANKER: I guarantee one good dekko would have
opened your eyes.

ALVIN: It's easy for women, they just have to be softies and
not do anything. It's always the man has to be hard and
go first.

MRS HANKER: Step back. You come second.

ALVIN: If at all.

MRS HANKER: I'll learn you. I'll gladly volunteer on
your behalf.

ALVIN: What for?

MRS HANKER: To set an example for you to emulate.

ALVIN: I can emulate on my own without your help
thank you.

MRS HANKER: No you can't. It takes two to emulate
properly. That's where I come in. That's what mothers
are for. Now. How about I'll be your guinea-pig?
Substitute me for the real thing and I'll observe and tell
you where you go wrong.

ALVIN: How do you mean?

MRS HANKER: Propose to me in her absence as though
she's here in my place. (*Taking up a pose with a magazine.*)

I am thumbing my way through this magazine when you decide. Go on. Decide.

ALVIN: (*Kneeling beside MRS HANKER.*) I have a proposal to make.

MRS HANKER: No wonder you're rejected.

ALVIN: Why?

MRS HANKER: You make yourself look obsolete.

ALVIN: Where do I go wrong?

MRS HANKER: They don't kneel down to it these days. That went out with the Bible.

ALVIN: How did my dad do it to you?

MRS HANKER: He didn't. I did. 'You're looking at the future Mrs Hanker,' I said.

ALVIN: 'You're looking at the future Mrs Hanker.'

MRS HANKER: *You* can't say it. She's the candidate for name changing, not you.

ALVIN: How would you do it?

MRS HANKER: I'd frame myself.

ALVIN: Show me. (*He pulls MRS HANKER into position.*) Go on. You know so much about it. Give me a lesson. (*He takes up the magazine.*) I know how to be her. I'm thumbing my way through this magazine like a guinea-pig when you come up to me with a decision.

MRS HANKER: Anna.

ALVIN: What?

MRS HANKER: Look at me.

ALVIN: I'm reading.

MRS HANKER: I asked you to look at me.

ALVIN: I'd rather not.

MRS HANKER: Look into my eyes.

(*ALVIN is persuaded to look at MRS HANKER. He laughs. She slaps him across the face. He is stunned.*)

Don't laugh till I've finished what I have to say.

ALVIN: I can't hit her.

MRS HANKER: We're getting married.

ALVIN: She'll say no.

MRS HANKER: I said, we're getting married.

ALVIN: Once I'm married I'll never be anything else.

MRS HANKER: You're going to be married.

ALVIN: She won't.

MRS HANKER: I can't live without you.

ALVIN: I can, though.

MRS HANKER: You know I'm lying, but you'll believe me because I'm persuading you by looking into your eyes and showing you the desire that only you can satisfy. The passion you can't afford to miss, this week's special offer while stocks last.

ALVIN: She'll look away.

MRS HANKER: I'm taking you in hand.

ALVIN: I've tried.

MRS HANKER: Bending you to my will.

ALVIN: I can't say that.

MRS HANKER: I'm determined.

ALVIN: So's she.

MRS HANKER: From whence cometh my strength? My strength cometh from you and I'm giving it back to you.

ALVIN: Aw, Mam.

MRS HANKER: I'm feeding you with my hunger and thirst.

ALVIN: Don't, Mam.

MRS HANKER: You'll be hungry and thirsty and my kisses alone will quench your appetite. You're famished, parched and dry. You're trembling on the brink of collapse… (*She kisses her hypnotised son.*) There you are, you see. Just dominate. It's easy if you persevere.

ALVIN: She won't agree to any of that.

MRS HANKER: You mean you haven't got my magnetism.

ALVIN: You'll have to see her yourself, then.

MRS HANKER: Very well. Stand aside, behind me.

(*They stand in the living-room doorway. ANNA appears, wearing a summer frock, carrying a magazine and a flower, then sits on the sofa.*)

ANNA: What do you want?

ALVIN: I've told my mother about you.

MRS HANKER: I expect you know why I'm here.

ANNA: To fight for your son. He can't fend for himself.

MRS HANKER: Because you've trifled with his affections.

ANNA: I'm the one who's been trifled with.

MRS HANKER: Listen you, I'm here to ask for my son's hand in marriage.

ANNA: He knows I won't accept.

MRS HANKER: If you refuse once more, I shall ejaculate.

ANNA: I'd better give my consent, then.

MRS HANKER: When's it to be?

ANNA: Three weeks from today at the registry office.

MRS HANKER: I thought you'd be against the match?

ANNA: Not at all. I'm thrilled to bits. You'll be very good for each other. Just what he needs, a mother to look after him. Excuse me now, won't you? I have to thumb through this magazine.

(She gets up, joins ALVIN and MRS HANKER's hands together, presents MRS HANKER with the flower, then leaves. They watch her go, then look at each other blankly.)

ALVIN: Now look what you've done.

MRS HANKER: I thought she agreed in a hurry.

ALVIN: I told you it was no use.

MRS HANKER: Never mind. If at first you don't win, try again. You stay here. I'll see what I can do a second time on my own. Don't go away. *(She goes after ANNA.)*

ALVIN: Don't come back. She's useless. *(He takes a photo from the album on the sideboard and addresses it.)* You could teach me. I have confidence in you. You look it, smiling at the camera, unblinking in the sun. If I could watch you, go about with you, maybe join your ship, go to sea with you... I could learn abroad where nobody speaks the language, then I wouldn't say the wrong things. I'll have to get you alone and ask you. Make up some lies and find out how to get with you. I'll have to be quick about it.

FEMALE ANNOUNCER: Will the train now standing in platform two please go to the stationmaster's office where a lost little boy will be found waiting for it.

(MAURICE appears below the living-room and remains downstage. He carries a rucksack and raincoat slung over his shoulder, but wears his bathing-suit, as in the photo.)

ALVIN: Excuse me. Aren't you Maurice Bowers?

MAURICE: Hello. Yes, I am.

ALVIN: Hello.

MAURICE: How did you know?

ALVIN: I'm Alvin Hanker.

MAURICE: Oh, I see.

ALVIN: (*Preventing MAURICE leaving.*) I know your sister. She gave me this picture. Don't walk.

MAURICE: I'm trying to get away from you.

ALVIN: You can't – I collect the stamps you stick on your letters. You know about me.

MAURICE: Of course I do.

ALVIN: I was just enquiring about the times of some trains, when they leave and arrive, and as I saw you I thought you looked like your photograph. I always happen to have this copy with me.

MAURICE: It's not very like me.

ALVIN: That's because I don't know you in the flesh.

MAURICE: That's why you came to meet me, isn't it?

ALVIN: Yes, I did. I came to recognise you and tried to make it look like an accident.

MAURICE: Why didn't Anna come?

ALVIN: I had to see you alone; I've wanted to for a long time.

MAURICE: Is Anna alright?

ALVIN: I want to talk to you about some things.

MAURICE: I half expected her to meet me.

ALVIN: Maurice Bowers…!

MAURICE: What?

ALVIN: I want to talk to you about my sex. I have to find out. You have to show me.

MAURICE: On the platform?

ALVIN: In private.

MAURICE: You're too young. (*He moves away, into the living-room.*)

ALVIN: (*Following.*) Thank you for the stamps.

MAURICE: My sister's waiting for me.

ALVIN: You're too early. Come with me to my house; it's very near. My mother's there, but she'll cook you

something – and there's my room. We can go into my
room and I can talk and ask and listen and watch the
answers you show me, if you like – and later – if you
like – we can go to the pictures, a musical film, and then,
if you like, we could go to a public house – I know you
like beer – and then, if you like, I'll take you up to
Byeways. To Stroggen Hill Road, where your sister lives.

MAURICE: Alright.

ALVIN: You'll like my mother.

MAURICE: How old is she?

ALVIN: Oh – between about thirty-odd and sixty-some.

MAURICE: How old are you?

ALVIN: I vary.

MAURICE: Sixteen?

ALVIN: Oh no, I'm a lot older than that before I start to vary.

MAURICE: How old?

ALVIN: I'm about twenty-four, or five, sometimes.

MAURICE: I thought you were.

ALVIN: Why did you say sixteen, then?

MAURICE: To make you blush.

ALVIN: I didn't, though.

MAURICE: You are now.

ALVIN: I'm hot. I'm sorry. All the fires are lit to warm the
house for when you get here.

MAURICE: It's charming. No need to apologise. I like it.
(*MRS HANKER appears from the spare room with her coat
and bag. She hangs her coat on the hall-stand.*)

ALVIN: I'm not hot. I do blush about my age level. I don't
know what to do about life, that's why, especially sex-
life. I know what to do about wild life and plant life at
different stages – but not my life at any time. That's why
I often go pink a lot quite easily.
(*MRS HANKER comes into the room, and is taken aback to
see MAURICE in his bathing-suit.*)

MRS HANKER: Oh, my God.

ALVIN: What is it now?

MRS HANKER: Spare my blushes... (*She puts her bag on the
sideboard.*)

ALVIN: (*To MAURICE.*) You'd better put your raincoat on. (*MAURICE does so.*)

MRS HANKER: Who is it?

ALVIN: Miss Bowers's brother, Maurice.

MRS HANKER: Travelling light, isn't he?

ALVIN: He's just got here from Spain.

MRS HANKER: Oh – very nice. Very hot, was it?

MAURICE: Sweltering.

MRS HANKER: Really – very nice. I'm glad you've brought your mac; you'll need it here.

ALVIN: He's just come up from Southampton.

MRS HANKER: Oh yes.

ALVIN: I met the train.

MRS HANKER: Oh. Very good, yes. I had one of my dizzy hot flushes when I saw you, but I've got the better of it now – for the moment, anyhow. (*Aside to ALVIN.*) Built like a prison wall, isn't he?

ALVIN: This is my mother.

MRS HANKER: How do you do, Mister Bowers. I'm Mrs Hanker. My husband's dead.

MAURICE: Pleased to meet you.

MRS HANKER: It's *Ivy* Hanker. (*She goes to MAURICE and shakes hands.*)

ALVIN: The clinging sort.

MRS HANKER: I was just saying to my son here, how much you resemble a prison wall. It's no wonder we jail birds are dreamers, for ever planning to escape. Solitarily confined as we are, sentenced to life imprisonment, each in our own little cells, is it small wonder we try to break loose? Many's the time I've knotted my sheets together in the early hours of the morning when the guards are asleep and crept out into the prison yard. There I've stood at your feet, looking up at your lofty granite front. Many a time I've climbed to the top in a bid for freedom, only to find, as I sit astride the spikes, there's nought but a sheer drop either way, back into nothing. A right let-down, as you might say. Still, you can't blame us for not trying; you've got to admire our pluck. One day we'll get away and be free. We'll get to the bottom of it.

ALVIN: Could you make some ham and eggs, please?

MRS HANKER: You can't be hungry.

ALVIN: He hasn't eaten on the journey.

MRS HANKER: (*To MAURICE.*) You must be ready for bed, I bet.

ALVIN: He's coming into my room with me.

MRS HANKER: Sleep's essential.

ALVIN: Did you see her wipe her hands on her apron?

MRS HANKER: I'll call you when it's ready.

ALVIN: We're going to talk heart to heart in my room.

MRS HANKER: I'll be in to join you directly.

ALVIN: We want to be left alone.

MRS HANKER: Speak for yourself. If Mister Bowers is not averse to my ham and eggs, he might like a bit of my company.

MAURICE: Not just now, thank you. (*Escorting MRS HANKER to the door.*) I'd rather be left alone with your son.

MRS HANKER: He's a problem child.

ALVIN: She's a big nuisance.

MRS HANKER: I'm a good cook, though. (*She leaves.*)

ALVIN: Thank you. I'm full of problems.

MAURICE: Don't break your heart. What's the most difficult trouble? In words of one syllable.

ALVIN: Yes. Well. That's it. There is one. I must tell you…

MAURICE: In monosyllables.

ALVIN: Yes. Plain and one at a time. One word on its own said one in front of the next, quite clear like steps in the snow, then you'll see them and the way I've gone and not lose me.

MAURICE: Good.

ALVIN: The plain thing, then, is this. I like her. She likes you. I'm not good at it. You are. I don't stay in her mind like you can. So you see? Where do I go wrong? Boys I went to school with don't. You don't. But I can't. I get hards on for her. And keep them up and keep up with them, too. They're a main part and some use, but not all. I take hards on in my stride as a must, just as they come. Life has its own ways and they're not for me to guess at. But when it boils down to the bloodstream as the one

thing in charge of you and what you are and do, I feel I
can't let it be that one thing. That's the thing, you see.
So where do I go wrong? Though I know my blood's in
charge and see there's no way round that, I still don't
think so, I have these grave doubts. As I'm not in charge,
I'm not free to feel free. Nor is she. I don't have faith in
the urge like you or my mam, so I must live on my own,
at a loss what to do for the best – or the worse, come to
that. I know I should want to make her let me make her
want me. All men do. And that's all I would ask, to be
the same as them. If I were her I'd know I'd have to want
to think I was forced to take things the way they were,
though I might not want to, for his sake. I'd know that
what I felt had not much to do with it in the long run but
that what he felt *did* and that I had to give in to that and
him, though I might not like him all that much, or he
me, that that was the law laid down from birth at the
start. That it was not right not to, that it would be wrong
not to in fact. But, in fact, when it comes to the point
with me, when I have to take things in hand, then I stop
– I don't want to go on. I can't want to. It seems wrong
to want to go on and yet just as wrong to stop 'cos I
know a man should press on. I see that. So where do I go
wrong? I've got to learn to cause pain and not stop and
not care or I'll be too late. I'll not know what it's like to
be in touch with the heartbeat, the pulse and the bloodstream that make up the rules for give and the laws of
take. Teach me. Once I know, I can't go wrong. I'll force
her till the pain gives way, and turn a blind eye. I'll
leave it at that. That will be all. Should it be? The girl,
hurt and put in charge of her needs by mine, the man,
male, and, lost for her to the end, gripped in the vice of
his own erection?

MAURICE: I can't answer for her.

ALVIN: I'll fake her if you show me.

MAURICE: Draw the curtains.

ALVIN: (*Doing so.*) I can't see to take notes in the dark, but
go slow in stages for me to remember and I'll write it
down after. Now – I want to know –

(*He shuts the kitchen door and the hatch, then wanders about the room. MAURICE follows, removing his mackintosh and ALVIN's pyjama top and putting them on the sofa.*)

– when to undress, what you have to say beforehand and whether I should undress first or second and should I leave the light on if it's dark or put it on if it's off and leave it or switch it out later on and if so when? Should I take her clothes off and if yes, how are they usually fastened and where, and if no, how should I wait till she has? Should I sit down on the bed or stand up and wait till she's ready, and, meanwhile, is it alright to watch? Should I hang them up or fold them with mine and how many times do you kiss and how long ought they to last and can I close my eyes and if I do, why? If she closes hers what does it mean? What is she thinking? Should I ask her? What do you say and ask in between and during? How do you know she'll like it if you put your tongue in her mouth and what can you do if she doesn't? How long should you leave it there if she does? What's the average length of time to allow for everything as a rule? Are you listening?

MAURICE: Yes – I'm listening.

ALVIN: What you doing?

MAURICE: (*Sitting ALVIN down and standing over him.*) Keep quiet. Students listen to learn. Do as I say.

ALVIN: Yes, alright.

MAURICE: First of all. You don't say anything about what you *want.* If you want the girl – don't say so, don't give her the *chance* to say no – or yes. And don't talk about anything else. Words are bad for the beginner, at the beginning. Now. I'm not a beginner, so I can chat to you. You're sitting there. You're a novice, let's say you've never been to bed with a man before, and you're wondering what it's like. You want to. Should you? She's sitting there, where you are, and you feel a warmth inside, abdominal warmth – Your blood flows slow. You wait. (*He unties ALVIN's pyjama bottoms.*) You're nervous. Your heart won't pump, and all the time you're listening

301

to me talking to her and she knows I'm the cause, I'm the reason you feel in such difficult trouble. Look at him, you are, you see he knows you're adrift. You stand up – (*ALVIN stands up, MAURICE lays his hand on his shoulder, and sits him down again.*)

– and my hand on her shoulder puts you back where you were. And your shoulder is small in my palm, like an emu's egg, and she lets him touch your throat – (*Carrying out his own directions.*) – and you feel – then – you feel his fingers at the side of your mouth move along to your ear and stay there for a time. Now her ear burns in the palm of my hand. He leans over from behind and takes hold of your wrist; lifting her fingers to his lips. You want to pull away – you do – and as your fingers were about to slip between his, he tightened his hold and trapped them. And now, he pulls your hand towards him and you have to stand up, though you pull away from him, you're drawn closer and closer and the closer you are the further you want to be. Say something. She's going to say something. She looks for a phrase, some words that will come between us but before they are put together and as you're about to speak he… (*He kisses ALVIN and then takes hold of his head.*) …and holding your head between his hands he takes control of your weakness and…

(*He kisses ALVIN again. ALVIN's pyjamas fall around his ankles. The kiss ends after some time.*)

ALVIN: Yes – I see. Thank you. (*He steps out of the pyjama bottoms and throws them onto the sofa.*) But what do you do if she pulls away and laughs at you?

MAURICE: But you didn't.

ALVIN: No. I didn't. I know. I'm only learning, though. One thing at once. Do it again. I'll do it this time. (*MAURICE kisses ALVIN once more. ALVIN tries to push him off, but gradually weakens and succumbs to the embrace. MAURICE breaks.*) It's not fair. You're stronger than me. You'd always be able to stop me pushing you off.

MAURICE: Your weakness overpowers me. I'm forced to go on.

ALVIN: Yes, I'm very weak. I have a very strong weak streak. That's why I can't hurt people properly.

MAURICE: Your weak side always holds you back.

ALVIN: Yes, it does. You haven't got one. Anyone can see you've been strong enough to hurt people since your very first orgasm. You knew straight away what was expected of you and grew up that way overnight. I bet you went to school the next day and had a stab at it without flinching. Picked a fight right left and centre, giving and taking it as good as you got. You might be a middleweight or a centre forward at first glance. There's no mistaking me like that. Not even if I wear football boots and boxing gloves.

MAURICE: Everyone has their weak side.

ALVIN: The trouble is with mine it overpowers my strong side. Perhaps you could teach me how to hurt people without feeling weak and hating myself. I'd always feel strong if I could do that once. I'd get on in life like I should. Yes. Just once would do me.

MAURICE: One more try, then. The third and last.

ALVIN: Kissing again?

MAURICE: With you pulling away and laughing at me.

ALVIN: Maybe. I'll try.

MAURICE: I might co-operate a bit more this time, help you a bit, let you push me off.

ALVIN: Yeah. Alright.

(*Once more they come together and kiss. After a short struggle ALVIN pushes MAURICE away. MAURICE stands a moment, waiting for ALVIN to laugh.*)

I don't want to hurt your feelings.

(*MAURICE chuckles and then starts to laugh uncontrollably at him.*)

Don't laugh at me. Please. There's nothing for you to laugh at.

MAURICE: You started me off.

ALVIN: I don't care.

MAURICE: I wouldn't mind going on with it either. Let's finish it off. It's a good game. Come on. Let's go into your room.

ALVIN: What for?

MAURICE: I like you. I fancy you. Come on.

ALVIN: No.

MAURICE: Please. Come on. We won't be long.

ALVIN: No. Let go.

MAURICE: I should have told you – I like a feller now and then, breaks the monotony.

ALVIN: You've been drinking.

MAURICE: I never have sex without a drink or two inside me first. Especially if I'm going with a woman.

ALVIN: What do you mean?

MAURICE: Well – don't tell anyone, but just between you and me, I prefer fellers to girls.

ALVIN: How can you do that?

MAURICE: Don't tell anyone.

ALVIN: You've told me.

MAURICE: Now we both know. It's our secret. If you don't tell anyone.

ALVIN: You mean all the time I was pretending to be a woman you weren't imagining I was?

MAURICE: No. Not in so many words.

ALVIN: How could you?

MAURICE: Easy. Come on. I'll show you. I'll straighten you out before Anna gets back.

ALVIN: No. Get off!

MAURICE: Oh no. No, no, not now. Too late. This way. Play your cards right, I'll fix you up. You'll like it.

ALVIN: No.

MAURICE: Yes – say yes to please me. Please yourself. Don't force yourself. I'll do that. Relax – I won't hurt you, promise – I really like you, see, you've got what it takes. I want you – smile...

(*He holds on to ALVIN, tantalising him with kisses. ALVIN pushes him away with tremendous force. MAURICE is thrown off balance. He turns away, cowering.*)

ALVIN: You filthy pig.

(*MAURICE slumps down.*)

Bastard. (*He spits at MAURICE.*) You dirty bastard.

(*MAURICE turns to look at ALVIN, who chuckles and then starts to laugh uncontrollably at him.*)

MAURICE: Don't laugh. Please. There's nothing to laugh at. You were the one who started it – you were the one. (*MRS HANKER breezes into the room carrying a plate of ham and eggs.*)

MRS HANKER: Ham and eggs for one. What's so funny?

ALVIN: Him.

MRS HANKER: What's this?

ALVIN: You can tip that in the dustbin.

MRS HANKER: What for?

ALVIN: We don't feed pigs in this house.

MRS HANKER: What's he done?

ALVIN: Never mind. (*He hurls MAURICE's bag at him.*)

MRS HANKER: What have you done to our Alvin?

ALVIN: Don't speak to him.

MRS HANKER: (*To ALVIN.*) What did you do?

ALVIN: Belted him once or twice. (*He opens the curtains.*)

MRS HANKER: His nose is bleeding.

ALVIN: He's bloody lucky that's all that is. Look, Mister Bowers, you're in a minority here. You know what I mean. Also. You're not wanted. So clear off before you get hurt some more. (*To MRS HANKER.*) You'd better take him or I'll put my knee in his groin. (*MRS HANKER goes forward.*) The back way. Don't foul up the front.

MRS HANKER: Come on, dear.

ALVIN: Mister Bowers.

MRS HANKER: Come on, Mister Bowers. You'd better do as he says.

ALVIN: Don't touch him. You'll need a bath if you do.

MRS HANKER: This way. (*MRS HANKER and MAURICE go into the spare room. The DOCTOR knocks on the front door. ALVIN pulls on his pyjama trousers back-to-front and hurries to open the front door.*)

DOCTOR: Ah – good morning.

ALVIN: Good morning.

DOCTOR: Doctor Franklyn.

ALVIN: Oh yes. You'd better come in.

DOCTOR: Thank you. Miss Bowers is at home, I take it?

ALVIN: Well – no, she isn't just at the moment, as a matter of fact.

DOCTOR: Oh – well there's no point in my coming in, then.

ALVIN: She won't be very long now, I should think. She just went to the shops. If you'd like to wait a few minutes.

DOCTOR: Oh no. If she's out and about, she must be feeling alright.

ALVIN: Has she been ill?

DOCTOR: Oh no, nothing out of the ordinary.

ALVIN: She looked alright when I got up.

DOCTOR: Did she? I see. Yes. Well, then, I'll be off.

ALVIN: She didn't have any breakfast, though.

DOCTOR: Oh.

ALVIN: Yes, that's right, she felt sick because she felt excited.

DOCTOR: That's only natural.

ALVIN: Because her brother's coming to see her.

DOCTOR: (*Going into the hall.*) Oh good. I'm glad she's seeing her relations.

ALVIN: (*Following.*) Shall I tell her to come and see you?

DOCTOR: Not unless she wants to.

ALVIN: Did she know you were coming to see her?

DOCTOR: No. I just happened to be visiting another patient not far down the road.

ALVIN: Oh.

DOCTOR: Er – I wonder if you could tell me what time it is. My watch is playing tricks.

ALVIN: Yes.

(*He goes back to the living-room and moves to within twelve inches of the clock face, on the wall, screwing his eyes up to see. The DOCTOR takes a step into the room, watching him.*)

It's five past eleven.

DOCTOR: Really.

ALVIN: I overslept. (*He picks up the raincoat and puts it on.*) Excuse me.

DOCTOR: You had a late night, I expect.

ALVIN: Not all that late. I got hot with this on.

DOCTOR: Do you wear glasses, by the way?

ALVIN: Glasses?

DOCTOR: To read, perhaps?

ALVIN: No, I've never worn glasses.

DOCTOR: I ask because you seemed to have to go very close to the clock to tell the time.

ALVIN: Oh.

DOCTOR: Can you tell the time from here?

ALVIN: (*Looking back at the clock.*) It's five past eleven.

DOCTOR: But can you see that it is?

ALVIN: No. I can see it's a clock, though.

DOCTOR: You're short-sighted.

ALVIN: Am I?

DOCTOR: Indeed. Who's your doctor?

ALVIN: I don't know.

DOCTOR: Might I suggest you find out and pay him a visit at once. He'll test your vision and fix you up. Will you do that?

ALVIN: Yes.

DOCTOR: If you're not on a GP's register, ask Miss Bowers to send you along to me on Monday evening, say. Here's my address. (*He gives ALVIN a card.*) And how long have you been short-sighted?

ALVIN: You just told me.

DOCTOR: Yes.

ALVIN: Since just now.

DOCTOR: You've not been aware of any difficulty?

ALVIN: Not about my eyes.

DOCTOR: Oh – you sound as though you have some other complaint.

ALVIN: Yes. I do have, but I don't think doctors can do anything for it.

DOCTOR: (*About to go.*) There's very little medical science can't cope with these days.

ALVIN: It's a sexual problem.

DOCTOR: Sexual. Oh. In what way?

ALVIN: I don't know how to put it.

DOCTOR: You can speak quite freely with me.

ALVIN: Thank you, but I'd rather not.

DOCTOR: (*Returning and sitting.*) It hasn't by any chance got anything to do with Miss Bowers, has it?

ALVIN: In a way. (*He sits.*)

DOCTOR: Oh. Then perhaps I can help you.

ALVIN: Oh...?

DOCTOR: At least, offer you my advice.

ALVIN: Yes, I like advice, I need it.

DOCTOR: Marry her.

ALVIN: Oh.

DOCTOR: That's the right thing to do in the circumstances.

ALVIN: Oh.

DOCTOR: Marriage solves many a problem besides.

ALVIN: I see.

DOCTOR: Yes, if you don't make it legal you'll never be happy. You want to be able to hold your head up, don't you?

ALVIN: Yes.

DOCTOR: Mark my words, I've seen couples who've tried to make a go of things outside the bonds of matrimony and it's never worked; one or other of them has always ended up in the gutter.

ALVIN: Oh.

DOCTOR: You see, they don't have the necessary respect for each other. And you won't get any from the community either unless you're legally united.

ALVIN: I see.

DOCTOR: No. From a tax point of view they're better off, but that's a mercenary consideration, unworthy of you both and outside your terms of reference, I'm sure.

ALVIN: It would be, I should think.

DOCTOR: For the child's sake, too. A child needs a stable house with a respectable well-defined relationship existing between the parents.

ALVIN: Yes.

DOCTOR: Marry her and the three of you will be much happier with the consent and goodwill of society behind you all the way. Oh yes.

ALVIN: Thank you.

DOCTOR: Not at all. Glad you mentioned it. I wouldn't have said anything if you hadn't intimated. It doesn't take much of a Sherlock Holmes to put two and two together.

ALVIN: No.

DOCTOR: Don't worry. That's the main thing. Many of my patients are obliged to take me into their confidence. They do so without hesitation, knowing they have my discretion and sympathy in return.

ALVIN: Thank you.

DOCTOR: (*Rising.*) Well, my boy – by the way, what's your name?

ALVIN: (*Rising.*) Alvin, Mister Alvin Hanker.

DOCTOR: So, Mister Hanky, I shall hope to see you on Monday evening. We'll look into your eyes then, unless of course you make other arrangements. Believe me, to lose your eyesight could be a far greater problem for you in life than anything that may be causing you anxiety now. You must attend to them right away. It would be doubly short-sighted of you not to – if you'll excuse the aptness of the cliché.

ALVIN: Oh yes.

DOCTOR: Well, Mister Hanky.

ALVIN: Hanker.

DOCTOR: I'm very glad we've met. Fortuitous, I think, is the word, in more ways than one. You'll doubtless tell Miss Bowers I called.

ALVIN: Yes.

DOCTOR: Good morning.

ALVIN: Thank you.

DOCTOR: Good morning.

ALVIN: Good morning.

(*The DOCTOR leaves through the front door. ALVIN sits on the sofa. ANNA comes from her room into the living-room. She is eight months pregnant. She stands in the doorway.*)

ANNA: Alvin.

ALVIN: Yes?

ANNA: You know your breakfast…

ALVIN: Yes.

ANNA: I wouldn't ask you normally.

ALVIN: Go on.

ANNA: If it weren't for the bending.

ALVIN: What about my breakfast?

ANNA: In future you can get your own.

ALVIN: I thought so.

ANNA: The kitchen's too small.

ALVIN: You're too big, you mean.

ANNA: I won't be when I've had it.

ALVIN: You wouldn't be when you get rid of it, either.

ANNA: I'm keeping it.

ALVIN: The world's overcrowded as it is. People take up too much room.

ANNA: That's why the kitchen's too small. The trays I prepare won't fit on the draining-board when I'm sticking out like this. They can't overhang when I do. There are by-laws and basic standards laid down by the local council forbidding housewives to go below a certain level.

ALVIN: You sunk below it some time ago.

ANNA: Now that you're responsible for me you could get a summons.

ALVIN: You're not married yet, you know.

ANNA: Meaning?

ALVIN: Don't push your luck.

ANNA: You will marry me?

ALVIN: If I don't?

ANNA: You must.

ALVIN: I will, then. If I must, I must.

ANNA: When?

ALVIN: Eager, aren't you?

ANNA: I'd just like to know.

ALVIN: I'm not good at making decisions.

ANNA: I thought you wanted to marry me.

ALVIN: I didn't know you were pregnant.

ANNA: I thought this would happen, that's why I didn't tell you.

ALVIN: (*Starting to get dressed.*) And I thought there was something funny about you, keeping me at a distance. You thought you'd be more sure of me if you played hard to get.

ANNA: Think that if you want to.

ALVIN: Oh yes, I can think what I like now it doesn't make any difference. Now I'm forced to marry you – don't pretend I'm not. I know I shall have to. You do look a mess. Imagine sleeping with you every night. I'd need to have pleasant dreams and even if I did they'd be nightmares when I woke up and turned over to face you. If you get much bigger you won't fit in the bathroom, never mind the kitchen. Oh – and by the way – since we got married last week and since your filthy brother decided to stay at home to look after his big, puffed-up sister, I'm leaving you both to it.

ANNA: You can't go away.

ALVIN: I can though.

ANNA: Alvin!

ALVIN: I thought you'd be pleased – alone with your big brother at last.

ANNA: (*Kneeling.*) No, please, see, as I go down awkwardly on my bended knees to implore you.

ALVIN: I can't live in the same house with my brother-in-law.

ANNA: I'll send him away.

ALVIN: If anyone gets out, it's me.

ANNA: No, no.

ALVIN: Anyway – you're too late. I've arranged to take his place, on his ship. Log book, vaccination marks, passport, all done legal. I'm joining his ship at Southampton on Wednesday. Cash on delivery. I've already kissed my mam goodbye. I haven't got very long before I have to catch the train I'm meeting. So, excuse me won't you, dear, while I put on something more suitable for life on board ship. I'll have to hurry. I don't want to be here when you get back if I can help it.

ANNA: Alvin – don't think things like that.

311

ALVIN: You do.

ANNA: Can't you see you're killing me.

ALVIN: I can't feel anything.

(*ANNA has a birth pang which ALVIN also feels. She collapses onto the sofa.*)

ANNA: Maurice.

(*MAURICE hurries in to help ANNA up.*)

It hurts.

MAURICE: It's supposed to. Come on. Come and lie down. The doctor's on his way. Everything's ready.

ANNA: Not today. Not now. Not yet.

MAURICE: Probably. You never know. If it has to be now, you can't stop it. Nearly there. Mrs Hanker has everything ready and waiting. Lots of hot towels. You'll be alright. It'll all be over in a twinkling.

ANNA: I hope so.

(*MRS HANKER comes from ANNA's room.*)

MRS HANKER: I'll take over now. Come along, dear. Nurse Harriet'll see to you. That's right. One in front of the other. Left, right. Didn't I tell you not to get up?

(*ANNA and MRS HANKER go into ANNA's bedroom. MAURICE faces ANNA's door. The clock chimes. MAURICE returns to the living-room. ALVIN finishes dressing.*)

MAURICE: How do you like it, then – being at sea?

ALVIN: Great, great.

MAURICE: Lucky you're home just as the baby's being born.

ALVIN: I didn't expect it to be yet.

MAURICE: Neither did anyone else. She's three weeks early. The doctor said it was too risky to take her to the hospital. She didn't want to go, anyway. Your mother's been very helpful.

ALVIN: Has she.

MAURICE: She's been coming up every day now for the last four weeks. Bringing things she's cooked, pies, cakes and shopping.

ALVIN: I didn't want to come up, I can tell you. I wasn't going to after what happened that weekend you came home. I've had enough of this place. Especially after sailing about for the last five months. It's bloody awful coming back to this dump after being with the lads, larking about in the places we've been, I can tell you. Course, you've been, I don't need to tell you.

MAURICE: Yeah. I've been to most places.

ALVIN: I needn't have come up if the silly bitch had left the key. I lost mine – huh – that was a night. We all got pissed. We had this great piss-up in a bar called the Black Panties. Black Panties! My mate, Len, got right pissed, worse than any of us and we dared him to have a couple of bluebirds tattooed on his tits, one on each, in a cubicle behind the bar. Huh – he passed out before the bloke had finished the second one, so he's got one bluebird, the left one, diving for his tit without a beak or a head on, just the body and the wings and tail, but no head. On board next day I said to him, 'Show us your tits then, Len, huh' – you should have seen his face when he saw it. I said 'Well, where were you last night? You must have been with a right hungry tart,' I said; 'she's made a meal of you; she's bitten your bluebird's head off, it's a wonder you've got a left tit left.' A great piss-up.

(*A baby cries in ANNA's room.*)

MAURICE: Sounds like you're a father.

ALVIN: Yeah.

MAURICE: What do you say? Boy or girl?

ALVIN: I couldn't care less. As long as I don't have to look after it.

(*MAURICE goes towards the hall. ALVIN stops him.*)

Eh – don't tell her I'm here, will you. I don't want her to be hurt or upset. She might be when she sees me. Tell her I'll call up tomorrow, or before I have to leave anyway. I'm here for five days.

MAURICE: Won't she be more upset if she knows you've been and gone away without seeing her and the baby?

ALVIN: That's not my funeral, is it?

MAURICE: I won't say you've been here, then.

ALVIN: Oh yeah. That's best, then I won't need to come up at all.

(*MAURICE goes into ANNA's bedroom. ALVIN rummages
through his mother's handbag, looking for the key. MRS
HANKER comes from the bedroom, cradling the baby in
her arms.*)

MRS HANKER: Well, then, and whose little baby are you?
Eh? Eh? Ooh, my God! Alvin – what are you doing here?

ALVIN: I came for the key. I can't get in.

MRS HANKER: I thought we had burglars, daylight
robbery.

ALVIN: Where is it?

MRS HANKER: What?

ALVIN: Key to home.

MRS HANKER: How should I know?

ALVIN: Oh, come on.

MRS HANKER: Look in my coat.

(*ALVIN does so and finds the key.*)
Come and see him. Isn't he lovely? Aren't you lovely?
Yes. Alvin, come and look.

ALVIN: Here it is.

MRS HANKER: Your daddy's come to have a peep at you
– sssh.

ALVIN: (*Looking.*) Christ!

MRS HANKER: Don't screw your face up at him.

ALVIN: I'm off. (*He moves towards the garden.*)

MRS HANKER: What about Anna? Stay a minute till she
comes round and have a word. Alvin – come back here!
Alvin!

(*ALVIN goes into the garden.*)
Well, the bloody bugger. Yes. Isn't he a bugger, your
daddy, eh? I expect you know that already, don't you, eh,
my little sweetheart, eh? Course he does, yes he does.
His daddy's a little sod and you're a little bastard – yes,
he is, he's a little bastard, aren't you, then? Aw, he's lovely.

(*MAURICE appears and calls.*)

MAURICE: Ivy – can you come in? The doctor's asking.

MRS HANKER: Right.

(*She joins MAURICE. He takes the baby from her as she goes
into the room. ALVIN looks in from the garden.*)

MAURICE: Anna's not very bright at the moment. She's still unconscious. Have you seen him?

ALVIN: Yes, thanks. I haven't come back to stop. I forgot to ask Mam for a pound or two. (*He picks up MRS HANKER's handbag, takes money out and pockets it.*) See you. Thanks for holding the baby and that.
(*MRS HANKER comes from the bedroom. The DOCTOR passes in front of her into the living-room.*)

DOCTOR: I'm afraid she's dead.
(*MAURICE, still holding the baby, goes into ANNA's bedroom. The DOCTOR and MRS HANKER follow. ALVIN goes into the extension when he hears the key being turned in the front-door lock. ANNA comes in, carrying shopping.*)

ANNA: Alvin... Alvin? He might have folded his blankets.
(*She goes into the kitchen. MRS HANKER comes from ANNA's room with the DOCTOR and helps him on with his coat.*)

DOCTOR: Well. Well, now, this is a grievous tragedy.

MRS HANKER: Yes, doctor. It is that.

DOCTOR: There'll be no need to send for the coroner, as she died in my presence.

MRS HANKER: No, no. I see.

DOCTOR: Will you be able to cope?

MRS HANKER: I know what to do.

DOCTOR: I'll leave things in your capable hands.

MRS HANKER: Thank you. That is kind.

DOCTOR: Good day.

MRS HANKER: Right. Thank you. Yes. Good day, doctor.
(*The DOCTOR leaves by the front door and MRS HANKER returns to the bedroom. ANNA comes in from the kitchen and picks up the blankets, pyjamas, paper and magazine.*)

ANNA: More washing. He could be here in five hours, five at the earliest. Lots of time...lots of time to get shipshape.
(*She goes into the kitchen with the things and returns with a lampshade, which she places on the table. She repositions a chair and turns on the radio. It plays the last duet from 'Aida'. She takes the rug from a corner, unrolls it, then positions the armchair. Cradling the baby, MRS HANKER comes into the living-room with MAURICE. ANNA removes*)

the dustcovers, takes them to the kitchen, and then returns.
During the following scene, ANNA plugs in the table lamp
and puts it on the coffee table. Then she places the standard
lamp behind the armchair and puts the shade on it. She goes
to the kitchen for a plant and a vase of flowers, places the
flowers on the sideboard and the plant on the table. She then
fetches the photograph album from the sideboard and puts it
on the table.)

MAURICE: I'd better go and see the undertaker.

MRS HANKER: In a bit. I'll go if you like. Shall I take him
off to my house? Look after him there? I am his granny.

MAURICE: I'm his uncle.

MRS HANKER: You could pop down when you feel like it.

MAURICE: No.

MRS HANKER: Have him here, then, and I'll pop up.

MAURICE: Why don't you move in?

MRS HANKER: Here?

MAURICE: If you want.

MRS HANKER: And my furniture?

MAURICE: Sell it.

MRS HANKER: You mean, why don't I move out.

MAURICE: Move out there, move in here.

MRS HANKER: Permanent?

MAURICE: If you like.

MRS HANKER: Why don't you say what you mean, then?

MAURICE: If I don't, you will.

MRS HANKER: Yes.

MAURICE: It would be more convenient here.

MRS HANKER: Oh, yes. Oh, very. Oh, it would be. Yes.

MAURICE: Save the journey backwards and forwards.

MRS HANKER: Morning and night.

MAURICE: That's settled, then?

MRS HANKER: We'll say agreed. It'll not be settled till
I've settled in, will it?

MAURICE: Better shake hands on it, hadn't we?
(*MRS HANKER and MAURICE shake hands. MAURICE*
keeps hold of her hand.)

MRS HANKER: You mean I can't trust you?

MAURICE: I wouldn't say that.

MRS HANKER: I like a man who's not to be trusted –
within reason.

(*ANNA goes into the kitchen. ALVIN comes in from the
extension, goes to the album and takes out a photograph.*)

You've come back, then, have you?

ALVIN: I haven't been as yet, have I?

MRS HANKER: You will be going, then?

ALVIN: Home to our house, you mean?

MRS HANKER: Off out to sea, you dope.

ALVIN: I can't decide.

MRS HANKER: Well, you'd better. It's up to you what
happens to us.

ALVIN: (*Looking at the photograph, then replacing it.*) I wish it
were up to you.

MAURICE: So do I.

ALVIN: No you don't. It's a good one of you.

MAURICE: Keep it.

ALVIN: Shall I?

MRS HANKER: Just do what you want.

(*ALVIN puts the photograph in his pocket.*)

ALVIN: I can't tell what I want as yet.

MRS HANKER: You mean after all this you're no nearer
now than you were to start off with before?

ALVIN: Well – I don't think I ought to go, that's all; not
just at this precise moment.

MRS HANKER: 'You don't think that's all precisely at this
moment...' Ohh – that's what I like, a man of positive
action. Did you ever hear.

ALVIN: You can go, though.

MRS HANKER: Eh?

ALVIN: Put him or her down and clear out.

MRS HANKER: Huh! (*She puts the baby down on the sofa.*)

ALVIN: You're not needed.

MRS HANKER: Indeed.

ALVIN: You've made your point.

MRS HANKER: How about your would-be brother-in-law?

(*She gets her coat and bag, then waits for MAURICE.*)

ALVIN: You both have to go. Miss Bowers has come back. (*To MAURICE.*) I'm sorry we didn't hit it off. I'll not be happy without you I don't suppose, but it's the thing to do, isn't it.

MAURICE: Is it?

ALVIN: What most people do must be right.

MAURICE: I wouldn't say that.

ALVIN: Neither will I, then. I won't ever forget you, though. I'll always wish I'd been like you.

MAURICE: Thanks. But if I were you I wouldn't tell anyone that – if I were you.

ALVIN: Thanks. But I'm not you, though, am I?

MAURICE: Cheerio, then.

ALVIN: So long.

(*He kisses MAURICE for the last time, authentic, slow and deliberate. MAURICE joins MRS HANKER outside the confines of the living-room. They leave. ALVIN takes off his raincoat, puts it over the baby and sits on the sofa. ANNA comes in with a tray of tea for herself.*)

ANNA: Oh, hello.

ALVIN: Hello.

ANNA: I thought you'd gone.

ALVIN: I was outside.

ANNA: Didn't you hear me call?

ALVIN: Yes.

ANNA: You like playing games, don't you? Want some tea?

ALVIN: No, thanks. I've not long had breakfast.

ANNA: I've done the shopping.

ALVIN: Good.

ANNA: Everything's tidy now. All in order.

ALVIN: Oh!

ANNA: What?

ALVIN: While I remember. You had a visitor while you were out.

ANNA: Oh. Who?

ALVIN: Er – (*He brings out the card.*) Doctor Franklyn.

ANNA: Oh.

ALVIN: He wanted to see you.

ANNA: Oh.

ALVIN: He said –

ANNA: Yes?

ALVIN: He said – well, I might have to wear glasses.

ANNA: Oh dear. Never mind.

ALVIN: He said I should go with you.

ANNA: Where to?

ALVIN: His surgery, next time you go.

ANNA: Oh.

ALVIN: When is it?

ANNA: What?

ALVIN: Your next visit.

ANNA: I don't have a regular appointment.

ALVIN: I'll make one for us both then, shall I?

ANNA: Alright, yes.

ALVIN: This Monday?

ANNA: Monday.

ALVIN: Seven o'clock, like last night?

ANNA: Seven o'clock.

ALVIN: You'd better be there this time.

ANNA: If you make the appointment, I'll keep it.

ALVIN: I shan't go in without you.

ANNA: I'll be there.

> (*ALVIN cradles the baby privately, momentarily content. ANNA has her tea. The last notes of 'Aida' play on the radio. No more.*)

The End.